# MEDIEVALIA ET HUMANISTICA

## STUDIES IN MEDIEVAL AND RENAISSANCE CULTURE

### NEW SERIES: NUMBER 34

Miscellany

EDITED BY
PAUL MAURICE CLOGAN

ROWMAN & LITTLEFIELD PUBLISHERS, INC.
*Lanham • Boulder • New York • Toronto • Plymouth, UK*

**ROWMAN & LITTLEFIELD PUBLISHERS, INC.**

Published in the United States of America
by Rowman & Littlefield Publishers, Inc.
A wholly owned subsidary of The Rowman & Littlefield Publishing Group,
Inc.
4501 Forbes Boulevard, Suite 200, Lanham, Maryland 20706
www.rowmanlittlefield.com

Estover Road
Plymouth PL6 7PY
United Kingdom

British Library Cataloguing in Publication Information Available

**The Library of Congress has cataloged this serial publication as follows:**
Medievalia et humanistica, fasc. 1–jan. 1943–;
New ser. No 1– 1970–
Totowa, N.J. [etc.] Rowman & Littlefield [etc.]
no. 29 cm
Annual, 1943–
"Studies in medieval and renaissance culture."
Vols. for 1970–1972 issued by the Medieval and neo-Latin society;
1973– by the Medieval and Renaissance Society.
Key title: Medievalia et humanistica, ISSN 0076-6127.

ISBN-13: 978-0-7425-6487-9
ISBN-10: 0-7425-6487-8
eISBN-13: 978-0-7425-6488-6
eISBN-10: 0-7425-6488-6
Library of Congress (8108)

Printed in the United States of America

∞™ The paper used in this publication meets the minimum requirements of
American National Standard for Information Sciences—Permanence of Paper
for Printed Library Materials, ANSI/NISO Z39.48-1992.

# MEDIEVALIA ET HUMANISTICA

# Contents

# Editorial Note

Since 1970, this new series has sought to promote significant scholarship, criticism, and reviews within the fields of medieval and Renaissance studies. It has published articles drawn from a variety of disciplines, and it has given attention to new directions in humanistic scholarship and to significant topics of general interest. This series has been particularly concerned with the exchange between specializations, and scholars of diverse approaches have complemented each other's efforts on questions of common interest.

*Medievalia et Humanistica* is sponsored by theModern Language Association of America. Publication in the series is open to contributions from all sources, and the editorial board welcomes scholarly, critical, or interdisciplinary articles of significant interest on relevant material. Contributors are urged to communicate in a clear and concise style the larger implications and the material of their research, with documentation held to a minimum. Text, maps, illustrations, diagrams, and musical examples are published when they are essential to the argument of the article. In preparing and submitting manuscripts for consideration, potential contributors are advised to follow carefully the instructions given on pages x–xi. Articles in English may be submitted to any of the editors. Books for review and inquiries concerning *Fasciculi* I–XVII in the original series should be addressed to the Editor, *Medievalia et Humanistica*, P.O. Box 28428, Austin, Texas 78755–8428. Inquiries concerning subscriptions should be addressed to the publisher:

Rowman & Littlefield Publishers, Inc.
4501 Forbes Boulevard, Suite 200
Lanham, Maryland 20706

## Manuscript Submission Guidelines

### Preparing Your Word File

- Double-space your file, except for extracts (lengthy quotes), which should be single-spaced with a line space above and below.
- Use only one space between sentences. Use tabs, not letter-spaces, to indent text.
- Type note callouts as superior numbers, then type out the notes themselves at the end of your document. Avoid the Notes feature of Word.

### Style Matters

- Spell out numbers up to one hundred—both cardinals and ordinals (e.g, "twentieth century).
- Use American punctuation and spelling: commas and periods go inside closing quotation marks.
- Lowercase biblical, medieval. Capitalize Bible, Middle Ages, West, Western.
- Style for literary works includes Book of Acts, Genesis (book of the Bible), *Genesis A* (poem), Gospel of Matthew.
- Short quotations: Put small quotations with translations in running text into parentheses: "Ipsa autem nocte vidit mulier . . ." ("That very night his wife saw . . .").
- Long quotations: For longer quotations with translations, set them off as extracts with the translation in brackets below. If the original text is poetry with half-lines, use only one tab between each half-line. Although the text will look uneven in your Word file, the tab will make the lines align exactly when typeset:

Cynewulf describes her as she sits on a throne while the Jews crowd around her:

| | |
|---|---|
| þrungon þa on þreate | þær on þrymme bád |
| in cynestole | casere mæg, |
| geatolic guðcwen | golde gehyrsted. |

[They crowded where the Caesar's kinswoman was waiting / in majesty upon a throne, / a magnificent battle-queenclad in gold] (329-331)

### Sample Notes

#### *Journal Article:*

1. Melinda Shepard, "The Church in Eleventh-Century Europe," *Medieval Studies* 15, no. 1 (1993), 211–226.

#### *Book:*

2. Shepard, p. 223. Shepard notes other similarities as well. See also R. A. Potter, *Church and Medieval State* (Chicago: University of Chicago Press, 1979), 301.

# Articles for Future Volumes

Articles may be submitted to any of the editors, but it would be advisable to submit them to the nearest or most appropriate editor for consideration. A prospective author is encouraged to contact his or her editor at the earliest opportunity to receive any necessary advice. The length of the article depends on the material, but brief articles or notes normally are not considered. The entire manuscript should be typed, double-spaced, on standard 8½-by-11 bond paper, with ample margins; documentation should be held to a minimum. The submission must also include a final copy of the manuscript in Microsoft Word, 3½-inch formatted diskette or CD-R. Endnotes, prepared according to *The Chicago Manual of Style*, fifteenth edition (University of Chicago Press), should be double-spaced and numbered consecutively, and they should appear at the end of the article. All quotations and references should be in finished form. Electronic submissions should be accompanied by two hard copies. Authors' names should not appear on manuscripts, but a cover letter with the author's name and address should be included with each manuscript.

The addresses of the American editors can be determined by their academic affiliations. The addresses of the editors outside the United States and their respective area of interest are as follows:

Francesco Bausi, Professor of Latinate humanism, Italian literature, and medieval saints' lives.   Università della Calabria (Cosenza), Dipartimento di Filologia—87036, Arcavacata di Rende (Cosenza), Italy; Piazza Giorgini 2, 50134 Firenze, Italia

Alcuin Blamires, Professor of English and comparative literature, Chaucer, fourteenth-century literature, and medieval women writers, Department of English and Comparative Literature, Goldsmiths College, University of London, Lewisham Way, New Cross, London, SE14 6NW UK

Jacques Dalarun, 3 rue du général Delestraint, 75016 Paris, France

Reinhold Glei,  Professor für Klassische Philologie, Seminar für Klassische Philologie, Ruhr-Universität Bochum, D-44780 Bochum, Germany

Yasmin Haskell, Professor of Latin humanism, School of Humanities (M205), University of Western Australia, 35 Stirling Highway, Crawley, WA 6009, Australia

David Lines, Professor of Italian, Centre for the Study of the Renaissance, University of Warwick, Coventry CV4 7AL, UK

Richard Madsen, Professor of English, School of English Studies, University of Nottingham, Nottingham, Nottingham, NG7 2RD, UK

Adriano Prosperi, Professor of history of the Reformation and Counter-Reformation, Scuola Normale Superiore, Pisa, Italia

# *Preface*

Unlike previous volumes in the new series, volume 34 is a miscellany, a collection of various and diverse articles in medieval and Renaissance studies today. It introduces unexpected polyphonies, a range of inter-texts, and dialogic entanglement. Seven original articles offer readers new histories in interstices. In addition, twenty review notices examine recent publications in medieval and Renaissance studies.

I am grateful to the editorial board for their expert advice and to the staff of Rowman & Littlefield Publishers for their helpful assistance in the production of the annual volume.

P.M.C.

# Boethius and the Consolation of the Quadrivium

## MICHAEL FOURNIER

Boethius's *Consolation* has suffered under many criticisms. Misunderstandings about the nature of the work have either led to its neglect or helped to cultivate prejudices about its philosophical importance. The fact that the *Consolation* draws upon such a wealth of sources leads some to question the originality of the work, while the apparent opposition of the positions represented leads others to question its philosophical merits. My own view is that the *Consolation* uses its sources in an original way, and the diverse arguments and methods are unified in a Platonic ascent. Boethius presents a logical progression from lower forms of knowing and being to higher forms, in a way that is essential to the integration of the form and the content of the work.

Scholars such as Thomas Curley and Elaine Scarry have argued for the unity and coherence of the *Consolation* on the basis of the formula in book 5, that things are known according to the mode of the knower and not the object known.[1] The form of the *Consolation* reflects the various modes of knowing. Sensation, imagination, reason, and intellect not only constitute the content of the various books but also give each book its formal features. Book 1 adopts the idiom of sensation, book 2 imagination, books 3 and 4 reason, and book 5 intellect. The diverse modes are related in a hierarchical order, with the lower modes contained within the higher.

Yet I think that Curley and Scarry do not go far enough with this interpretation. Neither makes clear the logic of the relation between the faculties or the nature of the movement from one to the next. I argue that the relation between the modes of knowing must be understood in terms of the presentation of the mathematical sciences found in the *Consolation*. The logical relation of sensation, imagination, reason, and intellect is elaborated and clarified in the relation between astronomy, music, geometry, and arithmetic.

*Medievalia et Humanistica*, New Series, Number 34 (Paul Maurice Clogan, ed.), Rowman & Littlefield Publishers, Inc., 2008.

The unity of the modes of knowing and the mathematical sciences is illustrated by the various forms of the circle (*orbis*) in the *Consolation*.[2] Book 1 presents sensation with the astronomical circle of the stars, book 2 presents the musical circle of Fortune's wheel to the imagination, books 3 and 4 present the circle of geometry to reason, and book 5 considers the paradigm of these forms in the simplicity of unity itself, which is the principle of the circle. The movement from the lower forms of knowing to the higher depends upon the forms of the circle presented to the Prisoner. Each form resolves a problem that hinders the progress of consolation. At the same time, each leads to the recognition of a new problem that compels the Prisoner to ascend to a higher mode of knowing. It is in virtue of the continuity between the various forms of the circle across the mathematical sciences of the quadrivium that the Prisoner is able to perceive the logical continuity from one mode of knowing to the next. For Boethius, the quadrivium is the key to philosophical pedagogy.

Philosophy qualifies the principle that things are known according to the capacity of the knower with a statement that clarifies the relation between the various faculties. Without this clarification, the modes of knowing would be opposed in an irreconcilable way. Sense, imagination, reason, and intellect would contradict each other with no means of arbitrating between them. For this reason Philosophy adds that "the greatest consideration is to be given to this: for the higher power of comprehension embraces the lower, while the lower in no way rises to the higher" (*Consolation* 5,4,31–34).[3] On the basis of this clarification the differences between the modes can be reconciled by recognizing the priority of the higher modes over the lower. Sense might contradict imagination, but imagination, as a higher and more comprehensive mode, must be regarded as revealing a greater truth concerning the same object.[4]

The question arises, however, how it is that the higher mode comprehends the lower. What does it mean to say that intelligence "knows the reason's universal, and the imagination's shape, and what is materially sensible, but without using reason, imagination or the senses, but by one stroke of the mind, Formally, so to speak, looking forth on all these things together" (*Consolation* 5,4,33)? How are the objects of the diverse modes not simply other?

A model for the relation between the faculties is found in the quadrivium. In fact, the quadrivium presents both sides, as the objects of the four mathematical sciences are for Boethius also related in virtue of being diverse forms of the same elements. Each science and its proper object is logically related to the others.

In the *Institutio arithmetica* Boethius states that arithmetic "holds the principal place and position of mother to the rest" (*Institutio arithmetica* 1,1,8).[5] It is an exemplar of God's thought, and "whatever things are prior in nature, it is to these underlying elements that the posterior elements can be referred" (*Institutio arithmetica* 1,1,8). Boethius argues that arithmetic is prior to geometry because without number there is no triangle, quadrangle, and so on. Remove the triangle and the quadrangle, still "3" and "4" remain. Similarly, arithmetic is prior to music because it is concerned with numbers in themselves, while music is concerned with the relations between numbers, the interval, and the harmonics, and so forth. Boethius goes on for the priority of arithmetic over astronomy, and the final logical order of the four sciences:

Arithmetic also precedes spherical and astronomical science insofar as these two remaining studies follow the third [geometry] naturally. In astronomy, "circles," "a sphere," "a center," "concentric circles," "the median," and "the axis" exist, all of which are the concern of the discipline of geometry. For this reason, I want to demonstrate the anterior logical force of geometry. This is the case because in all things, movement naturally comes after rest; the static comes first. Thus, geometry understands the doctrine of immoveable things while astronomy comprehends the science of mobile things. In astronomy, the very movement of the stars is celebrated in harmonic intervals. From this it follows that the power of music logically precedes the course of the stars; and there is no doubt that arithmetic precedes astronomy since it is prior to music, which comes before astronomy. (*Institutio arithmetica* 1,1,11)

Understood according to an analogy with the quadrivium, the faculties of sense, imagination, reason, and intellect are understood as related in virtue of being diverse modes of common elements. There is, however, more than an analogy. The *Consolation*, in order to console, must move from the lower mode of sense to the higher mode of reason. This movement is characteristic of the progression of the quadrivium. As Boethius asserts in an argument for the place of the quadrivium at the very foundation of philosophical education, it is "the *quadrivium* by which we bring a superior mind from the knowledge offered by the senses to the more certain things of the intellect" (*Institutio arithmetica* 1,1,7). The quadrivium provides steps (*gradus*) by which the mind is progressively illuminated and can raise itself from its immediate sensible circumstances to the certainty of intelligible truth. This movement is essential to the *Consolation*. Not only do the books of the *Consolation* correspond to the modes of sense, imagination, reason, and intellect, but there is also an important correspondence between the five books and the sciences of the quadrivium. The modes of knowing correspond to the objects of the mathematical sciences. In book 5 Boethius describes the objects of each faculty:

> For sense examines the shape set in the underlying matter, imagination the shape alone without matter; while reason surpasses this too, and examines with a universal consideration the specific form itself, which is present in single individuals. But the eye of intelligence is set higher still; for passing beyond the process of going round the one whole, it looks with the pure sight of the mind at the simple Form itself. (*Consolation* 5,4,28–31).

The figure in matter examined by sense is akin to the definition of astronomy as the science of mobile things—that is, matter in motion. The figure without matter examined by imagination is akin to the science of music, whose harmonic intervals are immaterial figures. The specific form examined by reason is akin to the objects of geometry, and the form itself examined by intellect corresponds to the number, which is the principal exemplar in the mind of the creator.

The relation between the modes of knowing and the mathematical sciences is first suggested by the fact that Philosophy's primary example of how the modes know the same object in diverse ways uses a sphere (*orbi*), known by sight and touch (*Consolation* 5,4,26). Each book, I argue, presents the mode of knowing with an object of the mathematical sciences. Book 1 relies on sensation's grasp of the astronomical, book 2 relies on imagination's grasp of the musical, books 3 and 4 rely on reason's grasp of the geometrical (the reason why geometry is given two books is explained below), and book 5 relies on intellect's grasp of the arithmetical. In this way, the Prisoner is led from his immersion in the sensible to his *patria* in the intelligible. The perspective gained from contemplating the highest things and perceiving the nature of the Good's rule depends upon the movement from sensation and imagination to reason and intellect.

## Book 1: The Circle of the Stars

Book 1 is the mode of sensation on the cognitive hierarchy. The Prisoner's senses are dulled and deficient, and as a result he is unable to see beyond the immediacy of sensation and the circumstances of his grief. Philosophy addresses sensation, the specific object of which is figure in matter, by adopting the practices of the science of astronomy. Astronomy, Boethius says in his work on music, is the science of "moveable magnitude"[6] and in the *Institutio arithmetica* he says that its object is the "movement of the stars themselves" (*Institutio arithmetica* 1,1,11). Thus while astronomy deals with the same elements as geometry (the circle, sphere, center, concentric circles), whose own elements derive from arithmetic, astronomy is distinguished in virtue of its relation to the material form of these elements. The circle of the stars is the first form of the *orbis* Lady Philosophy presents to the Prisoner. It is used to restore his senses, which leads to the recognition that there is a cause of his grief that cannot be understood from within sensation alone. The limit of sensation points beyond itself to the higher and more comprehensive mode of imagination. The movement between the modes is possible because of the continuity in the objects. Imagination too will be presented with an appropriate form of the *orbis*.

When Philosophy appears, the Prisoner is silent. She banishes the Muses, sits down on the bed next to him, and wipes away his tears, restoring his vision. This is the first step in the long process of consoling him. But how are we to understand the metaphorical restoration of his truer vision?

The answer is found in Philosophy's first words to the Prisoner. While she banishes the Muses in the first prose section, her first words to the Prisoner are in meter at 1m2. Her song is a response to the Prisoner's opening elegy, in which he recalls, "Verses [he] once made glowing with content" (*Consolation* 1m1,1). He believes that the Muses were the glory of his youth, that they comfort him still, and that they will never abandon him. To this false notion Philosophy opposes a true account of the Prisoner's youth. She recalls: "This man / Used once to wander free under open skies / the paths of the heavens" (*Consolation* 1m2,6–7). The Prisoner's youth was spent studying nature's secret causes (*Consolation* 1m2,22–23), in particular the science of astronomy.

When Philosophy appears, the Prisoner's gaze is downcast. When she approaches his bed she sees his face "cast down with sorrow" (*Consolation* 1,1,14), "his eyes cast down beneath the weight of care / seeing nothing / But the dull, solid earth" (*Consolation* 1m2, 26–27). The appearance of Philosophy makes him begin to turn his vision from the earth to the heavens. This is presented figuratively in the description of Philosophy. Philosophy has come from the pole (*cardine*) of the heavens to the Prisoner (*Consolation* 1,3,3). The image of the *cardo* in relation to the *orbis* of the heavens underscores the sensible aspect of book 1. The *cardo* is a pole—that is to say, it is a kind of center, but one that belongs to a complex figure, not a simple plane figure.[7] She is standing above his head (*Consolation* 1,1,1); the Prisoner must look up from the song he is recording, and he turns his gaze from the earth up to the sky. This change in orientation is required for the restoration of his sight. He is blinded by tears and cannot recognize Philosophy until she wipes them away with her dress. The recovery presented in these images represents what is accomplished philosophically by the presentation of the object of astronomy to his senses. The effect on the Prisoner's mind is equivalent to the figurative clearing away of fog that obscures vision. Philosophy's first song puts before the Prisoner the circle of the stars. The recollection of the study of the fixed and wandering stars (*stabilem orbem* and *varios orbes*) restores the Prisoner's vision by replacing an opaque and inscrutable object (the dull solid earth) with an object that is appropriate, one that can be "mastered and bounded by number and law" (*Consolation* 1m2,12).[8]

In the meter written with the help of the Muses, the Prisoner complains that his grief is due to a change in fortune. The first poem the Prisoner addresses to himself. The narrator describes the circumstances of the first poem saying, "While I was thinking these thoughts to myself in silence" (*Consolation* 1,1,1). The Prisoner's next meter is addressed to the "maker of the circle [*orbis*] of the stars" (*Consolation* 1m5,1). The Prisoner laments in verse that he is not simply afflicted by the feeling of loss. There is something that troubles him more deeply. He perceives that there is an incongruity between the order of the world and the disorder of human affairs. The maker of the circle of the stars has "a sure purpose ruling and guiding all" (*Consolation* 1m5,25), yet man's acts alone he will not constrain, though he rightly could. This opposition between the order of the heavens and the natural world on the one hand and the disorder and injustice of human life on the other leads the Prisoner to entreat the maker to "Look on this wretched earth, / Whoever you are who bind the world with law!" and "make the earth / Steady with that stability of law / By which you rule the vastness of the heavens" (*Consolation* 1m5,42–48).

When the Prisoner recovers the sight of the order in the heavens, he is forced to contrast this observed order with the chaos of his life. The articulation of his complaint about human affairs in 1m5 is possible only after he has looked upon the order of the heavens in virtue of the science of astronomy and seen the lack of this order in his own experience. It is also only after the Prisoner has articulated what he takes to be the cause of his grief that Philosophy can begin to properly diagnose him.

When he directs his sight toward the heavens, the Prisoner is able to perceive and articulate a deeper cause of his grief than the pain of losing fortune's gifts. The Prisoner feels the sting of the incongruity between the stars' order and the disorder of human life, and this is a necessary first step on the way to consolation. This step, however, is not sufficient to cure his ills. When Philosophy asks whether he thinks the world is governed by chance or reason, the Prisoner emphatically asserts that God indeed governs the world, and that he will never be moved from this opinion (*Consolation* 1,6,3–4). This opinion appears sound to Philosophy, despite the Prisoner's sickness. When, however, the Prisoner is asked if he knows how God governs the world (*Consolation* 1,6,7), what the end of all things is (*Consolation* 1,6,10), and who he is (*Consolation* 1,6,14), he cannot answer. These questions reveal the limits of the understanding he has from within his newfound perspective.

While he has gained an insight into the cause of his grief, he cannot find a solution for it. The Prisoner recognizes that there exists an order, but he cannot grasp the cause. The reason is that the science of astronomy considers matter in motion, and thus corresponds to the observations of the senses, whose object is "figure in matter" (*Consolation* 5,4,28). While the Prisoner can observe the order of the stars, he cannot give an account of the cause from the perspective of the senses. He has the true opinion that God rationally directs the world, but nothing more than opinion is possible from the observations of the senses that are involved in astronomy. This limitation is what compels the Prisoner to leave behind sensation and turn to what is above it. In book 2 the higher perspective of imagination will be considered.

## Book 2: The Wheel of Fortune

Book 2 is the mode of imagination. The Prisoner's imagination is deficient, and the result is that he has a false image of Fortune. His mistaken image of Fortune leads him to believe that it is the loss of her gifts that grieves him, and he would be happy again if her gifts were restored. Philosophy addresses his imagination, the specific object of which is figure without matter, by adopting the practices of music. Music here, broadly conceived, includes not only the mathematical ideas of harmony and ratio, but the art of the Muses in general. For Boethius, music is logically prior to astronomy (and therefore a step higher on the ascent) because "the very music of the stars is celebrated in harmonic intervals" (*Institutio arithmetica* 1,1,11). For this reason, poetry, which is part of music, is prior to astronomy.

Philosophy employs the poetic device of *prosopopeia*, a form of personification, to show the Prisoner a true image of Fortune. *Prosopopeia* allows

Philosophy to present the figures, without matter, of Fortune and her wheel. The imagination can grasp the *orbis* of Fortune's wheel in the understanding of her nature and the nature of her handmaids. The idea of the wheel grasped by the imagination allows the Prisoner to see that Fortune is not the real cause of his grief. Purged of a false relation to Fortune, whose gifts are external and contain no inherent good, he turns to the only stable center of happiness, the self. From the perspective of the imagination, only the goods of the soul are real. The Prisoner, however, is unable to perceive how these goods are related to the "love which moves the heavens" (*Consolation* 2m8,30).

Lady Philosophy must treat the Prisoner's imagination in book 2. Imagination can grasp something of the cause that eludes sensation. First, however, the imagination must be restored. Like his senses in book 1, the Prisoner's imagination is deficient because it is turned toward an unsuitable object. The Prisoner has set a false image of Fortune before himself, and this has led him to err concerning the cause of his grief. He imagines that Fortune has changed her attitude toward him (*Consolation* 2,1,9). For this reason he believes that if her gifts were restored, his former happiness would return. Philosophy recalls Fortune's real nature by presenting the Prisoner with a true image to replace this mistaken one. The image restores his imagination and allows him to glimpse the reason behind the chaos of human affairs. He can once again see the nature of Fortune's rule. He can recognize how she employs her handmaidens to raise men up, only to cast them low when she takes them away. The restored understanding of Fortune allows the Prisoner to discover the one thing that Fortune cannot change and the stable source of happiness: himself.

In book 1 the Prisoner imagined that Fortune was deceitful (*Consolation* 1m1,17) and that she ought to be ashamed of her actions (*Consolation* 1,4,19). In book 2 Philosophy corrects this idea of Fortune as random and unpredictable by showing the Prisoner an image of her true nature. Fortune is not at all random, but as regular and constant as a turning wheel (*Consolation* 2,1,19). As in book 1, when Philosophy turned the Prisoner's senses toward the heavens, here she directs his imagination to an image of Fortune by putting on Fortune's face and arguing in her words. In the *prosopopeia* of book 2, Fortune pleads her case, saying, "This is my nature, this is my continual game: turning my wheel [*orbe*] swiftly I delight to bring low what is on high, to raise high what is down" (*Consolation* 2,2,9). The order of the circle of the heavens, which seemed to be absent from human affairs governed by Fortune, is now seen in her wheel. The *orbis* of Fortune is as regular as the *orbis* of the stars. What is more, while the order of the heavens could only be observed, the reason for the motion caused by Fortune is presented in Fortune's own words. It is her nature. Her activity is what delights her.

Philosophy treats the Prisoner with music. The Muses banished in book 1 were replaced by Philosophy's own Muses ("my Muses," she calls them at 1,1,11), and in book 2 she employs music and rhetoric as the first, milder remedies appropriate to his condition.

There are three kinds of music according to Boethius: cosmic (*mundana*), human (*humana*) and that which rests in various instruments (*quae in quibusdam constituta est instrumentis*), including the human voice (*Institutio musica* 1,2). Human music "unites the incorporeal nature of reason with the body [by a] certain harmony and, as it were, a careful tuning of low and high pitches as though producing one consonance" (*Institutio musica* 1,2). It is human music that is employed in book 2. The cosmic music of the heavens "does not penetrate our ears" (*Institutio musica* 1,2). Human music does penetrate our ears, and "indeed no path to the mind is as open for instruction as the sense of hearing. Thus, when rhythms and modes reach an intellect through the ears, they doubtless affect and reshape the mind according to their particular character" (*Institutio musica* 1,1). The superficial character of music in book 2 has to do not with any imprecision in the mathematical science of music, but with our perception of a certain form. Philosophy does not present the Prisoner with a disquisition on the diatesseron, diapente and diapason (i.e., the way in which music is related to arithmetic in the *Institutio arithmetica*). She sings to him once his senses have been restored. She sings in order that the harmonies of her song might begin to unite the diverse elements of soul and body. Music, like the imagination, is intermediate between the two; thus it is music that treats the imagination.

This orientation to external, false goods is overcome by looking at the supposed goods and recognizing the contradictions they contain (*Consolation* 2,5 to 2,7). It is demonstrated that happiness cannot consist (*constare*) of these things, and the contradictions repel the mind and effect the turn to the self as the center (*cardo*) around which happiness turns. There is also a tension that emerges and propels the argument beyond these first attempts at a cure. The poem at the end of book 2 that ends "*amor quo caelum*" (*Consolation* 2m8,29–30) articulates this newfound isolation. The self-imposed exile of 1,5 has been replaced by an even deeper kind of exile, one in which the self seems to fall outside of the divine rule.

The *cardo* of the heavens in book 1, with its relation to the physical extension of the world, is superseded in book 2 by a new center, the self.

Philosophy reveals to the Prisoner "on what [his] greatest happiness really turns"—literally, the center of his greatest happiness, *summae cardinem felicitas* (*Consolation* 2,4,23). This *cardo* is contrasted with the *punctus* of the sensible cosmos, which is ultimately nothing. According to Ptolemy, in relation to the whole of the cosmos, even Rome is an insignificant point. The nullity of the worldly *punctus* is contrasted with the riches of the self as *cardo* (*Consolation* 2,7,3). Of this insignificant point that is the world, only a quarter is habitable, according to Ptolemy. Thus, Philosophy compounds the force of the demonstration when she asks,

Now is it in this tightly-enclosed and tiny point, itself but a part of a point, that you think of spreading your reputation, of glorifying your name? What grandeur or magnificence can glory have, contracted within such small and narrow limits? (*Consolation* 2,7,6)

In book 1 the diminished capacity of the senses was enough to prevent the Prisoner from perceiving the truth of his immediate circumstances. The problem in book 2 is that a similar failure of imagination keeps him from seeing the true nature of Fortune. Once the Prisoner perceives Fortune's impotence with respect to the stable center of his happiness—himself—he is freed from her influence. He is, however, now aware that the love that rules the heavens does not rule his heart, and the solution to this problem of governance cannot be found within imagination. The Prisoner must turn to what is above imagination, reason, to resolve this difficulty.

## Book 3: Creation as a Circle

Book 3 is the mode of reason. The Prisoner's reason is deficient, and the result is that he has mistaken the form of false happiness for the form of true happiness. Philosophy addresses his reason, which is the universal consideration of the specific form, by adopting the practices of geometry. Geometry speculates about fixed magnitudes (*Institutio musica* 2,3). Geometry is also the intermediate science. It spans the divide between the sensible and the intelligible. Geometry has a twofold orientation. The principles of geometry can be used as axioms in the investigation of the sensible world, and the sensible is known insofar as it is an image of the mathematical. Geometrical forms can also be investigated insofar as they are themselves images of higher intelligible realities. Book 3 deals with the first orientation, book 4 with the second. In book 3, the created world is understood as an image of the mathematical realities in the mind of the creator (3m9), and the created world is presented as reverting upon the creator, the good, who is the center around which all things turn. While the sensible is known qua image of the intelligible, the opposition between the motion of created natures and the unmoved creator is not reconciled in book 3 from this perspective.

Music and rhetoric, which were the milder remedies applied in book 2, are replaced in book 3 by rational arguments. Music and rhetoric were superficial preparations for the stronger remedies of reason, which are received internally (*Consolation* 3,1,3). Philosophy will show him what true happiness is, but for the moment his mind is too occupied by images (*Consolation* 3,1,5). Thus, she explains to the Prisoner: "I shall try to describe in words and delineate a subject better known to you, so that, when you have seen that clearly, you may, since you will then have turned your eyes on its opposite, recognize the appearance of true blessedness" (*Consolation* 3,1,7).

In addition to the use of deductive arguments, Philosophy employs the geometer's technique of drawing corollaries (*porismata*) from proven theorems. We know that Boethius wrote on geometry, specifically, a translation of Euclid's *Elements*.[9] We also know that he was deeply influenced by Neoplatonic notions about geometry.[10]

Book 3 corresponds to the first orientation of mathematical understanding, which takes mathematical principles as the axioms by which the sensible world is measured and stabilized. The central meter of the *Consolation*, 3m9 (which cannot of course be exhausted by any single interpretation), can be seen in one way as an understanding of the created world as an image of mathematical realities in the mind of the Creator. The material world is a moving image of a circular pattern of emanation and reversion. "Soul thus divided has its motion gathered / Into two circles, moves to return into itself, and the Mind deep within / Encircles, and makes the heaven turn, in likeness to itself" (*Consolation* 3m9, 15-17). Goodness is the center (*cardo*) (*Consolation* 3,10,38) and the created universe is a moving circle (*orbem mobilem*), which moves around this unmoved (*immobilem*) center (*Consolation* 3,12,37). Book 4 moves from contemplating the mathematical paradigms of the created world to a consideration of the nature of Fate and Providence, which are imaged in the relation of a circle to the center (*Consolation* 4,6,15).

By the end of book 3 all three questions involved in the diagnosis of book 1 have been answered. The Prisoner has remembered who he is (*Consolation* 2,4,22–26), what the end of all things is (*Consolation* 3,11,41), and how God governs the world (*Consolation* 3,12,22). There is nevertheless something inadequate about the conclusion of book 3, which compels the Prisoner to continue. His consolation is not yet complete, and the reason for this can be understood by looking at the argument of book 3 as it is presented in the final meter. Orpheus is permitted to descend into Hades to bring back his beloved Eurydice. The ruler of the shades permits Orpheus to lead Eurydice up from Hades, but puts a condition on this gift: Orpheus may not look back upon her until they are once again outside Tartarus. Orpheus cannot resist and loses Eurydice again. Philosophy concludes the meter with a caution. "To you this tale refers, / Who seek to lead your mind / Into the upper day; / For he who overcome should turn back his gaze / Towards the Tartarean cave, / Whatever excellence he takes with him / He loses when he looks on those below" (*Consolation* 3m12,52–58). The Orpheus poem stands between book 3 and book 4 and demarcates the border between the sensible world considered in books 1–3 and the intelligible which is treated in books 4 and 5. Although book 3 contains the theological hymn of 3m9, it is cast in terms drawn from the sensible world. Although book 4 considers human actions, the ideas of virtue and vice are considered according to their forms or as ideas. Thus, the Prisoner completes the ascent that Orpheus failed to complete. The Prisoner leaves the cave at the end of book 3 and, in a way, does not look back.

The final meter of book 3 depicts the separation between the multiple, divided, and imperfect created things and their single, unified, perfect creator. The myth of Orpheus is transposed and coordinated with the image of the Platonic cave.[11] The tale of Orpheus, who lost Eurydice by looking back down toward the cave and not upward to the light of day, is commended to all who are trying to raise their minds to the light of the Good. In a simple sense, Orpheus, in this Platonic presentation, is trying to have in the sensible what belongs only to the intelligible. The two worlds are separate, and Orpheus loses what belongs to the intelligible by trying to contain it in the sensible.

While the rational character of book 3 stands in clear contrast to the attempts at musical and rhetorical persuasion in book 2, it is not so clear how book 3 differs from book 4. In book 4, Philosophy also employs a rational, logical method. The argument about the power of virtue and the weakness of vice depends upon the logical contrariety of the two: "For since good and evil are contraries, if it is established that good is powerful, the weakness of evil is clear; and if the frailty of evil is evident, the strength of good is known" (*Consolation* 4,2,3). Book 4 also employs the geometrical image of the concentric moving circles of fate and the still center of Providence (*Consolation* 4,6,15).

The difference between the approach to reason in books 3 and 4 can be understood by referring to the intermediate place of reason on the Platonic line (*Republic* 510b–c). Reasoning, in particular reasoning about mathematicals, has a twofold orientation. Mathematical realities can be understood as those things of which things in the sensible world are images. In this way they are employed as principles in the investigation of the sensible world, and axioms whose truth is not investigated. The mathematical realities are in turn images of higher realities. By investigating mathematicals, the mind may ascend to a knowledge of the things of which mathematicals are only images. As Socrates notes, when the mind is turned toward the sensible, mathematicals are principles and the things of which sensible realities are images. Turned toward the intelligible, they are themselves images of higher ideas (*Republic* 510a–511b).

As O'Meara suggests, geometry is more important for philosophers because, while it has a presence in images and the sensible, "geometry reaches . . . up to true and divine being."[12] Thus, while geometry is not the first of the mathematical sciences, it is in a sense more accessible from the lower realm and it appears in a more immediate way to the human mind.[13]

It is fitting that the allegory of the cave should be taken as an image to describe the movement of book 3. The allegory uses an image drawn from the sensible world to describe the relation between the sensible and the intelligible and the way in which the ascent is possible. The sensible is an image of the intelligible, and this allows the mind to move to the intelligible from within the sensible.

## Book 4: The Geometry of Fate

Book 4 continues with the mode of reason, but moves to a consideration of geometrical realities not as they are reflected in the sensible, but as they are reflections of higher intelligible forms. The relation between the circle and the center is developed in an analogy that reveals the relation between Fate and Providence. The way that the moving sphere (*orbis*) or circle (*circulus*) is related to the still center (*cardo*) is an image of the relation of the motion of Fate to the immutability of Providence. The opposition at the end of book 3, which presents the imperfect and divided created world as simply other than the perfection and unity of God, is resolved in book 4. With this opposition

overcome, however, it is no longer possible to see how there is anything other than the good of Providence.

The Prisoner interrupts Philosophy to praise her arguments to this
point. There is, however, work to be done. In fact, the greatest cause of
his grief remains: that "although there does exist a good ruler of the universe, evil can exist at all and even pass unpunished" (*Consolation*
4,1,3–4). The Prisoner cannot reconcile the arguments that show that
the Good is the end and ruler of all things with his experience, which
seems to teach that virtue goes unrewarded and vice seems to prosper
with impunity. Philosophy promises the Prisoner, "By the help of the
same God of whose kingdom we are now speaking you will learn that the
good are always powerful, while the bad are always abject and weak, nor
are vices without punishment, nor virtues without reward" (*Consolation*
4,1,7). This argument returns to the world of human affairs, which was
in a way left behind in the ascent to the highest good and unity itself in
book 3. The appearance that the Good is simply other than the divided
and created natures whose end it is must be overcome.

While it might appear that book 4 is a descent from the heights
reached in book 3, it is in fact a continuation of the ascent. The glimpse
of the "creator of heaven and earth" (*Consolation* 3m9,2) allows the Prisoner to delve into the inner logic of virtue and vice, and grasp their effect upon human nature. Book 4 considers the effects of virtue and vice
on the soul, and shows how they can transform the human into a god or
a beast. The logical method of book 3, by which the understanding of
the false form of happiness leads to the recognition of the true form, is
continued in book 4. Philosophy explains to the Prisoner that "since
good and evil are contraries, if it is established that good is powerful, the
weakness of evil is clear; and if the frailty of evil is evident, the strength
of good is known" (*Consolation* 4,2,3). Not only does Philosophy establish the impotence of vice, she argues that "those who leave aside the
common end of all things that are, at the same time also leave off being"
(*Consolation* 4,2,32). The contrariety of virtue and vice is akin to the opposition of being and non-being.

Philosophy argues that good men can never be without their rewards
and adds the remarkable notion that the vicious man is happier if he
does not escape punishment (*Consolation* 4,4,36). These notions emanate from the very *ideas* of virtue and vice. When the Prisoner is reluctant to concede these conclusions, Philosophy reminds him that prem-
ises granted, he must accept the conclusions (*Consolation* 4,4,11). The
Prisoner consents to the truth of the arguments about virtue and vice,

but sets them against the popular idea of fortune, "for none of those who are wise would prefer to be an exile, poor and disgraced, rather than to flourish staying in his own city, powerful because of his riches, respected for his honours, and strong in his power" (*Consolation* 4,5,2).

From this perspective virtue does go unrewarded and vice unpunished. For this reason, the nature of God's governance is still unclear to the Prisoner, who laments once again, "Since he frequently grants delights to the good and unpleasant things to the wicked, and on the other hand frequently metes out harshness to the good and grants their desires to the wicked, unless the cause is discovered, why should his governance seem to be any different from the randomness of chance?" (*Consolation* 4,5,6). With the forms of virtue and vice having been established, it is now necessary to reconcile the appearances to these forms. Philosophy attempts to pass over the arguments necessary to explain why the clarity observed in the logical relation of the forms of virtue in vice is obscured and almost inscrutable in the world. The Prisoner is not satisfied with her assurances, and insists on knowing the causes of hidden things (*Consolation* 4,6,1). Philosophy acquiesces to the Prisoner's vigorous and forceful demand.

Philosophy explains that the reason for her reticence is the Hydra-headed character of the problem (*Consolation* 4,6,2–3). She then sets out the arguments about Fate and Providence as if she were beginning "from a new starting point" (*Consolation* 4,6,7). The central image that captures the arguments is that of the nested spheres. The way that the mutability of Fate is related to immutable Providence is to be understood in terms of a geometrical image.

For just as, of a number of spheres (*orbium*) turning about the same centre (*cardinem*), the innermost one approaches the simplicity of middleness and is a sort of pivot (*cardo*) for the rest, which are placed outside it, about which they turn; but the outermost one, turning with a greater circumference, the further it is separated from the indivisibility of the central point, the wider spaces it spreads over; and if anything is joined or associated with that centre, it is gathered into its simplicity and ceases to spread and diffuse itself: in a similar manner, that which is furthest separated from the principal mind is entangled in the tighter meshes of fate, and a thing is the more free from fate the more closely it moves towards that centre of things (*Consolation* 4,6,15).

The opposition between the form of virtue, considered in itself, and its appearances in the world lead the Prisoner to question the nature of God's governance. The cause of this apparent opposition, as well as a number of others, is explained using the image of the sphere as an image of higher realities opaque to human understanding. The relation of

Fate and Providence has parallels in a series of oppositions that cannot be reconciled by reference to an image drawn from the sensible such as the Platonic cave. Philosophy explains that "as reasoning is to understanding, as that which becomes is to that which is, as time is to eternity, as the circle is to its centre, so is the moving course of fate to the unmoving simplicity of providence" (*Consolation* 4,6,17). The geometrical image works in virtue of the place of geometrical realities between the sensible and the intelligible. They are easily grasped by the mind through images, but it is not the image but the idea of the sphere, contemplated by reason free from images, that allows the mind to glimpse the relation of the multiple spheres turning around a single center. With all of the oppositions set up by the image of the cave in book 3 (perfect/imperfect, being/becoming, divided/unified, time/eternity, etc.) having been reconciled, it appears at the end of book 4 that the greatest cause of the Prisoner's grief has been addressed. The conclusion is that God "removes all evil from within the bounds of his commonwealth by the course of the necessity of fate" (*Consolation* 4,6,55). This consolation, however, is not complete. In book 5 it appears that with evil, Philosophy has also banished contingency and freedom by making Providence absolute. This appearance is overcome by the proper understanding of knowledge and the relation of the various faculties.

## Book 5: The Unity of Center and Circumference

In book 5 Philosophy turns to intellect to solve the problem of the relation of free will and Providence, which vexes reason. As Philosophy notes, "reason belongs only to humankind, as intelligence only to the divine" (*Consolation* 5,5,4). For this reason, intellect can only be sketched according to reason's ability to comprehend it. In order to present the divine mode of knowing to reason, Philosophy adopts the methods of the science of arithmetic. Arithmetic is to the other mathematical sciences as intellect is to the other modes of knowing. Arithmetic is logically prior and contains the elements of all the other sciences in a more perfect and complete way. As Boethius writes in the *Institutio arithmetica*, "from the beginning, all things whatever which have been created may be seen by the nature of things to be formed by the reason of numbers" (*Institutio arithmetica* 1,2,1). The principle of number itself is unity, for "it constitutes the primary unit of all numbers which are in the natural order and is rightly recognized as the generator of the total extended plurality of numbers" (*Institutio arithmetica* 1,7,5–6). Thus, number is the principal archetype of creation, and unity is the archetype of number.

In book 5 Philosophy adopts the language of arithmetic to present the final form of the *orbis*. In book 1 the *orbis* of the heavens, the object of astronomy, was adopted to conform to sensation's grasp of figure in matter. In book 2, the *orbis* of Fortune, drawn from the art of the Muses, was appropriate to the imagination's grasp of figure without matter. The ever-moving wheel of Fortune was shown to turn around an unmoving center (*cardo*), the self. In books 3 and 4, the two orientations of the geometrical *orbis*, as the paradigm of the sensible (3m9) and the image of higher intelligible realities (*Consolation* 4,6,15), were adopted for their conformity to reason. The *orbis* in book 5 is that which belongs to arithmetic. The sensible, imaginative, and rational forms are superseded in book 5 by the paradigm of the *orbis*: unity itself. As Boethius explains,

> Unity in both power and force is a circle and a sphere. As often as you multiply a point by itself, it always ends in itself from which it began. If you multiply one by one, one remains; and if you multiply it again and again, it is still the same. If there is one multiplication of a number, it gives a plane figure, which is a circle; if you multiply it a second time, then a sphere is created. (*Institutio arithmetica* 2,30,4–5)

Philosophy describes the highest intelligence as a point (*cacumen*) and describes the highest knowledge as simplicity (*simplicitas*) (*Consolation* 5,5,12). The simplicity of the divine mind is identified with unity (*Consolation* 4,6,10), and the discussion of the nature of the divine intelligence is therefore likened to the paradigmatic relation of the center to the circle. The arithmetical unity in geometry is the center of the circle, and contains within itself in an unextended way all that belongs to the circle. What is present in the circle as extended and complex (circumference, radii, center, etc.) is present in the point or unity in an unextended and simple way. This relation is described by Proclus and can be usefully set forward here to illuminate the power inherent in the unity described by Boethius.

Proclus, in his commentary on Euclid's geometry, describes not only the elements of the circle, but from these elements moves to a consideration of the causes of the circle. After considering the various sensible, imaginative, and rational forms of the circle, he writes, "Now that it has been made precise what is meant by a circle (*kuklos*), its center (*kentron*), the circumference of the circle (*periphereia*), and the figure (*skēma*) as a whole, let us move once more and ascend from these details to the contemplation of their paradigms" (*In primum Euclidis*, 153). The paradigm of the circle is the unified possession of all the elements at once. Proclus explains: "As in the circle the center, the distances, and the outer circumference all exist at the same time, so also in the paradigm there are no parts that are earlier in time and others that come to be later, but all are together at once—rest, procession, and reversion" (*In primum Euclidis*, 153). The various extended and complex forms of the circle originate in the simplicity of the paradigm.

But the figures differ from the paradigms in that the latter are without parts or spatial intervals, whereas the figures are divided, the center being in one place, the lines from the center in another, and the circumference that bounds the circle still another. But up there they are all in one. If you take what corresponds to the center, you will find everything in it; if you take the procession coming out of the center, you will find that this also contains everything; and likewise if you take the reversion. (*In primum Euclidis*, 153–154)

Everything is found in the simplicity of the center.[14] As the numbers 3 and 4 are the conditions of the triangle and the square (*Institutio arithmetica* 1,1,9), so unity is the condition of the circle and the sphere. Philosophy has moved from the geometrical image of the nested spheres in book 4 to the simple paradigm of this image found in arithmetic. The arithmetical unity that is the principle of geometry is adduced to expound an analogy of the divine intellect's relation to contingent actions, for "God possesses this present instant of comprehension and sight of all things not from the issuing of future events but from his own simplicity" (*Consolation* 5,6,41).

Philosophy presents the Prisoner with this image of the simplicity of the divine intellect. The Prisoner cannot ascend to share in this perspective. Instead, it can be glimpsed from within human reason. This glimpse is achieved when the geometric image of the nested, concentric circles of book 4 is considered, as far as possible, according to the principles of the circle. The glimpse of unity considered in book 5 is achieved by collapsing the extended idea of the circle into its center. The procedure of simplification is analogous to that followed in the movement from book 1 to book 2, book 2 to 3, and 3 to 4.

In book 1, the circle of the stars is composed of the figure of the circle and matter. This complex is simplified in book 2, which leaves aside the matter for the figure alone. This figure is merely an image in book 2, the image of Fortune's wheel. While the sensible matter is left behind by the imagination, there is still composition in the figure in the imagination. The mind imagines a particular circle, a wheel, and whatever attends the particularity of this image. The wheel is not a circle—rather, it is circular. In book 3 the particularity is stripped away, and the idea of the circle itself is seen under the aspect of its role as a paradigm of the created world. This paradigm, which is grasped through its images in the created world, is purged of those images and contemplated according to its own nature as an image of the highest intelligible.

By following the progressive logic of increasingly simplified forms of the circle, Philosophy can point the Prisoner's mind to the idea of God's grasp of Providence, which contains human freedom. The circle can be simplified by reducing it to its center, which contains in an almost ineffable way the fullness and plurality of the geometric shape. The fecundity of unity is akin to the fecundity of the circle's center, which contains in the extensionless point at its center the infinite number of radii and the endless line (without a determinate beginning or end) of the circumference.

## Conclusion

The books of the *Consolation* form a step-by-step ascent from the lower part of the soul to the higher. For Boethius, the ascent passes from sense (book 1) and imagination (book 2) to reason (books 3–4), but it ends with a glimpse of what is beyond reason (book 5). Intellect and not reason characterizes the divine life and is its mode of knowing all the lower modes in a simple way. Boethius moves the reader from the lower modes of knowing to the higher by showing the limits of each mode. At the end of each book there is an opposition or a contradiction that cannot be resolved by the mode and points to the need to adopt a higher mode of knowing.

The *Consolation* not only advances from lower modes of knowing to higher, but also presents an ascent through the levels of being. When Philosophy appears to the Prisoner her height is ambiguous (*Consolation* 1,1,1), and she appears at one moment to "confine herself to the ordinary measure of man" (*Consolation* 1,1,2), while at another moment it appears that "the crown of her head touched the heavens" (*Consolation* 1,1,2) and at yet another she appears to have "penetrated the heavens themselves" (*Consolation* 1,1,2) and passed beyond the reach of human vision. The three heights of Lady Philosophy represent the terrestrial world of process, the spheres of the heavens that circumscribe the natural world, and the transcendent divinity. For Boethius, consolation requires an ascent from the lower, human perspective to the highest, divine perspective, even if this divine perspective is only intimated or adumbrated.

## Notes

1. Thomas F. Curley, "How to Read the *Consolation of Philosophy*," *Interpretation* 14 (1986); Elaine Scarry, "The External Referent: Cosmic Order; The Well-Rounded Sphere: Cognition and Metaphysical Structure in Boethius's *Consolation of Philosophy*," in *Resisting Representation* (New York: Oxford University Press, 1994). My own view is that Curley and Scarry do not adequately recognize the nature of the distinction between book 3 and book 4. The two books do, as Curley argues, operate at the level of reason. There is, however, a significant difference between the modes of each. It is not, as Scarry argues, that book 3 does not fall into the linear progression of the ascent. I argue that it is because book 3 demarcates the division between the sensible and the intelligible, and the reason that bridges this divide necessarily shares in the features of both. This is the nature of geometry.
2. On the many circles found in the *Consolation*, see Jean-Luc Solère, "Bien, cercles et hebdomades: formes et raissonnement chez Boèce et Proclus," in *Boèce ou la chaîne des savoirs* (Louvain: Peeters, 2003): 55–129; John Magee, "The Boethian Wheel of Fortune and Fate," *Mediaeval Studies* 49 (1987): 524–533; H. R. Patch, "Fate in Boethius and the Neoplatonists," *Speculum* 4 (1929): 62–72.
3. English translations of the *Consolation* are from the Loeb Boethius, *The Consolation of Philosophy*, translated by S. J. Tester (Cambridge, Mass.: Harvard University Press, 1997). Book, section, and line references are to the Latin text of *De consolatione philosophiae*, edited by Claudio Moreschini (Leipzig: Teubner, 2000).
4. On the importance of this relation between the faculties, see Stephen Blackwood, "*Philosophia*'s Dress: Prayer in Boethius' *Consolation of Philosophy*," *Dionysius* 20 (2002): 146.
5. All references to the text of the *Institutio arithmetica* are from *L'institution arithmétique*, edited with a translation by Jean-Yves Guillaumin (Paris: Les Belles Lettres, 1995). English translations from Michael Masi, *Boethian Number Theory: A Translation of the* De Institutione Arithmetica (Amsterdam: Editions Rodopi B. V., 1983).
6. *De institutione musica* 2,3. All references to the Latin text are from Boethius, *De institutione musica*, edited by G. Friedlein (Leipzig: Teubner, 1867). English translations from Boethius, *Fundamentals of Music*, translated with introduction and notes by Calvin Bower (New Haven, Conn.: Yale University Press, 1989).
7. Proclus describes the pole and the center in this way: "Of necessity, therefore, [Euclid] adds at the end that this point which lies within the circle and from which all the lines drawn to the circumference are equal is the center of the circle. For there are only two such points, the pole and the center, but one is outside the plane, the other within it. If you imagine, for example, a gnomon standing at the center of the circle, then its extreme point is the upper pole, and all the lines drawn from it to the circumference of the circle are demonstrably equal to one another. Likewise in a cone the apex of the whole figure is the pole of the circle at its base." Proclus, A *Commentary on the First Book of Euclid's Elements*, translated by Glenn R. Morrow (Princeton, N.J.: Princeton University Press, 1970), 121. For the Greek text see Proclus, *In primum Euclidid elementorum comentarii*, edited by G. Friedlein (Leipzig: Teubner, 1873).
8. In addition to the explicit reference to astronomy and natural philosophy, 1m2 contains a striking resonance with Ovid's account of Pythagoras in *Meta-*

*morphoses* XV, 60–75. There Pythagoras is described as living in exile because of a tyrant, yet continuing to approach the gods with his thoughts. This connection to Ovid's Pythagoras is to be contrasted with the striking allusions to the *Tristia* that mark the Prisoner's opening elegy. On the relation of 1m1 to 1m2, see Thomas Curley, "The *Consolation of Philosophy* as a Work of Literature," *American Journal of Philology* 108 (1987): 343–367.

9. See David Pingree, "Boethius' Geometry and Astronomy" in *Boethius: His Life, Thought and Influence*, edited by Margaret Gibson (Oxford: Blackwell, 1981), 55–161; Henry Chadwick, *Boethius: The Consolations of Music, Logic, Theology, and Philosophy* (Oxford: Oxford University Press, 1981), 102; and Max Lejbowicz, "Cassiodorii Euclides: Eléments de bibliographie Boécienne," in *Boèce ou la chaîne des savoirs* (Louvain-Paris: Peeters, 2003), 301–339.

10. Henry Chadwick notes that "Proclus uses the word *porisma*, exactly as in Boethius, to mean an 'incidental gain arising out of the demonstration of the main proposition' (*In Eucl. Elem.* I, 212, 16; 301, 22 Friedlein)," *Boethius*, 106–107. For the more general influence of Proclus on Boethius, see Wayne J. Hankey, "*Ad intellectum ratiocinatio*: Three Procline logics, *The Divine Names* of Pseudo-Dionysius, Eriugena's *Periphyseon* and Boethius' *Consolatio philosophiae*," in *Studia Patristica*, vol. 29, edited by Elizabeth A. Livingstone (Leuven: Peeters, 1997), 249.

11. On the Orpheus poem and its central importance for the *Consolation*, see Eileen Sweeney, *Logic, Theology, and Poetry in Boethius, Abelard, and Alan of Lille: Words in the Absence of Things* (New York: Palgrave MacMillan, 2006), 48–49; Gerard O'Daly, *The Poetry of Boethius* (London: Duckworth, 1991), 188–207; Seth Lerer, *Boethius and Dialogue: Literary Method in the* Consolation of Philosophy (Princeton, N.J.: Princeton University Press, 1985), 154–165; Anne Astell, *Job, Boethius, and Epic Truth* (Ithaca, N.Y.: Cornell University Press, 1994), 53–60.

12. Dominic J. O'Meara, *Pythagoras Revived: Mathematics in Late Antiquity* (Oxford: Clarendon Press, 1989), 173.

13. Chadwick notes that for the Neoplatonisits, "Mathematics in general and geometry in particular therefore occupy a half-way house between the material world and the purely abstract world of concepts" (*Boethius*, 106). On the intermediate position of geometry, see also Annick Charles, "Sur le charactère intermédiaire des mathématiques dans la pensée de Proklos," *Les études philosophiques* 22 (1967): 69–80; Ian Mueller, "Iamblichus and Proclus' Euclid Commentary," *Hermes* 115 (1987): 334–348; Ian Stewart, "Mathematics as Philosophy: Proclus and Barrow," *Dionysius* 18 (2000): 151–181; Jean Trouillard, "La puissance secrète du nombre selon Proclos," *Revue de philosophie ancienne* 2 (1983): 227–241; and Stanislas Breton, *Philosophie et mathématique chez Proclus* (Paris: Beauchesne, 1969).

14. Cf. Plotinus's *Enenads*, where the geometry of the circle is employed to illuminate the nature and character of One, *Nous*, and Soul: 5,1,11; 6,5,5; 6,8,18; 6,9,8.

# Language, Power, and Holiness in Cynewulf's Elene

LAURENCE ERUSSARD

Cynewulf's *Elene*[1] has not awakened favorable comments and has not fared well among modern critics. Both the poem and the title[2] character have been considered unpleasant and anti-Semitic. Twentieth-century critic James Doubleday summarizes the general consensus by writing that "with her threats, her torture, and her arrogant self-righteousness," Elene "seems to be one of the most unpleasant saints of the calendar."[3] Such a negative evaluation may come from the fact that Elene stands in contrast to the expected stereotype of the holy woman. She could not be further away from the typical young, holy virgin who eventually becomes a martyr after many bodily hardships and spiritual trials. On the contrary, Elene is an older woman, an impressive, powerful, ubiquitously respected, feared, and obeyed queen. Focusing on these aspects of her character, recent and feminist scholars have drawn a more generous portrait; Hennessey Olsen describes her as a "strong, autonomous figure";[4] Damico describes her as echoing the Anglo-Saxon character type of the "Germanic warrior-woman,"[5] while Chance orients her commentaries toward the motherly function of the queen and converts her into an allegory[6] of the *Mater Ecclesia*.[7] Even these positive critical comments centered on allegorical and heroic qualities recognize that, unlike Juliana, Judith, or even Judas, Cynewulf's Elene never awakens the sympathy of the reader. She remains an imposing *cwen* (queen), a representation that corresponds to the historical situation and explains that readers can find her "too business-like, curt, efficient, purposeful . . . but distant."[8] Using artistic and numismatic evidence, Kenneth Holum argues convincingly that, starting with Helena, the Theodosian empresses (379–455 C.E.) exercised a specifically powerful *basilia* (female dominium) and were elevated to the rank of *Augusta*.[9] This title and the qualification of *basilia* did not mean that these women had actual political power but that they were listened to while they encouraged their husbands and sons to exercise power virtuously.[10] With

*Medievalia et Humanistica*, New Series, Number 34 (Paul Maurice Clogan, ed.), Rowman & Littlefield Publishers, Inc., 2008.

the growth of Christianity, these empresses became emblems of the Christian virtues of self-restraint and pious dedication to others;[11] they were seen as inspiring members of the ecclesiastic institution, as "pillars of the Church."[12] Their social and hierarchical grandeur and privileges were perceived as the reflection of their authority and moral superiority: In his *Vita Constantini*, Eusebius praises Helena for "her pious deeds and for the towering and wonderful plant that sprang from her."[13]

The function of the empress as "pillar of the Church" fits the static, formal, insensitive, unemotional depiction of Cynewulf's female hero. She is described with impersonal, generic terms, and the text surrounds her systematically with symmetrical figures of style and puns such as *chiasmus* and *paronomasia*, which reinforce the impression of static impersonality. Elene stands like an icon, towering over the Jews, and her own language reflects her characterization. When she talks, she limits herself to demand information, state rules, inflict punishment and even torture, in a constantly matter-of-fact, detached, impersonal tone. This attitude can be explained by the fact that Elene acts as instrument of her son Constantine's mission, but her linguistic style is also an iconographic expression of holiness, which will be adopted by Judas upon his conversion. By the end of the poem, Judas and Elene's common hieratic and impersonal style stands in drastic contrast with the devil's personal language.

\* \* \*

Right from the beginning of the poem, Elene's stately and impersonal dimension appears in the language that defines her. She is a stern commanding *guðcwen* (battle queen), the only woman in a world of soldiers and Hebrew elders. Before her spiritual superiority is asserted, before the dialogue actually begins, the text displays her secular position of power. The *scop* (poet) tells that she came to the Holy Land with a numerous army; with awe, he exclaims, in the first person: "Ne hyrde ic sið ne ær / on egstreameidese lædan, / on merestrætemægen fægere" ("Neither before nor since have I heard of a woman leading a finer army on the ocean-tide, the sea-road") (240–242).

Elene dominates the poem because of her hierarchical supremacy as queen. Cynewulf uses the substantive *cwen* (queen) in reference to Elene twenty-one times, alone or as part of a compound. In contrast, her personal name can be found only sixteen times in the text. This preference underlines the secondary importance of personal identity; it illustrates the insistence on Elene's status rather than on her person. This point must have been essential to the author since it implies an additional difficulty of composition: Cynewulf stretches the possibilities of Old English prosody to find ways to keep alliterating with *cwen* or to integrate the substantive into an alliterating compound. The use of "Elene" would have been easier for the poet since, in alliterative prosody, a vowel may alliterate with any other vowel. The noun *cwen* is also modified by adjectives that enlarge the glorious dimension of the heroine: She is a *guð cwen* (warrior queen) (254, 331), *sigecwen* (victorious queen) (260), *rice cwen* (mighty queen) (411), a *tireadig cwen* (glorious queen) (605), an *æðeleðcwen* (noble queen) (662), a *þeodcwen* (queen of the people) (1155). *Sige* is actually a masculine noun; this compound noun *sigecwen* (victoryqueen) echoes another compound noun, *sigedrihten* (victoryruler), which is a recurrent phrase in the Anglo-Saxon corpus; it is almost a kenning, used to define God.[14] It is used only twice to describe secular power in reference to specific individuals,[15] once in reference to Hroðgar in *Beowulf* (391) and once in reference to Eadgils in *Widsith*.[16] It seems therefore reasonable to infer that the term tends to express spiritual rather than secular power. This hypothesis is reinforced by the fact that the compound is also used twice in the case of saints when their lives/battles on earth are over and they leave this world to be received gloriously in heaven: Guthlac is called *sigedrihten* after his death (b. 1375) and Andrew, at the end of the *Menologium* when he is dying (215). This vocabulary suggests consequently that Elene's power does not come only from her secular royal position, but also from her religious zeal and authority.

Additional emphasis on Elene's social status rather than personal identity comes from the repetition of the impersonal two words that can be translated as "lady," which is used four times (*ides*: 229, 241, 405, and *hlæfdige*: 656). In contrast Elene is called a *modor* (mother) only once (214), at the beginning of the text, while the generic terms *wif* or *mæg* (woman) recur five times (*wif*: 223, 286, 1131; *mæg*: 339, 669). The terms underline the femaleness of the queen and are conventionally used in Anglo-Saxon poetry to refer to women. The use of *modor* occurs to introduce Elene as the one chosen by her son to go on the mission of the recovery of the True Cross. However, the noun does not appear because Cynewulf wishes to define Elene in relationship to her son, as mother. When *modor* is introduced in the text, it is the object of the verb *het* (ordered), whose subject is Constantine for whom Elene is primarily a mother.[17] Other defining terms include two non-gendered phrases, *seo æðele* (the noble one) (300, 545) and *seo eadige* (the blessed one) (619).

The reiteration of the term *cwen* (queen) seems to reduce Elene's individuality to her social status and power; it defines her and it stresses her historical importance. All the language that surrounds her characterization evokes her majestic importance and her static, unchangeable qualities.[18] Before anything else, Elene is the queen, the impressive *Augusta*, the precursor of three generations of Theodosian empresses showing them the way to manifest their mission in the growth of Christianity in the Roman Empire. Recognizing her Eastern characteristics, Lee defined Elene as "a rather stylized Byzantine creation."[19] The term "Byzantine" seems particularly felicitous when applied to both Cynewulf's representation of Elene and of the structure of the poem, for both appear to be mapped on the model of Byzantine icons.[20] As has been observed by Michael Roberts, "comparisons between poetry and the visual arts were a commonplace of literary criticism in antiquity."[21] It appears that Cynewulf is applying the system of the critics of antiquity to the poetic style of *Elene* by mapping the literary elements of the poem on Byzantine iconic representations. Cynewulf's hagiography might be defined as a literary icon; his narrative and poetic approaches may be summarized by the expression "iconographic style."[22]

Elene's mission is to confront the Hebrew wise men, to force them to reveal the emplacement of the true Cross and to unearth the relic. As observed by Jacques Le Goff, whenever a pictorial icon expresses any type of confrontation—whether in time, ideas, or state—it tends to articulate disparity by showing a space divided either horizontally, vertically, or obliquely or else to symbolize the division through the use of colors or symbols.[23] The lines of visual composition indicate a separation in the ideologies of the opponents. In Byzantine illuminations, whenever saints are depicted, their similar language, beliefs, or authority are represented by similar objects. This sign may be a book or a scroll that symbolizes the law, and/or it can also be a kinetic indication—a gesture of the index, for instance. When a change is represented, the same character may be reproduced in sequence to show that he or she is no longer the same. In *Elene* these patterns are represented by the linguistic style of the characters and the structure of their speeches.

Elene's speeches and the poem itself reproduce iconographic designs and conventions used in art forms. The very structure of the poem is twofold. Duality is basic for two intertwined reasons. First, the poem articulates the difference between the Christian *cwen* and the Jews and, consequently, between two ideologies and their symbolic emblems: the Christian Church and the Synagogue. Second, the poem is actually a double hagiography. In the beginning Elene is the only saint, but at the end, she has converted Judas, who becomes the second holy character. Furthermore, these two main characters, Elene and Judas, who at the beginning of the poem represent the two distinct ideologies, become united in a common faith through the discovery of the True Cross. Throughout the poem, the constant dialogue pattern reinforces the duality and creates an iconographic composition similar to the ones observed in illuminations. Le Goff observes that, in iconography, duality is often expressed by special distance and clear organization of the two parts. One of the images selected by Le Goff shows Saint Francis as he preaches to the birds.[24] The saint stands at the left of the image with two monks; the birds are at the right of the image and occupy more than half of the total space; an empty space separates Saint Francis from the static dark birds that face him, which are organized in five unrealistically superposed rows of six. These rows of barely traced, identical birds give the impression of infinite number. The composition of this image is identical to the poetic image created by Cynewulf's description of Elene as she confronts the Jews.

Elene arrives at Jerusalem with the secular might of an army and the religious power of the "true faith." Yet, as she talks, she draws strength from her religious authority rather than from her military superiority. She stands static, solemn, and alone in the face of many: After summoning all the Hebrew wise men to Jerusalem, she addresses three thousand of them. As pointed out by Jean-Claude Schmitt, the descriptions of movements and situations in medieval illuminations and texts "are supposed to correspond to and express the quality and movements of the soul."[25] The "frontality"[26] of her situation may be imagined as the one represented in many medieval illustrations that place the speaker at the center, in the position called in "majesty," like an image of wisdom. This unchanging frontality distances her from the other characters and gives her a timeless, otherworldly dimension that is expressed in the unchanging patterns of her speeches. She is crowned and majestic; Cynewulf describes her as she sits on a throne while the Jews crowd around her and await her words:

> þrungon þa on þreate          þær on þrymme bád
> in cynestole                  casere mæg,
> geatolic guðcwen              golde gehyrsted. (329–331)

[They crowded where the Caesar's kinswoman was waiting / in majesty upon a throne, / a magnificent battle-queen clad in gold.]

Line 329 is significantly longer than most surrounding verses and the usual poetic line; it introduces the grandiose description of the queen on her throne in a way that does not fit the typical four-stress verse of Old English prosody. This verse comes very close to the occurrence of the longer six-stress line in *The Dream of the Rood*, which, according to Michael

Alexander, "seems to be used at particularly solemn moments."[27] The length of the verse adds solemn intensity to the image of the queen as she gets ready to speak; it echoes the gilded emphasis of an icon in which the most important character is often not only at the center of the picture, but taller than the others, and whose head is enlarged by the width of the halo that surrounds it.[28]

The iconographic quality of the setting of Elene's discourse is reinforced by the iconographic pattern of her rhetorical style itself, as if Cynewulf conceived his literary composition in visual terms. Elene's utterances are built according to an iconographic symmetry coherent with the overall aesthetics of the poem. Much of the symmetry of the stylistic figures used in *Elene* depends upon the reproduction of Socratic paronomasia. Systematic paronomasia is used to establish contrasts between concepts centered on themes that are relevant to hagiographic writings: the questions of holiness, sin, and mankind. Cynewulf does not use these puns only in *Elene* but also in *Juliana*, as it has been pointed out by Roberta Frank in her study of *Juliana* and *Elene*.[29]

In *Elene*, whose main theme is obviously the Cross or *rod*, Cynewulf transforms this word in the hinge of the poem's diction. The most prominent paronomasia in *Elene* is, quite fittingly, a play on the words *rod* (cross) and *rodora* (heaven). The instrument of redemption and the boon of redemption are linked in a linguistic icon. This pun recurs regularly as a pictorial motif; it can be found twelve times throughout the poem.[30] Furthermore, this pun has a dogmatic function: It states the relationship between the Cross and salvation in heaven; it summarizes the dogma of redemption. To reinforce the link between the two terms and the iconographic efficiency of the pun, the two terms are systematically juxtaposed in the same line and they alliterate.

In addition to the *rod/rodora* motif (or any of its grammatical variations), several other puns recur and stress further the systematic use of paronomasia as a relevant rhetorical figure of style. The other cases are *man* (sin) and *mann* (man) in line 626 and at the very end of the poem. In the first case the religious message implied by the juxtaposition of the two terms states man's innate relation to sin. As the two words are linked, man appears as naturally predestined to sin. In that first passage, the *man/mann* pun occurs in the same sentence as the *rod/rodora* coupling; the juxtaposition implies that, because of man's predestination to sin, the redemption for the atonement of the sins is a necessity. Complicating the design is the fact that this first grouping of *man* and *mann* paired with *rod* and *rodora* happens right at the climax of the dramatic moment, at middle point of the poem. The sophistication of this stylistic design is close to a type of conceit penned by a metaphysical poet:

| | |
|---|---|
| Gif ðu in heofonrice | habban wille |
| eard mid englum | ond on eorðan lif, |
| sigorlean in swegle, | saga ricene me |
| hwær seo **rod** wunige | **rador**cyninges, |
| halig under hrusan | þe ge hwile un |
| þurh morðres **man** | **mannum** dyrndun. (621–626) |

[If you want to have an abode in heaven with the angels, a reward of victory in the sky, and life on earth, tell me quickly where is the Cross of the king of heaven, holy under the ground, which you have hidden from man for some time now on the account of the sin of murder.]

Two other words are paired through the same kind of figure, but in diametrical oppositions to the *man/mann* (sin/man): the recurring pair *hæleð* (man, hero) and *halig* (holy).[31] While *man/mann* suggests man's predisposition to sin, this new pair stresses man's capacity for holiness as long as he abides in the true faith. It states that man's holiness depends upon his recognition of the Cross, which symbolizes Christianity. Represented iconographically, the statement would show the cross at the center, man on the left still laden with sin, and on the right freed from sin. This icon, which the paronomasia of the text sets in the imagination of the reader, is precisely an illustration of the spiritual evolution experienced by Judas. Before he recognizes the Cross as symbolic object, as testimony of Christ's divinity, and in his own heart, Judas is in the pit of inequity; he is a simple *hæleð* blinded by the sin of the Jews' murder of Christ. But, as soon as he reveals the emplacement of the Cross and identifies it, Judas converts and becomes an inspired and enlightened *halig*. The process between *hæleð* and *halig* shows that the text stresses hope and faith in man's capacity to bring remedy to his sinful condition.

Cynewulf demonstrates this hope by using again, at the end of the poem, the pair *man/mann* in an iconographic way that resolves the tensions between the two terms. The proximity of the two words and the fact that they both alliterate with *morðres* (murder), in line 626 quoted above, suggests that man and sin are irrevocably tied to each other; it is man's condition to be connected to sin. The three alliterating terms follow one another in an uninterrupted continuum going from (murder) to (sin) to (man). The meaning of this continuum can be seen and heard as creating a unity through the homophonic attraction of *mann* and *man* and their alliteration with *morðres*.[32] This pattern transcends the literal purport of the individual terms and reveals an iconographic pattern: The physical proximity of the three words constitutes an icon that illustrates on the page the dogmatic situation of unredeemed man. As he disrupts this continuum at the end of the poem, Cynewulf applies to the poetic construction of the last two sentences a convention that belongs to iconographic representation: the distance between objects. He separates the two terms *man* and *mann* by several lines. The homophonic attraction disappears. *Mann* (1312) stands by itself, at the beginning of the first sentence of this closing section, totally disconnected from *man* (1317)—away from "sin." Just as in an image elements that are physically far away from each other are conceived as unrelated, *man* and *mann* (sin and man) stand far from each other, stating that through the recovery of the Cross mankind has recovered the possibility of his original innocence. Sin and man are no longer connected with murder; rather, *man* has been *forsawon* (despised) and *mann* can alliterate with *milde* (mild). The resulting pattern is the felicitous fitting together of the two effective words within the discourse and as a design on the page. The linguistic icon of the dogmatic message of man's atonement through Christ's sacrifice on the Cross shows man and sin physically disconnected and separated by punctuation.[33] A period is set symmetrically, exactly halfway between the two words. The text stands as a shadowless image that lacks realism because it does not look to this world but toward the otherworldly reality of the *Wuldorcyninges* (King of Glory) kingdom. So, each one among men will be separated, held aloof from each of their

|  |  |
|---|---|
|  | Swa bið þara **manna** ælc |
| deopra firena, | þurh þæs domes fyr. |
| Moton þonne siðþan | sybbe brucan, |
| eces eadwelan; | him bið engla weard |
| **milde** ond bliðe | þæs ðe hie **mana** gehwylc |
| forsawon, synna weorc | ond to suna metudes |
| wordum cleopodon; | forðan hie nu on wlite scinaþ |
| englum gelice, | yrfes brucaþ, |
| wuldorcyninges | to widan feore. Amen. (1312–1321) |

[guilts, of deep sins, through the fire of judgment. Then, they will be allowed to enjoy peace, eternal well-being; to them, the guardian of angels will be mild and kind because they despised each sin, the work of evil, and called in words to the Son of the Creator; therefore, they now shine in beauty like the angels and enjoy forever the heritage of the king of glory.]

This final pattern of paronomasia corresponds to the ultimate goal of Elene: the separation of man from sin announced by the conversion of Judas.

This iconographic style, which can be recognized in the poetic patterns and in the presentation of the poem's message, corresponds to the type of the *sermo humilis* analyzed by Auerbach: It develops deep theological concepts about faith, redemption, and atonement but it uses a story and symbols rather than a theological discussion.[34] *Elene* remains an example of vernacular storytelling, but its skillful iconographic style invests the text with a highly sophisticated artifice both as an overall narrative and in its details. The passage quoted above is a good example of how the icon of the big narrative, of the story and its purport, resolves itself in the micro-narrative of the last two sentences. This final passage and the symmetric use of *man* and *mann* show verses that are shaped and carved as a religious image, according to the principles of laconic frontality and symmetrical patterns found in the elaboration of manuscript illuminations.

In addition, Elene handles language as if it were a sword. Her long discourses show perfect linguistic expertise and control of rhetorical styles.[35] Her systematic approach might have the same strategic qualities as her son's use of the art of war. Her first talk to the Hebrews, for instance, is divided into three distinct parts. First, Elene presents her theme in an introduction that praises the Jews and therefore disposes them to wish to listen to her:

| | |
|---|---|
| Ic þæt wearolice | onwiten hæbbe |
| þurg witgena | wordgeryno |
| on Godes bocum | þæt ge geardagum |
| wyrðe wæron | wuldorcyninge, |
| dryhtne dyre | ond dædhwæte. (288–292) |

[I have thoroughly learned through the written secrets of the prophets in the books of God that in former days you used to be precious to the King of Glory, dear to the Lord and courageous].

After she has made sure that the Jews are not on the defensive, Elene takes them by surprise: She attacks and insults them. The passage is then much longer:

| | |
|---|---|
| Hwæt ge þæresnyttro | unwislice, |
| wraðe wiðweopon | þa ge wergdon þane |
| þe eow of wergðe | þurh his wuldres miht, |
| fram ligcwale | lysan þohte, |
| of hæftnede. | Ge mid hour speowdon |
| on þæs andwlitan | þe eow eagena leoht |
| fram blindnesse | bote gefremede |
| edniowunga | þurh þæt æðele spald |
| ond fram unclænum | oft generede, |
| deofla gastum. | Ge deaþe þone |

|                          |                          |
| ------------------------ | ------------------------ |
| deman ongunnon           | se ðe of deaðe sylf      |
| woruld awehte            | on wera corþre           |
| in þæt ærre lif          | eowres cynnes.           |
| Swa ge modblinde         | mengan ongunnon          |
| lige wið soðe,           | leoht wiðþystrum,        |
| æfst wið are,            | inwitþancum              |
| wroht webbedan;          | eow seo wergðu forðan    |
| sceðþeð scyldfullum.     | Ge þa sciran miht        |
| deman ongunnon,          | on gedweolan lifdon      |
| þeostrum geþancum        | oð þysne dæg. (293–312)  |

[Listen, you foolishly, fiercely threw away wisdom, when you cursed the one who wanted to free you, through his glorious might, from damnation from the torment of fire, from imprisonment. Filthily you spat on the face of him who found remedy against blindness for the light of your eyes, afresh with his noble spittle, and [who] often saved you from the unclean spirits. You condemned to death him who himself woke the world from death among a multitude of people, in the previous days of your nation. So, spiritually blind, you confused error with truth, light with darkness, evil with mercy; with guile, you invented a false accusation. So, this curse will crush you, the false ones. You condemned the light-giving power And you have dwelt in the error of your dark thoughts until these days.]

Elene's linguistic expertise includes the phonic, rhythmic hammering of the alliterations over several lines. These regular, recurring phonic rhythms add to the iconographic style: They can be interpreted as linguistic elements that reproduce the patterned precious stone inlays found in some icons such as the ones depicting Saint Eudocia[36] or the gold, gilded silver, and enamel bust of Saint Michael.[37] The insistence on blindness, mentioned twice in seven lines (299 "blindnesse"; 306 "modblinde"), also brings to mind the iconic representation of Synagogue as blind, with her eyes covered with a blindfold. The idea of "blinding" mankind is also, in Cynewulf's poems, one of the favorite weapons of the devil.[38] Since the eyes are the perceived as windows of the soul, blinding the eyes corresponds to keeping the soul in darkness.

Once Elene has crushed and frightened her opponents with these accusations, she offers to them the solution to their collective damnation. She places herself as the one who knows, judges, and can bring a remedy to their otherwise hopeless situation. The third part of her discourse is, therefore, the solution. She changes the tone of her sentences and the tense of the verbs. After the accusations in the past tense she switches to the present, to refer to the Jews' present state and the future for their everlasting damnation. Now, she uses the imperative to give the orders and demand that they obey:

|                     |                    |
| ------------------- | ------------------ |
| Gangaþ nu snude,    | snyttro geþencaþ   |
| weras wisfæste,     | words cræftige,    |

| | |
|---|---|
| þa ðe eowre æ, | æðelum cræftige |
| on ferhðsefan | firmest hæbben |
| þa me soðlice | segan cunnon, |
| andsware cyðan | for eowic forð |
| tacna gehwylces | þe ic him to sece. (313–319) |

[Go quickly now and with wisdom consider wise men, talented with words, who, talented by lineage, most firmly have your laws in their minds, who can truly tell me, reveal before you, the answer to every one of the mysteries I seek from them.]

This first speech introduces a linguistic style that remains Elene's own through the whole poem; it does not change and consequently creates a very static image. This particular style includes the triadic construction just pointed out and finishes with a kind of recapitulation, the use of chiasmus as in *þæt ge geardagum / wyrde wæron wuldorcyninge, / dryhtne dyre ond dædhwæte* (290b–292)], and of the imperative. The triadic structure of Elene's rhetorical style becomes a constant pattern in five of Elene's seven major speeches (288–319, 333–376, 386–396, 643–654, 1073–1092); there are only two exceptions (574–584, 670–682). Chiasmus recurs in six of the seven speeches (all except 574–584) and even three times in her second speech. Recapitulations through the introduction of *þæt* clauses are also found in four of the seven long speeches and in two of the short ones. The occurrence of chiasmus is particularly felicitous as expression of iconographic style in that poem, since the function of chiasmus is to set clauses in a symmetric pattern forming a cross. Imperative, which is found in most of Elene's long speeches, becomes almost a constant in the shorter ones, whose main purpose is to give such orders as "tell, say, go." (406–410, 605–608, 621–626, for example).

The result of these stylistic devices is an intricate pattern that is repeated each time the saint speaks. This sophisticated regularity gives a static sense of artificiality and predictability that fits the stable presence of the saint. The patterns elaborate a highly static, majestic, impersonal, intricate, and official style. Such a constant, impersonal linguistic form fits the idea that Elene is speaking as an embodiment of the Church. This stability also reflects the concept that the Truth is one and immutable. The complex but regular and predictable design of Elene's speeches seems to be a linguistic reproduction of such material remains as many Anglo-Saxon crosses, such as the Ruthwell cross or the Farr Stone.[39]

These ideas are reinforced by the contrasting analysis of Judas's early speeches, of the devil's speech, and, finally, of Judas's speeches after his conversion. Judas's first four speeches (419–535, 611–618, 632–641,

656–651) contrast sharply with Elene's; they show a very personal, agitated style punctuated by first-person pronouns. Elene's use of the triadic construction and of the imperative are totally absent, while rhetorical questions recur. The first speech may be quoted as a reference; to the elaborate, impersonal use of paronomasia in Elene's discourse between lines 621 and 626 (quoted above), Judas answers:

| | |
|---|---|
| Hu mæg **ic** þæt findan | þæt swa fyrn gewearð |
| wintra gangum? | Is nu worn sceacen |
| tu hund oððe ma | geteled rime; |
| **ic** ne mæg areccan | nu **ic** þæt rim ne can ; |
| is nu feala siðþan | forð gewitenra, |
| froda ond godra | þe **us** fore wæron |
| gleawra gumena; | **ic** on geogoðewearð |
| on siðdagum | syððan acenned |
| cnihtgeong hæleð; | **ic** ne can þæt **ic** nat |
| findan on fyrhðe | þætswa fyrn gewearð. (632–641) |

[How can **I** find something that has grown so distant in the course of the years? A long time has gone by now, amounting to the number of two hundred years and more; I cannot even say since I do not know that number. Many wise men, knowledgeable and good, who lived before **us**, have passed away since then. I came into my youth during later days, as a young man born after. I cannot find in **my** heart that which I do not know, that which happened so long ago.]

None of Elene's stylistic devices appear in this speech. At this point, Judas's linguistic style and personal mood of complaint are far from the patterns of Elene's linguistic sophistication, but they are close to the later devil's discourse. A (gloomy and fevering spirit oppresses his heart) in such a way that Judas's mode of expression reflects the agitation of his heart and his anguish.[40] However, as soon as Judas converts, he readily adopts Elene's style and constructs his speeches exactly like hers.

Judas's crucial long speech (725–801) may be considered as the dramatic climax of the poem, since it calls for, precedes, and introduces the first miracle of the poem. In that speech, which gives expression to his conversion, Judas conforms to the structure of Elene's speeches; it may be taken as an example of Judas's new mode of expression. It is formed by an introductory invocation that is a ten-line-long succession of clauses pausing in a semicolon, and whose content is a praising prayer that acknowledges God's power (725–734a). Accordingly, the prayer starts with God's attributes of power, *Dryhten Hælend, þu ðe ahst doma* . . . (Lord Savior, you who have the power . . . ). A dogmatic section follows to show that Judas has been enlightened and understands the faith. This statement of faith is divided into three sections, like all of Elene's speeches. The first passage is dedicated to the description of the good angels (734b–759a); the second deals with the fallen angels (759b–771) and the third tells about Christ's imminent rule of earth as soon as the True Cross is discovered (772–792a). Judas ends with a recapitulation, which is a petition prayer asking God's help in the *Inventio* (792b–801) so that the rule of Christianity may take place.

The overall construction of this speech is an amazingly intricate and sophisticated iconographic design. The introduction starts at the beginning of verse 725 but ends in the middle of verse 734. The first section of the second part begins and ends in the middle of a line; but the second section about the fallen angels finishes at the end of line 771 with a period, as if to separate completely evil from Christ, who is the theme of the following verses. However, Christ's linking with the Father is revealed by their sharing of line 792. The petition prayer, which recapitulates the whole speech by announcing its full motive, is introduced by an invocation parallel to the initial call: *Forlæt nu, lifes Fruma* . . . (Let now, Author of life . . .). God listens to the petition prayer and grants the miracle asked for.

The length of this speech creates an impression of suspense and expectation that prepares the reader to witness the miracle. A smoke rises from the spot where the Cross is hidden and Judas continues speaking, delivering another speech which starts, in all logic, with a thanksgiving prayer and resolves itself with another petition prayer. This shorter speech, as the previous one and like Elene's, is formed of three parts and contains the patterns observed earlier in Elene's: the use of the imperative and of the chiasmus. However, this similitude in style does not mean equality between Elene and Judas; the two saints have a very different way of using the imperative. Elene remains the queen; her imperatives reflect her imperial status and the supremacy of the Church; she gives orders, commands. On the other hand, Judas's imperative reflects the mood of submission, hope, and prayer, even when he addresses the devil as in "wite ðe þe gearwor/ þæt ðu unsnyttrum anforlete/ leohta beorhtostond lufan dryhtnes" ("May you recognize most clearly that you have lost foolishly the brightest of existence and the love of the Lord") (945b–947).

The triadic division of the speeches, in itself, can be interpreted as an iconographic representation of the Trinity, and for that reason was not allowed to Judas until his conversion. This radical change in style illustrates Judas's human condition and free will, with the capacity to choose sinfulness, but also the ability to resist wickedness and embrace holiness. For the same reason, the devil cannot use this type of speech; he repeats the patterns and personal tone that were also characteristic in the speeches of Judas prior to his conversion. Consequently, it may be argued that in this poem, Cynewulf gives to the devil the function of validating Judas's new voice by means of contrast. The devil begins by depicting himself as a victim and shows the personal style by repeating the first-person pronouns:

Hwæt is þis, la, manna          þe **minne** eft
þurh fyrngeflit                        folgaþ wyrdeð,
iceð ealdne nið,                      æhta strudeð?
þis is singal sacu;                    sawla en moton,
manfremmende                     in **minum** leng
æhtum wunigan;                    un cwom elþeodig
þone **ic** ær on firenum          fæstne talde,
halað **mec** bereafod             rihta gehwylces,
feohgestreona;                       nis ðætfæger sið. (902–910)

[Listen! What man is this who once more through old strife destroys **my** retinue, increases the old enmity, robs **my** belongings? This is endless strife; sinful souls may no longer dwell within **my** realm; now a stranger has come, one who before **I** thought was bound fast by sins, has taken away each of **my** rights, of **my** treasures; this is not fair].

The speech continues using first-person pronouns, eight in total within the eighteen lines. The pronouns are also stressed by alliteration in several lines along the speech (902, 906, 915, 917, 929). The alliteration with the first-person possessive, on line 929b, is particularly poignant since the first-person pronoun alliterates with sin: "ond **manþeawum-minum** folgaþ" ("and will follow my sinful way"). The shift of tone from the praying mood of Judas, who went from praise to petition and thanksgiving prayers, to the devil's personal complaint surprises; the contrast underlines the change that has taken place in Judas. The parallelism between the devil's speech and Judas's pre-conversion style demonstrates that Judas was inhabited by demoniac forces; he was not master of his own potential for goodness; the devil governed his whole being, was guiding his language and his thoughts; he was on the earth what the damned are in hell. Since the devil's style resembles Judas's "pre-Christian" initial speech, it can be seen as emblematic of evil and points out Judas's spiritual growth. The devil has lost his power over Judas, while both Elene and Judas have gained a power; each of the two saints at the end of the poem brings recognition and *lof* in this world, but this *lof* will also "siþþanlifge mid englum / awa to ealdre, ecan lifes blæd, / dream mid dugeþum" ("will live with the angels forever and ever, in the glory of eternal life, joy among the hosts").[41]

    Direct speech in this poem has often been judged too intensely didactic, having "virtually no dramatic or narrative function."[42] Yet this apparent platitude is very carefully crafted according to meaningful and sophisticated patterns; it might not be in tune with the tastes of the modern age, but it was probably pleasing to the Anglo-Saxon religious audience. Mostly, this impersonal, structured style develops and displays one of the characteristic of holiness. The omission of all first-person pronouns expresses the negation of self-interest and personal desires, and therefore, the surrender of the self. *Elene* is not the only poem to display personal style as a mark of evil and impersonal speech as indicative of holiness. The same personal, defiant characteristics appear in Satan's speeches in *Genesis B* (356–438). Even more striking is the case of the devil in *Juliana:* In this poem, the devil's speech contains some forty first-person pronouns; in addition, the comparison with Juliana's prayers, in Cynewulf's version of the hagiography and in his source, reveals that the Anglo-Saxon poet avoided all the petition prayers and that the saint never asks God to protect her against the torments of torture. It may be concluded that the negation of the self is one of Cynewulf's main points, which explains that the language of the holy ones is systematically structured and impersonal but seems as stable and organized as the stones used to build a church; it leaves no room for personal desire and expression, but it celebrates the timeless and Divine. Cynewulf's intensely iconographic language adds to the timelessness of this message as the poem, like a material religious object, imprints its message on the eyes as much as on the ears of the reader.[43]

## Notes

1. Even though nothing is known about Cynewulf, it can be asserted that he is the chronological and literary successor of Caedmon. But, unlike Caedmon's, his identity and existence remained unknown until the middle of the nineteenth century. He appears in no extant contemporary report and, in spite his effort to sign his poems and be identified, his name was not noticed until the 1840s. Grimm's edition of *Elene* and Kemble's almost simultaneous work on the *Vercelli Book* led these two scholars to the discovery of Cynewulf's acrostic signature. The runes of Cynewulf's acrostic signature appear in four Anglo-Saxon poems: *Juliana, Christ, The Fate of the Apostle,* and *Elene.* The primary sources for *Elene* are as follows:

   (a) Pamela Gradon, ed., *Cynewulf's Elene* (New York: Appleton-Century-Crofts, 1966). *Elene* occupies from folio 121 to folio 133 of the manuscript called *Vercelli Book* because it was mysteriously found in the little town of Vercelli, in northern Italy. In addition to *Elene,* the manuscript contains a number of homilies on traditional themes of meditation: *Andreas,* Cynewulf's *Fate of the Apostles,* the poem called *The Soul and the Body, The Dream of the Rood,* and the prose *Life of Saint Guthlac. Elene* appears towards the end of the book, after some homilies and before *Guthlac,* which is the last text in the manuscript. The *Vercelli Book* is relatively well preserved and protected by a nineteenth-century leather cover that bears the following inscription: "Homiliarum liber ignoti idiomatic" ("Book of homilies written in an unidentified language").

    (b)  *Acta Cyriaci* in *Acta sanctorum Junii, ex latinis et græcis aliarumque gentium monumentis, servata primigenia veterum,* 1743. Facsimile edition published in Brussels by Société des Bollandistes.

    (c)  Rosemary Woolf, ed., *Cynewulf's Juliana* (New York: Appleton-Century-Crofts, 1966).

    (d)  Charles Kent, ed., *Elene, an Old English Poem* (Boston: Gin, 1891).

    (e)  G. P. Krapp and E. V. Dobbie, eds. *The Anglo-Saxon Poetic Records,* vol. 2, *Vercelli Book* (New York: Columbia University Press, 1935).

2. The title of the poem was bestowed by Jacob Grimm in 1890. This title has sometimes been judged improper. Rosemary Woolf argues, for instance, that "it is necessary to stress the inappropriateness of the title" because the structure of the poem becomes "clear if the subject is taken to be either the Cross or Judas" (Woolf, *Cynewulf's Juliana,* 46).

3. James Doubleday, "The Speech of Stephen and the Tone of *Elene,*" in *Anglo-Saxon Poetry: Essays in Appreciation for John C. McGalliard,* ed. Lewis Nicholson and Dolores Warwick Frese (Notre Dame: University of Notre Dame Press, 1975), 116–123.

4. Alexandra Hennesey Olsen, "Cynewulf's Autonomous Women: A Reconsideration of Juliana and Elene," in *New Readings on Women in Old English Literature* (Bloomington: Indiana University Press, 1990), 222–234.

5. Helen Damico, "The Valkyrie Reflex in Old English Literature," in *New Readings on Women in Old English Literature* (Bloomington: Indiana University Press, 1990), 176–190.

6. This allegorical interpretative model has been defended as well by other critics, such as Earl Anderson, Thomas Hill, and Jackson Campbell.

7. Jane Chance, *Woman as Hero in Old English Literature* (Syracuse, N.Y.: Syracuse University Press, 1986).

8. Jackson Campbell, "Cynewulf's Multiple Revelations," *Medievalia et Humanistica* 3 (1972).

9. Kenneth Holum, *Theodosian Empresses: Women and Imperial Dominium in Late Antiquity* (Berkeley: University of California Press, 1988).

10. The title of *Augusta* was created by the first Roman emperor, Augustus, for his wife Livia.

11. Once Christianity became the official religion of the Roman Empire, historians began to record the generous deeds of the empresses. Theodoret of Cyrrhus, for instance, describes how Flacilla visited the poor. Gregory of Nyssa writes long commentaries on Flacilla's "zeal for the faith"; he sees her as "the image of philanthropy . . . the pillar of the Church, decoration of altars, wealth of the needy, the right hand which satisfied many, the common haven of those who are heavy laden." From "Oratio funebris Flacillam Imperatricem," in *Patrologia Graeca,* vol. 46, *The Writings of Saint Gregory of Nyssa: Patrologiae cursus completes,* ed. J. P. Migne (Cambridge: Chadwyck-Healey), 877–892.

12. Martin Garruchaga, ed. and trans., *Vita,* vol. 3, in *Eusebius of Caesarea: De vita Constantini* (Madrid: Gredos, 1994), 47, 1.

13. Garruchaga, *De vita Constantini,* 47, 1–2.

14. *Sigedrihten* used in reference to God may be found in the following poems and lines: *Andreas* 60, 877, 1453; *Christ* 128; *Descent into Hell* 92, 111; *Genesis*

523, 778; Guthlac B 1238. *Sigedrihten* defines God also in the *Metrical Charms* and in the *Meters of Boethius.*

15. *Drihten,* on the other hand, seems to be referring to both secular and spiritual lords. Commenting on the *Seafarer,* Orchard points out the "dual sense of certain words, both Christian and heroic, most notably *drihten,* which in the space of three lines refers to lords both secular and spiritual." Andy Orchard, *Pride and Prodigies* (Toronto: University of Toronto Press, 2003).

16. The use of *sigedrihten* in reference to Hroðgar and Eadgils surprises the reader for two reasons. First, both kings, being pagan, are not expected to be associated with a compound usually reserved to refer to the Christian God. Second, while Eadgils may be considered victorious when he is called *sigedrihten,* in line 391 of *Beowulf,* Hoðgar is not even engaged in any battle and may be considered defeated by Grendel since he is ready to welcome Beowulf's help against the monster whose attacks he has been unable to control. As pointed out by Andy Orchard, before the arrival of Beowulf, "the utter helplessness and impotence of the Danes in the face of Grendel's predations are stressed twice in practically identical terms" (*A Critical Companion to* Beowulf [Rochester, N.Y.: D. S. Brewer, 2003]). It is consequently surprising that at this point, Hroðgar should be called *sigedrihten* by one of the followers. The situation may suggest that pagan kings can be perceived as *sigedrihten* when they are considered to have fulfilled their earthly duties toward the members of their *comitatus.*

17. It is remarkable that Cynewulf never defines Elene in reference to a male, even to her son in spite of his political importance as the emperor and the one who sends her on the mission. In contrast, in *Beowulf,* seven of the women who are mentioned have no name and are defined only in terms of their relationship to a male: Healfdene's daughter, Beowulf's mother, Ongentheow's wife, Hygelac's daughter, and so on. Even Grendel's mother, whose actions are central to the poem, remains unnamed and is defined in relationship to her son.

18. These observations obviously favor the allegorical interpretation of Elene as an image of the Church.

19. Alvin Lee, *The Guest Hall of Eden: Four Essays on the Design of Old English Poetry* (New Haven, Conn.: Yale University Press, 1972).

20. Since before the time of Bede, exchanges with the Eastern part of the Roman Empire had been frequent in Anglo-Saxon England. In the seventh century, for instance, Theodore of Tarsus was sent to Britain as archbishop. More influentially for the arts, Benedict Biscop, abbot of Wearmouth and Jarrow, brought back from Rome "many holy pictures of the saints" (Bede, "Lives of the Abbots of Wearmouth and Jarrow," in *The Age of Bede,* trans. D. H. Farmer [New York: Penguin Classics, 1983]). These art pieces were, according to art historians, Byzantine-style icons painted on small wooden panels, such as the seventh-century Roman icon of the Virgin and Child with angels in Santa Maria in Trastevere (164 x 116 cm).

21. Michael Roberts, *The Jeweled Style* (Ithaca, N.Y.: Cornell University Press, 1989).

22. This expression was first employed in Thomas Hill, *Old English Poetry and the Sapiential Tradition* (Ithaca, N.Y.: Cornell University Press, 1967), 59.

23. Jacques Le Goff, *Un moyen âge en images* (Paris: Hazan, 2007).

24. Le Goff, *Un moyen âge,* 148. Even though this image comes from a later period, it retains all the iconographic characteristics of previous art.

25. Jean-Claude Schmitt, *La raison des gestes dans l'occident médiéval* (Paris: Editions Gallimard, 1990), 38.
26. Konrad Onash, *Icons* (New York: A. S. Barnes , 1963).
27. Michael Alexander, *The Earliest English Poems* (London: Penguin, 1991), 85.
28. Not only does this description echo Byzantine iconography, it also reproduces images from illuminated manuscripts of the period such as the Anglo-Saxon representation of Saint John in the *Lindisfarne Gospels* and many of the portraits of the *Book of Kells*.
29. Roberta Frank, "Some Uses of Paronomasia in Old English Scriptural Verse," *Speculum* 47 (1972): 207–226.
30.

| | | |
|---|---|---|
| Line 147: | rice under **roderum** | þurh his **rode** treo. |
| Line 206: | on **rode** treo | **rodora** waldend . . . |
| Line 482: | of **rode** ahæfen | **rodera** wealdend . . . |
| Line 624: | hwær seo **rod** wunige | **rador**cyninges . . . |
| Line 631: | rice under **roderum,** | gif he ða **rode** ne tæhte . . . |
| Line 855: | on **rode** treo; | **rodor** eal geswearc . . . |
| Line 886: | **rod** arǣred | **rodor**cyninges beam . . . |
| Line 918: | ræd under **roderum;** | ic þa **rode** ne þearf . . . |
| Line 1022: | reod of **roderum;** | heo þa **rode**heht . . . |
| Line 1066: | mid þam on **rode** waes | **rodera** wealdend . . . |
| Line 1074: | **rode roder**cyninges | ryhte getæhtesð . . . |
| Line 1234: | **rode** under **roderum** | þa se ricesða . . . |

31.

| | | |
|---|---|---|
| Line 679: | **hæle**ð**um** to helpe | þæt me **halig** God . . . |
| Line 935: | **hæle**ð hildedeor- | him wæs **Halig** Gast. |
| Line 1011: | **hæle**ð**um**to helpe | þær sio **halige** rod . . . |
| Line 1203: | **hæle**ð**a**cynnes, | to þære **halgan** byrig . . . |

32. Strictly speaking, *man* and *mann* are not perfect homophones because the former has a long "a" and the latter a short "a." Consequently, there would have been a phonic difference for an Anglo-Saxon speaker. However, the two words are definitely a pun that works at the aural, visual, and alliterative levels and fit the conscious graphic, lapidary quality of Cynewulf's language.
33. It is always dubious to stress the punctuation of an Anglo-Saxon text because punctuation is more often than not an addition of the editor of the poem. However, such additions are carefully introduced and most likely represent the author's intensions. In this particular case, the structure of the sentences fit perfectly the punctuation introduced by the editor.
34. Erich Auerbach, *Literary Language and Its Public in Late Latin Antiquity and in the Middle Ages*, trans. Ralf Manheim (Princeton, N.J.: Princeton University Press, 1965).
35. The fact that direct discourse represents over 40 percent of *Elene* (538 lines out of 1321) and 63 percent of *Juliana* (460 lines out of 730) supports the hypothesis of the importance of the analysis of the speeches in Cynewulf's poems.
36. Wife of Theodocius II (408–450) who became a devout Christian. Like Elene, she is remembered for going to Jerusalem to get important relics. She brought back to Constantinople the chains of Saint Peter and the relics of Saint Stephen. The marble intarsia representing Saint Eudocia is found

in Istanbul; reproduced in Kurt Weitzmann, *The Icon: Holy Images—Sixth to Fourteenth Century* (New York: George Braziller, 1978), plate 10.

37. This icon of Saint Michael is found in Venice; reproduced in Weitzmann, *The Icon*, plate 14.

38. In *Juliana*, the devil himself confesses to the holy Virgin that "oft ic syne ofteah, / ablende bealoþoncum beona unim / monna cynnes, misthelme forbrægd / þuh attres odeagna leoman / sweartum scurum" ("Often have I deprived of vision, blinded with wicked thoughts, a great number of mankind; I obscured the light of their eyes with dark mist with dark showers of poisonous arrows").

39. The Farr Stone, an eighth-century cross-slab, may be taken as an example. The comparison between Elene's predictable speeches that repeat again and again the same intricate patterns shows similarities in the reproduced designs of the crosses. Similarities extend even to the details; for instance, the chiasmus, as a symmetric figure of speech and rhetorical emblem of symmetry, can be compared to the two at the center of the Farr Stone, as their intertwined necks make an X shape.

40. "Him wæs geomor sefa / hat æt heortan (627b–628a); Iudas . . . gnornsorge wæg" (655).

41. *The Seafarer* (78b–80a), in Bruce Mitchell and Fred C. Robinson, *A Guide to Old English*, 7th ed. (Hoboken, N.J.: Wiley-Blackwell, 2007).

42. Barbara Raw, *The Art and Background of Old English Poetry* (London: Edward Arnold, 1978).

43. Cynewulf's iconographic style and his appeal to the eyes indicate, as does his acrostic signature, that he was expecting his texts to be read and appreciated visually.

# A Precarious Quest for Salvation: The Theophilus Legend in Text and Image

JERRY ROOT

The legend of Theophilus—his spiritual rescue from the hands of the devil by the Virgin—obviously resonated well with medieval audiences of the twelfth through the fourteenth centuries. It was represented frequently in a variety of media, including literature, sculpture, stained glass, and manuscript illuminations.[1] Rutebeuf's "stage" version of the story, *Le Miracle de Théophile,* embodies many of the key textual and visual features of the legend and illustrates well why this particular story, from outside the canon of saints' lives and biblical types, could take on such prominence in the medieval imagination. Rutebeuf's play is a deeply humanist reaction to and interpretation of the new economy of salvation that the Catholic Church put forth with its institutionalization of the sacrament of confession, begun in 1215. This economy of salvation is also present in the Theophilus story that Rutebeuf inherits from Gautier de Coinci and in the visual representations of the Theophilus story that precede Rutebeuf's play, in sculpture at Souillac, in stained glass at Beauvais and Laon, and in the Parisian manuscript illustrations of the Ingeburg Psalter. Perhaps not surprisingly, the visual representation of the Theophilus story that most matches Rutebeuf's interpretation is the near-contemporary sculpted version by Jean de Chelles on the north transept portal of the Cathedral of Notre Dame in Paris. These two representations of this popular medieval story clearly resonate with one another. They both interpret the general thrust of the Church's institutionalization of confession, broadly conceived here as repentance, as a new path to individual salvation. The context and content of Jean de Chelles's sculpted relief of this story make clear that he sees this new path mainly as institutionally sanctioned and controlled. His relief nonetheless also gives evidence of a tension in the individual's relation to the institutional path to salvation. Rutebeuf's representation of the

*Medievalia et Humanistica,* New Series, Number 34 (Paul Maurice Clogan, ed.), Rowman & Littlefield Publishers, Inc., 2008.

story is clearly less institutionally focused but equally complicated. It relegates the institution of the Church to a secondary role and emphasizes the struggle of the individual to exert control over his own salvation. His Théophile finds himself existentially stranded by this responsibility; he ultimately chooses a more private and idiosyncratic path out of his spiritual despair.

In this paper I will focus on these two representations of the Theophilus story as interpretations of a new way of thinking about individual salvation. In particular I will look closely at the way the individual character of Theophilus is portrayed and at the way both representations create a dynamic of figuration to convey his story. The new economy of salvation seems to demand a new, or at least rethought, relation of literal to figural, of individual to type, of inner disposition to outer appearance. I think that Rutebeuf and Jean de Chelles struggle with rather than resolve the issues surrounding a representation of a new relation of the individual to his or her own salvation. Their struggle is surely aesthetic, religious, and personal. In this sense it captures the shifting technology of the self brought about by the legislation of 1215 toward a greater sense of individual responsibility in the path to salvation.[2]

As extensive and pervasive as the Theophilus legend was in medieval representation, it is somewhat surprising that a longer, synthetic study of the legend in different media has not been undertaken.[3] While this paper cannot be the broad synthesis of visual and textual aspects of the Theophilus legend that is needed, I do hope to make this synthesis between the Rutebeuf play and the Jean de Chelles relief. Ultimately, I think that this comparison of visual and textual representations of this story will illuminate the way both work formally and aesthetically as well as the way they engage with the social and religious context in which they appear.

I would like to turn first to the visual representation of the Theophilus story at Notre-Dame de Paris. The figurative dynamic of salvation is more uniformly hierarchical here than in the *Miracle*. The Theophilus story was sculpted in the center tympanum of the north transept of the Cathedral of Notre Dame in Paris, sometime between 1245 and 1250.[4] The literature on this relief has discussed the three-tiered image in a piecemeal fashion.[5] Fryer's exhaustive census of the visual representations of Theophilus discusses and mentions only the middle register. Most other discussions concentrate on the middle and upper registers. Only Williamson discusses the lintel, which clearly makes for a third register, visually part of the tympanum image. All three registers are important for my reading.

Legend of de Theophilus, north transept portal, Notre Dame, Paris,
c. 1245–50. Photo courtesy of visualtravelguide.com.
Reproduced with permission.

The Theophilus relief is located in the tympanum of the door of the
north transept, which is dedicated to the life of the Virgin. This context figures importantly in any understanding of the Theophilus story.
It is, after all, an example of a "miracle" of the Virgin, of *her* works, of
*her* intervention in human life. Theophilus exemplifies her goodness.
I think this exemplary status of his story must condition the way we
view this version of it. This larger context clearly informs also the representation of the nativity that forms the base of the Theophilus story.
While the content of the lintel (the Nativity, Presentation in the Temple, Massacre of the Innocent, and Flight into Egypt) is not particularly significant in relation to the Theophilus story above, its figurative
function is significant. We are clearly meant to see this "miracle" of the
Virgin as a type, a model, of which the miracle of Theophilus above is
just another variant.[6]

The figuralism works two ways here. First, we see the story of the Virgin's immaculate conception as a figure for her intervention in
Theophilus's life. Second, we see the story of the birth of Christ as a figure for the Theophilus story portrayed above. Both interpretations put

Theophilus's story into the larger context of biblical typology so typical of medieval sculpture. In the first case, we would be led to think of both the lintel and the relief of Theophilus as stories of the Virgin's supernatural powers. In the second case, we would be led to see the incarnation of Christ as the ideal form of supernatural intervention.[7] Both interpretations would urge the viewer to think of the Theophilus story as hierarchically determined by a higher form. That is, his "miracle" does not belong to him but is instead an instance of Christian charity generally and of Christ's and the Virgin's intermediary role in the salvation of individuals. This larger context compels us to see Theophilus's story as rather insignificant, or at least as no more than a discrete realization of the salvific powers of Christ and the Virgin.

The middle register of the tympanum (with the four traditional scenes of Theophilus's story) can indeed be read as the confrontation of the Virgin and the devil. Facing this tympanum, one is struck by its elegant symmetry. This is especially the case if one contrasts the twelfth-century image of the Theophilus story at Souillac (and in particular after reading Shapiro's analysis of it). From the viewer's left, the devil in triumph over the sinner Theophilus is balanced to the far right by the Virgin in triumph over the devil. Each of the four scenes depicted juxtaposes two characters facing each other simply—the middle scenes depict exchange, the outer scenes confrontation. The outer scenes clearly juxtapose good and evil as much as they juxtapose the devil and the Virgin. The figure of the devil frames the whole register. The sculptor further emphasizes symmetry by having the devil face inward in both of the outer images. As the more crowded nativity scene on the lintel gives way to the four images here, so too these four images fold into the singular frame of the upper register. Visually the vertical economy is typological and didactic. The story of the Virgin and the birth of Christ are types that the individual sinner, like Theophilus, would like to but cannot really follow. The middle register, framed by the devil, is clearly the fallen world where the "Anemis m'a enchantei" ("devil tricked me"), as Rutebeuf says in his *Repentance* (40). This register represents man's inevitable turn to evil—in spite of the positive models he has been given by Christ and the Virgin. The upper register is clearly the didactic "sentence" that provides a resolution to the perils of the middle register and the fallen world. The unity of the upper image could not be more apparent. It has only one "frame" or episode, in a sense resolving the particularities of the middle register, in another sense shifting the life of Theophilus to exemplary status: He is the fallen and yet saved sinner. He is no longer the individual with multiple particularities, trials, sins; he has himself be-

come one, a type. This status is reinforced in his and the other characters' posture. Three of the four characters surrounding Theophilus mirror his gesture of repentance with their heads placed in their hands.
They are spectators of and participants in his repentance, now shifted
from the individual, private act to an exemplary, public act through the
bishop's sermon. The middle register announces this shift and invites
the viewer to read vertically with several key signs. The pointed steeple
and sharp vertical columns of the church lead the viewer upward. And
so too does the sword/cross that the Virgin uses to threaten the devil.
Each of these signs belongs to the church, like the open nave of the
church where Theophilus prays. We are invited clearly to choose this institutional portal, this pathway, this opening to pursue salvation and flee
from the devil. The bishop and the admiring figures in the upper register seem the fulfillment of having chosen the path of the Church for salvation—a kind of peaceful, sacramental, ecclesiastical symmetry.

The symmetry and context of the Theophilus tympanum suggest that
Jean de Chelles and certainly the thirteenth-century Church believe that
salvation is available to the individual only with the help or intervention
of the Church itself. The figure of the Church in the middle register is
a mirror of the north transept portal for the individual penitent: He or
she (like Theophilus) must pass through this doorway, through the institution and through the sacraments, to find salvation. While I think
this message of Church control could not be clearer, I also think it is not
the whole story. And, I think that one of the reasons the Theophilus
story is so widespread and powerful in the medieval imagination is because it also hints at another path to salvation.

In order to glimpse this other path, we must reread the middle register. Alongside the more obvious ecclesiastical signs (the church spire,
columns, and sword/cross that point upward), Jean de Chelles embeds
another quieter, more horizontal set of signs: the hand gestures of
Theophilus and the devil. The hands in this register tell a slightly different story than the one we saw above and point the viewer to a more subtle interpretation of this middle register. The first image of the series
shows Theophilus paying homage to the devil. The "joined hands" image is a traditional sign of homage, an indication of equality and dependence between vassal and lord.[8] This is a horizontal gesture, one that
keeps the viewer in the middle register and the secular world. The
devil's and Theophilus's arms extend in an even parallel plane and reinforce the horizonality here, even if the devil is standing and
Theophilus is kneeling. The Salatin figure further reinforces the sense
of horizontal (and feudal) bond by wrapping his left arm and hand

around Theophilus's back. His right hand sits prominently on his chest, holding the contract that Theophilus has signed. The hands all reinforce horizontal, human, fraternal relations. They enfold and embrace evenly. They symbolize the proximity and intimacy of feudal and human relations. Of course, this impression of fraternity is supposed also to be undercut by other subtle signs. Theophilus, in a sinister manner, faces left. The Salatin figure envelops him with his left hand. The face in the loin of the devil peers down menacingly at the viewer to suggest that all this fraternity and horizontality are false appearances.

The second episode in the middle register is very similar to the first. Here we have Theophilus to the left, now facing right, with an unidentified character sitting opposite (and facing left). Behind and to the side of Theophilus there is a small figure of a devil. This image copies and continues the story of the first image. Hands and arms again embrace and enfold. Theophilus and the character opposite extend their arms in a parallel and horizontal fashion that repeats the feudal ceremony of the first image. In this case, they are not performing a ceremony of homage, even if their relation is symbolically similar. Theophilus hands money to the character, displays his newfound wealth to the world, puts on an appearance of charity. The clasped hands and exchange of money suggest fraternity, proximity, human bonds. But again the falseness of this impression is signaled by the now largely symbolic devil whose left hand reaches across Theophilus's body to put coins in Theophilus's left hand. The devil's left arm extends to Theophilus's left arm and effectively wraps up Theophilus.[9] He is caught in the embrace of the devil. But he is obviously active himself in this fraternal relation as he has visually taken the place of the devil from the first image. It is now Theophilus who embraces, beguiles, and extends the reach of the devil's grip.

The third image in the middle register constitutes an abrupt shift and in many ways stands on its own. The devil is gone. Of the four images in the middle register this is the only one with just two characters and the only one where we do not have the figure of the devil. The frame of the church building indicates clearly a geographical shift in position away from the first two images. The figure of Theophilus and in particular the position of his hands provide the viewer with a constant thread to help make sense of the continuity. Clearly the "joined hands" image here resonates with those of the first two images. The gesture of prayer is, of course, also the gesture of feudal homage.[10] But in this case, the joined and praying hands do not link with any other hands. This image of hands on their own, unconnected to someone else, suggests that the feudal bond, the bond with the devil, has been broken. Likewise, this image breaks with the theme of proximity and fraternity of the first two images. The Theophilus figure is clearly alone, isolated. His arms are not extended in a parallel and horizontal fashion to link with someone else. On the contrary, this is an image of distance and separation, of isolation. Indeed, as the gesture of prayer suggests, it is an image of supplication. The Virgin seems to be visualized as Theophilus's only source of help, but she remains distant, small, symbolic. She is represented by a statue in the church, thus very much remaining within the frame of the institution, symbolically an extension of its power. Unlike the devil of the first two images, she does not embrace Theophilus. Nor does she appear to coexist horizontally with him. On the contrary she remains at a distance and sits, symbolically, high up in the towering church edifice. It is as if by merely walking into church and joining his hands in supplication to the Virgin, Theophilus could undo the feudal bond that this same hand gesture signaled in the first image.

While this image seems to reinforce the message of Church control in matters of salvation, it also hints at a different, more idiosyncratic economy of salvation. In the first place, Theophilus's isolation here can be read as an undoing of the feudal bonds of the previous images, but it can also be read as independence, autonomy, as a realization that he must (and can) take his salvation into his own hands. If we look at the position of the hands in all of the first three images, we could read them as an allegory of an individual sinner's fall and repentance. The position is nearly identical in all three images. In the first, it is the devil's hands, pointing ever so slightly upward, that entrap Theophilus in sin. In the second, it is Theophilus's hands, pointing ever so slightly upward, enjoying the fruits of ill gain, focused on the horizontal world. In this third image, Theophilus's hands break free from the bonds of this world to focus, symbolically, inward on himself and upward to the Virgin. Perhaps the most notable shift in this third image is the reversal of Theophilus's kneeling position from the first image. The staging in the second image showed us a Theophilus indeed facing in the right direction but nonetheless seated high in all the pride of his worldly, ill-gotten gain. This third image clearly implies that Theophilus has really turned, has "converted" himself from evil to good. The statue of the Virgin and the church seem to sanction this conversion, but the shifted position is clearly one of the only means that Jean de Chelles has to signal an inner turn as well. The relatively diminished size of the figure of Theophilus here also suggests a kind of symbolic attitude of repentance. If this is the case, then the absence of the devil is quite significant. For it suggests that Theophilus's conversion took place even before the Virgin has had a chance to take any action—as she will in the fourth scene. In other words, simply turning—sincerely, independently, on the inside—is sufficient to ban the devil and put the sinner on the road to salvation.[11]

It seems quite clear that for Jean de Chelles the remainder of this path to salvation must pass through the institution. The fourth scene supports this interpretation of institutional control. But it does so in a fairly idiosyncratic way that does not necessarily negate the possibility that Theophilus's own, inner conversion was what made all this possible. In the first place, Theophilus himself retains the very same position of scene three, but it is as if his conversion and supplication have allowed him to grow. The Virgin similarly has miraculously, fantastically, taken flesh, moved into action, and now towers over the devil. The absence of the church edifice from the preceding scene may simply suggest a change in location, but it also suggests a far less dominant image of institutional surveillance. The sword she holds clearly is meant to resemble a cross and points upward to the exemplary scene. But this does not necessarily negate Theophilus's role in his own conversion. Finally, to pick up again on the narrative of the hands, it is clear that the Virgin stands between Theophilus and the devil, keeping their hands, which are in a very similar (almost praying) position, apart. The devil no longer holds sway—physically or spiritually—over Theophilus. We have come full circle from the first scene of the devil's power, symbolized by Theophilus's kneeling gesture of homage, to a scene of the devil humbled and supplicant to the Virgin and Theophilus. Indeed, the devil's hands seem to mirror Theophilus's—both are raised and joined in prayer. The line from the one to the other creates a parallel line, pointing upward, like the Virgin's sword, to the upper register.

One additional detail of this middle register seems worth noting. The second scene, depicting Theophilus's false charity, is raised as if on a pedestal. This odd detail sets this scene apart from the others in the middle register. It seems to go along with the symbolic function of the small devil figure and to tell the viewer: Beware—this scene of charity is false, it is merely a "staged" representation of charity. This symbolic function seems to fit with the larger message of the tympanum. The "stage" here clearly parallels the pulpit of the upper level where the bishop preaches Theophilus's example. By equating these two scenes, Jean de Chelles seems to be suggesting again a vertical and figural economy. The power that the individual has in this world is an illusion. The lower image looks like charity but in fact points to the gap between appearance and reality. The upper image converts the stage to a pulpit and its didactic message and ecclesiastical frame in effect close the gap between appearance and reality. This correspondence reinforces the message of institutional control. The "stage" highlights and exacerbates the gap between appearance and reality. The pulpit closes that gap and tells things as they really are, or should be.

Jean de Chelles's version of the Theophilus story clearly sets it within a typological framework that folds his individual fall and repentance into the larger context of Christ's incarnation and the Virgin's miracles. In this sense, Theophilus and the whole middle register are mere examples of larger forces of Christian charity. The Virgin's intervention and, above all, the institution's path to salvation seem paramount in this story of sin and redemption. The story that the bishop of the upper register is telling is one of Christ's charity, of the Virgin's charity and intervention, and ultimately of Theophilus's good fortune to have been the object of these benevolent forces. The middle register tells a somewhat naturalistic narrative of Theophilus's encounter with evil and conversion to good. Most of the details of this narrative can be recuperated by the broader figural dynamic to serve the message of institutional control.[12] It is possible that the third scene, depicting Theophilus's moment of repentance and conversion, resists this typology. But it does so timidly. Other visualizations of this moment, including the prostrate Theophilus at Souillac and the confessing/penitent Theophilus in the Ingebourg Psalter, might have served Jean de Chelles better if he had wanted to reinforce the responsibility and power or the interiority of the individual, through confession and repentance.[13]

It is tempting therefore to conclude that Jean de Chelles envisions the story as a negative exemplum of Theophilus's fall and a positive exemplum of the Virgin's intervention. This message would be supported by the typological reading we have done above. The underlying message of institutional control of repentance and salvation would also fit with this conclusion. One final detail, however, troubles this interpretation. The quieter narrative of the hands that we saw in the middle register is maintained in the upper register. Here, as in the last two scenes of the middle register, hands are not joined in feudal homage or fraternal bonds. The bishop's right hand points horizontally at a paper that he holds in his left hand. The horizontal position of his arm echoes and parallels the horizontally positioned arms of the middle register. But now the illusion of feudal power has been transformed into an example of the pitfalls of the fallen world. The paper he holds is the contract that the Virgin has taken back from the devil. This pointing hand seems to underline the exemplarity and didacticism of the upper register. Theophilus's contract with the devil has become an example of his recovery from sin, of his repentance, of the Virgin's miracle. In a sense it is no longer Theophilus's story; it belongs to the Church, to the bishop, to the community. The message of exemplarity is further underlined by the community members who all sit, apparently listening to the "miracle of Theophilus." Three of the four have the same hand gesture; they rest their chin quite noticeably in their hand. This gesture clearly mirrors, indeed, imitates Theophilus's. For he too rests his chin in his hand. The traditional interpretation of the head-in-hand gesture is a "man of sorrow." [14] And it is imaginable that Theophilus would hear his story with sorrow. Likewise, following the logic of exemplarity, it would make sense that all the listeners would immediately put their heads in their hands, sharing the sorrow of Theophilus and his story. But the head-in-hand gesture can also be interpreted as a penitential gesture.[15] If Theophilus's gesture is supposed to indicate repentance, then the message of the upper register is quite different than one of institutional control or typologically conceived salvation. Following the hand narrative that began below, we have to see the head-in-hand gesture as one that defies typology. It does not signify a feudal bond, nor does it imply a link to the devil; but it also does not point upward to a higher power (as the devil's hands and the Virgin's cross in the final scene of the middle register clearly do). This hand gesture seems to indicate the idiosyncrasy and interiority of repentance. If this is the case, then the seated Theophilus in the upper register is the transformation through penitence of the seated and sinful Theophilus of the lower register. It is possible, then, that Jean de Chelles's relief of the Theophilus story subtly contains a message that is a bit more hopeful and optimistic about the individual's role in his or her own salvation than appeared at first glance.

One final consideration of this relief will help us fine-tune our understanding of its message and will position us to move comparatively to Rutebeuf's version of this story: the question of intended audience. Cothren argues persuasively that the Theophilus story in glass was not for a popular audience: "By arguing for the didactic structure of the Theophilus window recension, I do not mean to imply any sort of popularizing movement. This was in no sense an attempt to educate an unlettered multitude. . . . The story, after all, concerns the sort of sin whose commission was a privilege of this class alone [wealthy and powerful men who wielded secular, temporal authority], . . . a focused message about hypocrisy and misuse of power."[16] Shapiro notes that the Theophilus story does not come from the "people": "The protagonist is a secular functionary of the Church."[17] Williamson concurs with Shapiro and Cothren.[18] If the intended audience is aristocratic and clerical, then we might be led to favor a message of institutional control of salvation and repentance, based in a figurative dynamic of biblical typology. If this had been the audience Jean de Chelles intended, he might have chosen a scene of "aristocratic," penitential scourging to represent Theophilus's repentance. Such scenes were well established and known from the Bibles Moralisées and from the Theophilus story in glass at the Cathedral de Beauvais.[19] But I do not think Jean de Chelles's version of the Theophilus story had such a narrow audience in mind or such a "focused message."

This is not to say that the Theophilus story did not lend itself to a well-defined message aimed at a clerical elite. In fact, I think the power of the Theophilus story was that its representation of fall and recovery, of pride and humility, of supernatural intervention and the individual capacity to turn and repent allowed it to be focused narrowly and broadly. Michael Davis's fine reading of the fourteenth-century Theophilus story sculpted on the cloister wall of Notre Dame of Paris proves this point clearly. Davis argues that this more sequestered image, set within the cloister and destined to be seen by a community of fewer than 250 men, was indeed aimed at an elite clerical audience. This setting differentiates the fourteenth-century relief from Jean de Chelles's on the north facade of the cathedral which, like the west facade, "aimed to communicate to the people an essential outline of sacred history and to popularize clerical culture."[20] The chapel relief compresses the story into three scenes: the pact with the devil, the prayer to the Virgin, the Virgin's retrieval of the contract. It excises all reference to feudal and worldly bonds, the representation of the church edifice, the repentant Theophilus, and the exemplary sermon. Davis finds that this compression "takes the action out of the communal realm to concentrate instead on the Virgin's decisive response to a sinner's change of heart."[21] Davis's argument indirectly underlines the broad, communal, and more popular audience intended in Jean de Chelles's version of the Theophilus story. I think it is this broadly intended audience that explains the tension that we discovered in the image and the possibility of two different, potentially competing, messages.

Rutebeuf's play is conceived with a similarly broad audience in mind and will also exhibit the tensions that we have seen in Jean de Chelles's version of this story. Ultimately, Rutebeuf will come closer than Jean de Chelles to "solving" these tensions. In stanza V of the *Repentance Rutebeuf,* the poet/narrator acknowledged the possibility of salvation through the intervention of the Virgin but neither took action to make this happen nor narrated the story of intervention. *Le Miracle de Théophile* will take this next step and provide us with a fuller picture of how the Theophilus story represents the thirteenth century's new economy of salvation. Given his general pessimism, it may indeed be the case that for Rutebeuf the Theophilus story serves him better than his own more personal poetry as a vehicle for the representation of the individual's path to salvation. While *Le Miracle de Théophile,* like the *Repentance,* makes individual salvation seem problematic, unlikely, and idiosyncratic, it will nonetheless intimate that the individual sinner can be saved.[22] But he has much to overcome before this will happen. Theophilus, like the poet/narrator of the *Repentance,* makes clear in his prayer to the Virgin that he has always moved himself in another direction: "En enfer . . . dont la porte est ouverte" ("toward Hell . . . where the door is open") (480–481).[23]

This is the contradiction that the Theophilus story wants to resolve: In spite of the overwhelming odds of the individual falling into sin and going to hell, another possibility exists—one that, especially with the onset of auricular confession, seems available to the individual. Rutebeuf's version of the story highlights this contradiction and the bind that it puts the individual in. In a confessional economy of salvation, the individual has the capacity and responsibility to turn himself or herself from sin. For Theophilus here, as for the poet/narrator of the *Repentance,* individual initiative cannot make this turn happen. Jean Dufournet calls *Le Miracle* above all a story of conversion.[24] The question is how to initiate it. The broad appeal of the Theophilus legend, as Cothren and Shapiro have shown, seems to be that it captures a social preoccupation with new relations between the secular and religious realms and a new access to salvation. Rutebeuf's dramatization of this preoccupation illustrates the dilemma that it poses for the individual sinner.

Critics have emphasized the abruptness of Theophilus's repentance in *Le Miracle.*[25] I think, on the contrary, that Theophilus's repentance is a long extended movement—from dark to light, from ignorance to knowledge, from distance to proximity.[26] This journey is not unlike the one depicted on the tympanum of the north transept of the Cathedral of Notre Dame. But it is clear that Rutebeuf envisions the journey in more existential terms; it is the rough passage of one individual through the obstacles of this world. The five scenes on the Notre Dame tympanum form the worldly backdrop for this passage through the world and for Theophilus's conversion. This inner conversion is harder to visualize than the other scenes on the Notre Dame tympanum. We will have to look for it, as Michel Zink has suggested, in the psychological terms of Theophilus's monologues.[27] The play is really about the psychological distance that Theophilus travels.[28] This distance also manifests itself as the distance between appearance and reality. This gap is what deceives the individual and occasions his or her fall. It results in additional distances or gaps: between God and the sinner, between the sinner and his worldly acquaintances, between the sinner and himself. Rutebeuf's version of the Theophilus story will dramatize the individual spiritual journey it takes to close this gap. It is, indeed, a "dramatisation du moi" ("drama of self").[29]

The beginning of the *Miracle* sets us in a figurative economy reminiscent of the biblical typology we saw earlier. Rutebeuf himself sketches out a similar typology in his earlier *Repentance*. There Rutebeuf imagined serving God perfectly (6) and being made in his image (28), but he was not able to achieve this perfect service or realize this resemblance. The *Miracle* starts out quite similarly. The play begins with Theophilus's lament that he has been rejected by the new bishop, left alone and penniless (6–10). Even his family will be without resources (11) unless God provides for them (12), but clearly this God is distant. If Theophilus's family wants help from God, "en autre lieu les covient trere" ("they will have to get themselves to another place" 14), for "on ne puet a lui avenir" ("one cannot reach this God" 23)—"il s'est en si haut leu mis" ("he has placed himself high up out of reach" 27). In a typically Rutebeufian annominatio, the position of God is inscribed as the counter opposite to Theophilus. God is physically and comfortably high up, "lasus": "Or est lasus en son solaz" ("he is happy up above" 33); Theophilus is spiritually and uncomfortably low down, "laz": "Laz, chetis, et je suis es laz" ("wretched, miserable, I am caught" 34). Even more than in the *Repentance*, Rutebeuf palpably marks a physical distance that will become an opposition between God and his main character.

This distance will be exacerbated before it will be diminished. We begin *in medias res* with the new bishop's rejection of Theophilus. It would not have been difficult to move quickly to the pact with the devil that figures so prominently in Theophilus iconography. But Rutebeuf really seems interested here in dramatizing Theophilus's spiritual and psychological fall. The opposition set up in the word play "lasus" and "laz" of lines 33 and 34 foretells the inevitable. Theophilus no sooner acknowledges the distance between God and himself than he begins to increase that distance. Salatin in effect sets the contrary movement in motion: "Voudriiez vous Dieu renoier / Celui que tan solez proier" ("Would you renounce the God to whom you so frequently pray?" 81–82). The rhyme "renoier/proier" indicates two key discourses (denial or apostasy and prayer) that move in opposite directions. For now, Theophilus will choose the first, and this moves him further away from

God very quickly. He is quite aware of this distance and imagines himself in the "hideus manoir" ("horrible house" 112) and "mesons" obscure (118) of the devil. In this space, one that is clearly more mental than physical, he imagines himself stranded, exiled ("m'avra Diex issi estrangié" "God will have expelled me" 124), even before he has committed any sin. Once he commits to visit the devil the sense of a downward movement is reinforced. The devil describes his own place as in a valley ("en cel val" 190), and Salatin instructs Theophilus to descend ("Va la aval" 215) to visit the devil.

This emphasis on and dramatization of physical and psychological distance brings Theophilus to the scene of feudal homage with the devil. This scene is clearly meant to be one of the lowest of the play. It is worth recalling that this is where Jean de Chelles began his version of the Theophilus story. The difference between these two versions of the story highlights Rutebeuf's desire to depict not just the "fall" of man but the fall of one individual man and, in particular, the psychological journey that such a fall entails. He wants us to know that Theophilus has chosen to sin, and is aware and regretful of his choice. He shows us a sinner devastated by his unfortunate decision. When we arrive at the scene of homage in the *Miracle*, the figurative economy of salvation has already been established. This does not mean that the feudal bond is not at least a manifestation of Theophilus's fall, but it does mean that the real plunge here has already taken place before this visual and social worldly gesture. The real fall is psychological; it is the "renoier," the inner desperation that pushed the main character to negate and turn away from God. Indeed, it takes approximately 240 lines to get to the feudal ceremony and only five to get through it. By the time Theophilus has put his hands in the devil's the downward trajectory has already been completed and is confirmed rather than initiated. The feudal pact with the devil and the subsequent illusion of a return to power that it implies are, in effect, a static space in the *Miracle*. In other words, it is not through the feudal pact itself or the abuse of Thomas or Pinceguerre that Theophilus buries himself further in sin. Theophilus's illusion of worldly power is unlike the second scene of the Notre Dame tympanum. Here, the gap between the illusion of power and the reality of the devil's presence and support is constant and little emphasized. This is because for Rutebeuf the real gap (and journey) is a psychological one that began even before the feudal ceremony and will not end until the play is over.

Theophilus's spiritual journey in the *Miracle* manifests itself quite differently both spatially and psychologically than the image of prayer and repentance in the third scene of the Notre Dame tympanum. In the first place, as has been mentioned, the spiritual journey begins earlier. It is also more evident in the text and more evenly spread throughout the play. Finally, and importantly, it is a more anguished and less hopeful trajectory than the one we see on the Notre Dame tympanum. As we have already seen, Rutebeuf opens the play by reinforcing the gap between God and Theophilus. Theophilus is aware of this gap and of himself as alienated from God. This awareness in some sense constitutes his psychological journey and is most acutely felt in the monologues.[30] The first one takes place before he has visually hit bottom and put his hands in the devil's. Early on, after having spoken with the devil's intermediary, Salatin, Theophilus has a moment of anguished self-awareness that lasts from verses 101 to 133. The opening words, "Ha! laz" ("alas" 101), echo the annominatio of lines 33 and 34 that we examined earlier. Theophilus's unhappiness is clearly connected to the distance between himself and a God who is "lasus" ("up above" 33). He asks immediately "que porrai devenir?" ("what will become of me?" 101). This simple question is an important indicator of self-awareness. Theophilus is preoccupied with the consequences of the particular decision he is about to make. He is aware of his misery and, more importantly, of where he is headed with the choice that he has made to join forces with the devil. He goes on to state quite lucidly that if he renounces the saints and the Virgin, his soul will be burnt in the flames of hell (104–110). He acknowledges that he knows that the flames of hell are eternal (114) and that hell itself is a well filled with "ordure" ("garbage" 120) and that he is headed there (121). He knows that God will exile him for what he is about to do: "M'avra Diex issi estrangié" ("God will have expelled me" 124). This exile will clearly make him a stranger to himself. No one is as miserable about this as he is: "Si esbahiz ne fu més hom / Com je sui, voir" ("No man has ever been so troubled as I truly am" 127–128). This monologue is a psychological "descente aux enfers." It is important to note that it occurs before Theophilus makes his fateful decision. This anticipation gives a specificity and lucidity to his upcoming sin. When he decides a few lines later, "Diex m'a grevé: jel greverai" ("God affronted me: I'll affront him" 133), there is no doubt for the reader that this is a premeditated and self-aware decision. For Rutebeuf, a key part of Theophilus's "drama" is this inner struggle. This first monologue dramatizes a psychological fall, but it does so with enough regret and self-awareness that it also constitutes the beginning of the spiritual trajectory that will culminate in the repentance.

The repentance proper, lines 384–431, seems unanticipated and indecisive. It may be, as Lope has suggested, that Theophilus's attitude of contrition or repentance was less abrupt on the stage as it could be anticipated by gestures.[31] But I think it is very much Rutebuef's intention to spread Theophilus's "conversion" over a broader psychological space. His conversion neither begins nor culminates in the "repentance" proper. The first line of the repentance, in fact, takes us right back to the beginning of the play and repeats line 101 of the first monologue: "Hé! laz, chetis, dolenz, que porrai devenir?" ("Alas, wretched, miserable, what will become of me?" 384).[32] We hardly expect this line in the middle of a dialogue with the character Thomas, but it is not unexpected or unprecedented. It is very much a continuation of the self-examination that Theophilus began at line 101. When he asks, rhetorically, "Sire Diex, que fera cist dolenz esbahis[?]" ("My Lord, what will this sad and troubled man do?" 396), we are clear because of the repetition of "esbahis" from line 127 that this is a continuation of the psychological journey that began in the earlier monologue. With the word "esbahis," Theophilus acknowledges less his surprise than his inability or incapacity to understand. As in the *Repentance*, so here, the world is full of trickery, the devil is always setting traps. Theophilus acknowledges that he has fallen into these traps: "des maufez d'enfer engingniez et trahis" ("I've been tricked and betrayed by devils" 398). In this sense, "esbahi" indicates a kind of ignorance of the world, the kind of ignorance that he recognized would not help him in the *Repentance* (22–24). Here Theophilus says in a tone that feels more confessional and more self-aware than in the *Repentance* that this ignorance has in fact played a big role in his spiritual downfall: "Hé! las, com j'ai esté plains de grant nonsavoir" ("Alas, how full of ignorance I was" 400). There is clearly a contradiction between the heightened self-awareness these monologues suggest and the "grant nonsavoir" that Theophilus seems to claim. This is less a contradiction in Rutebuef's logic than a kind of medieval aporia. It is very similar to the contradiction in the *Repentance* that the only way to renounce poetry is through a poem. As Andrew Cowell has said, it shows that "poetic redemption in Rutebeuf lies finally in the conscious realization of the impossibility of full self-expression."[33] Theophilus seems to combine confessional self-awareness with the conviction that his own conversion and salvation can only be effected by some higher power. He is, by now, hyper-aware of his sinfulness but still clearly ignorant of the way out of this state. The "repentance" in the *Miracle* shows him quite stranded in this negative self-awareness: "Enfers ne me plest pas ou je me voil offerre; / Paradis n'est pas miens, que j'ai au Seignor guerre" ("Hell, where I was happy to offer my services, is not pleasing to me; Paradise is not for me, because I am at war with God" 422–423). As in the *Repentance,* Rutebeuf seems to paint a picture here of the fallen sinner, terribly self-aware that he is headed toward sin and hell, yet terribly incapable of turning himself around. There is not much evidence in the repentance section that suggests conversion. Two lines imply a rather feeble hope that turning to a higher power is the only alternative (414–415 and 431).

The last line of the repentance section invokes this higher power, the Virgin, and shifts from a discourse of confessional and pessimistic self-awareness to a discourse of prayer and more hopeful supplication: "Se je li cri merci, nus ne m'en doit blasmer" ("If I ask her mercy, none could blame me" 431). This shift clearly makes way for the long prayer to the Virgin that will follow. It is also, I would argue, the most significant moment of the play and of Theophilus's spiritual journey. We would do well to recall the key rhyme that signaled Theophilus's spiritual downfall. Salatin asked him if he would be willing to deny the God to whom he had so often prayed: "Voudriiez vous Dieu renoier / Celui que tant solez proier" (81–82). With the rhyme "renoier/proier" Rutebeuf juxtaposes two discourses that embody two stances toward God and toward salvation. One obviously points away from God, the "renoier." The repentance section uses this word repeatedly to acknowledge Theophilus's greatest sin (386, 388, 401). The other discourse, the "proier," points toward God. It will be used repeatedly in the remainder of the play.[34] This simple juxtaposition of denial and prayer recalls the middle register of the Notre Dame tympanum, where the image of Theophilus in homage to the devil contrasts symmetrically with the image of Theophilus in prayer.

It is rather odd that the "repentance" section of the *Miracle* does not give us a more distinct image of confession, repentance, or contrition. Theophilus articulates the same sins, the same self-awareness, and the same self-loathing that we saw earlier in the play. He does say "Or ai Dieu renoié, ne puet estre teü" ("I renounced God, this cannot be kept quiet" 388), and that it has been seven years that he has pursued the path of sin (404). These lines give a sense of urgency and renewal to his current "repentance." They mark too the distance that he has come from his first moment of regret and self-awareness prior to denying God. There he spoke with self-awareness and trepidation about a sin that he anticipated committing. Now he speaks with the knowledge of experience that has confirmed his original fears. The "repentance" here then strikes a very similar tone to the one in the *Repentance Rutebeuf.* Like the poet/narrator there, Theophilus does not have that much confidence in his own words, in his own confession and repentance. These words can at best reaffirm his exile and impotence: "Or n'ai je remanance ne en ciel ne en terre. / Ha! las, ou est li lieus qui me puisse souffere?" ("I no longer have a place in heaven or on earth. Alas, where is the place that could tolerate me?" 420–421). In terms of his salvation, ultimately Theophilus's repentance brings him to something of a spiritual dead end. At best, the impotence of the "repentir" serves to transition him to another form of discourse.[35]

This pessimistic interpretation of the power of a sacramental discourse brings to mind and is supported by the relative absence in Rutebuef's play of images of the Church. While the legend and the iconography greatly emphasize the Church as an institution, edifice, and path to salvation, Rutebuef barely mentions the Church.[36] In the stage directions he indicates that Theophilus enters into a chapel to repent (between verses 383 and 384). We assume that Theophilus's prayer is in front of a statue of the Virgin as she tells him, in her moment of hesitation, to get out of her chapel (553). But this quiet scene of prayer and supplication does not bring to mind the towering presence of the Gothic church from the Notre Dame tympanum or the other church images from Theophilus iconography. Finally, the Virgin again tells him that his contract with the devil should be read "Devant le peuple en sainte yglise" ("Before the people in the church" 593). These minor and indirect references to the Church suggest that Rutebeuf did not choose to emphasize, either through the sacrament of confession or the building of the church, an institutional path to salvation.[37] Instead, Rutebeuf seems to choose a more private and idiosyncratic pathway for his main character.[38] This choice sets his version of the Theophilus story quite apart from all the others.

In the *Miracle*, then, no single moment depicts a contrition or confession that announces the conversion of Theophilus. The "conversion" of Theophilus is more subtle and more extended. It is a psychological and discursive journey that takes the main character from the language and attitude of provocation—"Se or pooie a lui tancier" ("If I could threaten him" 30)—to the language and attitude of supplication and prayer—"Or vieng proier" ("I come to pray" 545). Within the repentance section there is some evidence of this shift. We have seen that Theophilus admits three times that he has denied ("renoier") God. After this admission, he then claims twice that he does not dare call out to God, the saints, or the Virgin. Both times (424 and 428) he uses the verb "reclamer," translated as "invoquer" but clearly giving the impression of calling out, calling back. Verse 429 rhymes "amer" with "reclamer" and makes it clear that Rutebeuf is announcing a shift in discourses, from

the negation and rejection of Theophilus's "renoier" to the call for help
that will lead to the love and charity of the Virgin.[39] The rest of the poem
builds off this shift and works toward closing the gap that we saw early
on between God and Theophilus. Within the prayer to the Virgin, Rutebeuf uses annominatio again to mark and bridge the antithesis that
prayer will allow Theophilus to overcome.[40] "Li proieres qui proie /
M'a ja mis en sa proie: / Pris serai et preez, / Trop asprement m'asproie. /
Dame, ton chier Filz proie / que soie despreez" ("The raptor that hunts
has got me in his trap : I'll be caught, prey, too bitterly he attacks. Lady,
pray to your dear Son that I might be released" 528–533). Like the object ("proie") of a bird of prey ("proieres"), the main character has been
trapped ("pris" and "preez"). He will only be freed ("despreez") if the
Virgin prays ("proie") to Christ for him. This passage nicely substanti-
ates Mickle's idea that antithesis manifests itself thematically and linguis-
tically in the play. It also shows his claim that "in the same word form one
can find both positive and negative values."[41] Here the message seems to
be that prayer is the only way to escape being "pris" by the rapacious
claws of the devil. Rutebeuf's emphasis on prayer is in no way limited to
the Virgin. Even after she has returned his contract from the devil, he
approaches the bishop with this same discourse: "si vous vueil proier,
com mon pere" ("I come to pray to you as to a father" 627). The discourse of prayer culminates at the end of the play with the *Te Deum.*

     This prayer to God that only begins in the last lines of the play is a
sure sign that we have come full circle from the beginning of the play
and closed the gap between God and Theophilus.[42] On the one hand
this circle takes him through the scenes and characters of the
Theophilus legend that are familiar to us from the Notre Dame relief:
Salatin, the devil, anonymous characters of the world (Thomas and
Pinceguerre), the Virgin, and the bishop with his parishioners. On the
other hand, this circle has been less imageable and has taken
Theophilus from the psychological distance and isolation that resulted
from his "renoier," through the self-awareness and self-loathing that develops almost from the beginning of the play and culminates in the repentance section, to the more hopeful proximity to the Virgin, to the
bishop, and to God that comes from his shifting to a discourse of prayer.
The psychological and discursive journey from negation to prayer is subtle and evolves over the course of the whole play. It does not require an
extraordinary, momentary contrition or conversion. Nor does it require
an intervention from the Virgin, at least certainly not an unprecedented, even unsolicited, intervention like the one in Gautier de
Coinci's version of the Theophilus story.[43] Theophilus's psychological

journey seems above all concerned with finding the right discursive stance, the language that will penetrate the "oreille sorde" ("deaf ear" 15) that he imagines in God at the beginning of the play. He tries railing against God (30–32), denying him (133), praying to the devil (237), speaking with irony and derision to Thomas and Pinceguerre, speaking in repentance, and finally praying. More than anything the discourse of prayer allows Theophilus to speak in a language that will be heard. He says his prayer to the Virgin (432–539), asking her specifically to listen to him: "car entent ma proiere" ("Please listen to my prayer" 500). She clearly hears him and wastes little time in recognizing him: "Theophile, je t'ai seü / Ça en arriere a moi eü" ("Theophile, I've known you, you once belonged to me" 567–568). This is a more positive version of the resemblance to Christ that the *Repentance Rutebeuf* mentions but cannot fully realize. It is not a supernatural intervention in Theophilus's sinful life. It is a more humanistic recognition that Theophilus himself participates in by taking the initiative to speak out ("reclamer") and by speaking in the discourse of prayer.

Rutebeuf's *Miracle* ends on a note that is quite similar to the exemplary upper register of the Notre Dame tympanum. The bishop announces to his parishioners that they will hear "la vie de Theophile" ("Theophilus's life" 633–634). This "life" is clearly a reference to the exemplary genre of saints' lives and makes of Theophilus's story a lesson. The bishop sums up the gist of the story: "Marie, la virge pucele, / Delivré l'a de tel querele" ("Mary, the virgin, delivered you from your plight" 659–660). But this "miracle" of the Virgin was neither as easy nor as quick nor as certain as these lines and the exemplary genre might imply. While Rutebeuf has significantly shortened the version of this story that he got from Gautier de Coinci, he increased the main character's anguish, his deliberations, and his psychological journey.[44] He also increased his initiative. Unlike the poet/narrator of the *Repentance Rutebeuf*, Theophilus does speak out here, in prayer, to seek the help of a higher power. But by the time he has pronounced his plea for help, which is itself a long prayer (432–539), and asked the Virgin to turn him around, to "change his heart" ("mon corage varie" 457), he has in effect saved and converted himself. The Virgin's quick recognition of him supports this interpretation. There is nothing institutional or exemplary about this recognition; it is very much a private exchange between Theophilus and the Virgin. She recognizes him because of his own particular goodness, which she recalls from his past service to her (568). After the Bishop has read the letter from the devil at the very end of the play, he concludes: "Issi ouvra icil preudom" ("this good man has acted" 656). The reference to Theophilus as a "preudom" clearly indicates that he has shifted from bad to good. The verb "ouvra" is translated by Zink as "comportement" and similarly by Dufournet as "voilà l'histoire." It implies acts, action, what Theophilus did. But it seems that one could also read this line to mean that what Theophilus did implies what he accomplished. In this sense, his "oeuvre" would be the "life" we have just heard, the language that he has spoken, and the psychological journey that he himself has just undergone.

This latter interpretation would make a place for the *Miracle de Théophile* in the economy of salvation that Rutebeuf sketched out in the *Repentance Rutebeuf.* Somewhere between *Renart Repentance 79* and *Sainte Marie L'Egyptienne Repentance 57*, the *Miracle* is a positive example of language, and moreover literature, being used to bring the poet/narrator closer to his own salvation. The discourse of prayer that Theophilus learns to embrace and initiate would, in this reading, be a small step from the discourse of rhyme and poetry that the poet/narrator of the *Repentance* so denigrates. Likewise in this reading, *Le Miracle de Théophile* would itself be an example of Rutebeuf converting not just the main character but poetry itself to the service of God and the Virgin. Theophilus's accomplishment has been to find a language that will allow him to be heard and recognized for the good in him rather than the bad. Rutebeuf's accomplishment has been to convert his own poetry into an "oeuvre" that moves him toward instead of away from God, an "oeuvre" that allows him "to serve God perfectly" ("A Deu servir parfaitement" *Repentance* 6) with what he knows best, his own poetry.[45] David Kuhn has claimed for the *Repentance* that Rutebeuf manages to use the theme of confession to convert language from a profane to a sacramental use.[46] Our reading suggests that in the *Miracle* Rutebeuf weighs the discourse of confession against the discourse of prayer and finds greater hope or salvific efficacy in the latter.

The broad comparative reading of Jean de Chelles's and Rutebeuf's versions of the Theophilus legend shows a very similar set of preoccupations and figurative economies. They both imagine the character of Theophilus as worldly and in some sense vulnerable. He is more a common man or everyman than the haughty and ambitious clerk that the legend would have allowed. They both insist on the feudal nature of the pact with the devil. This link to an important contemporary model of social and power relations makes the Theophilus character a potential symbol of all characters caught in these relations. In Jean de Chelles's version it also adds a rich subplot, as the hands that come together to seal the feudal agreement metamorphose into the gesture of prayer that will rescue the individual from that very same feudal agreement. Indeed, an important correspondence that we have yet to draw attention to exists between this subplot of hands in the Notre Dame tympanum and the discourse of prayer in the *Miracle*. Both characters seem to seek a vehicle to lead them to salvation. For the sculptor it is a gesture of prayer embodied in a silent narrative of hands. For the poet, the vehicle is language, embodied also in a shift to a discourse of prayer. In either case, the idea that Theophilus has the capacity to take his salvation into his own hands introduces a tension into the exemplary logic of the Theophilus legend. While Jean de Chelles's relief seems to imagine more worldly power and therefore greater hypocrisy coming from Theophilus's pact with the devil, both the sculpture and the play see this pact as pushing the main character into a period of isolation that leads to repentance and prayer. In Jean de Chelles's version this moment of repentance and prayer is carefully inscribed in a tight, institutional setting. Rutebeuf depicts this same moment with more isolation, estrangement, and anguish. It is clearly more desperate, more individual and private than what we see in the Notre Dame relief. In effect, for his Theophilus, simply getting to the chapel is not enough. The institutional path remains uncertain for Rutebeuf. Through his emphasis on language, on different discourses and even different verse forms, Rutebeuf can portray a more idiosyncratic, psychological journey in which the individual must play some role in the accomplishment of his salvation or conversion.[47]

# Notes

1. Grace Frank lists over fifty literary versions (twenty-five in Latin, at least six in French, many in English, three narrative poems and three plays in German, one play and several narrative versions in Italian, at least four in Spanish, two in Dutch, one in Anglo-Saxon, three in Icelandic, one in Swedish) (*Le miracle de Théophile: Miracle du XIIIe siècle* [Paris: Champion, 1967], xii–xiv). Michael W. Cothren lists nine stained-glass recensions and eleven manuscript illustrations of the Theophilus story in the thirteenth century ("The Iconography of Theophilus Windows in the First Half of the Thirteenth Century," *Speculum* 59, no. 2 [1984]: app. A and B). Alfred C. Fryer lists four sculpted versions in France and one in England ("Theophilus, the Penitent, as Represented in Art," *Archaeological Journal* 92 [1936]: app. 11 and 3).
2. See in particular Jean Charles Payen, "La penitence dans le context culturel du XIIe et XIIIe siecles," *Revue des science philosophiques et theologiques* 61, no. 3 (1977): 399–428; Thomas Tentler, *Sin and Confession on the Eve of the Reformation* (Princeton, N.J.: Princeton University Press, 1977); *Faire Croire: Modalités de la diffusion et de la réception des messages religieux du XIIe au XVe siècle*, Table Ronde organisée par l'École française de Rome, en collaboration avec l'Institut d'histoire médiévale de l'Université de Padoue (Rome 22–23 juin 1979), Collection de l'École française de Rome 51 (Rome: École française de Rome,

1981); Michel Zink, *La subjectivité littéraire* (Paris: Presses Universitaires de France, 1985); and Jerry Root, *"Space to speke": The Confessional Subject in Medieval Literature* (New York: Peter Lang, 1997). For studies that link specifically the visual and verbal representation of self, see Michael Camille, *Mirror in Parchment: The Luttrell Psalter and the Making of Medieval England* (Chicago: University of Chicago Press, 1998), 124, 140–150; Suzanne Lewis, *Reading Images: Narrative Discourse and Reception in the Thirteenth-Century Illuminated Apocalypse* (Cambridge: Cambridge University Press, 1995), 16; and Ann Eljenholm Nichols, *Seeable Signs: The Iconography of the Seven Sacraments, 1350–1544* (Woodbridge, UK: Boydell Press, 1994).

3. Two wide-ranging art historical studies exist. Alfred Fryer's 1936 article gives a broad census of visual representations (sculpture, manuscript illuminations, stained glass) of the various aspects of the Theophilus legend ("Theophilus, the Penitent"). Michael Cothren's 1984 article argues persuasively that stained-glass representations encompass a broader social and visual context than other representations ("Iconography of Theophilus Windows"). Meyer Shapiro's interpretation of the Theophilus relief at Souillac brilliantly works out the formal dynamics of the relief and the religious and social context that it reflects. Shapiro limits his study to this one sculpture (Romanesque Art [New York: George Braziller, 1977]).

4. Fryer lists the date as between 1250 and 1260 ("Theophilus, the Penitent," app. 11); Minnie B. Sangster lists it as between 1265 and 1270 ("Envisioning *Le Miracle de Théophile* in France: Stained Glass, Sculpture, and Stage," *Medieval Perspectives* 14 [1999]: 194); E. Faral and J. Bastin also give 1265–1270 as the date of the sculpture (*Oeuvres complètes de Rutebeuf* [Paris: Picard, 1960], 2:169, n. 3). Paul Williamson notes: "Although the north doorway is not dated by documentary evidence it has been convincingly demonstrated that it was executed first, probably in around 1245–50" (*Gothic Sculpture, 1140–1300* [New Haven, Conn.: Yale University Press, 1995], 151). Because Sangster and Faral and Bastin give such a late date, they also attribute the Theophilus tympanum to Pierre de Montreuil. I follow Williamson in attributing it to the earlier Jean de Chelles. Dieter Kimpel further nuances the attribution of the north transept to two sculptors, a "Master of the Virgin" and a "Master of the Childhood Scenes" (Dieter Kimpel, "A Parisian Virtue," in *The Brummer Collection of Medieval Art*, edited by Caroline Bruzelius with Jill Meredith [Durham, N.C.: Duke University Press, 1991], 130–131). According to Kimpel, the "Master of the Virgin" did the two upper bands of the Theophilus tympanum, while the "Master of the Childhood Scenes" did the lower band.

5. The Jean de Chelles relief of the Theophilus story has not been extensively interpreted. Dieter Kimpel discusses it briefly in his 1991 article and in more detail in his doctoral dissertation Die Querhausarme von Notre-Dame zu Paris und ihre Skulpturen (Ph.D. diss., Bonn, 1971). Emile Mâle gives a brief account (*L'art religieux du XIIIe siècle en France* [Paris: Armand Colin, 1948], 468–473). Williamson gives an informative discussion with an explanation of why the Theophilus story appears here (*Gothic Sculpture*, 150–153). Alain Erlande-Brandenburg mentions it in passing (*Notre-Dame de Paris*, translated by John Goodman [New York: Harry Abrams, 1998], 164). One study, by Minnie Sangster ("Envisioning *Le Miracle*," 1999), has done a rapid comparative and historical overview of the Theophilus legend in text (Rutebeuf), sculpture, and stained glass.

6. In addition to the obvious visual connection of the lintel to the tympanum, the nativity story is linked to Theophilus's story in the Gautier de Coinci

version (line 2060). Rutebeuf's *Un Dit de Notre Dame* itself recounts the nativity (35–60). The De Brailes Psalter's manuscript image of the Theophilus story is encircled by a series of images telling the story of the "rise and fall of man from the cradle to the grave" (Fryer, "Theophilus, the Penitent," 318). This juxtaposition of type and exemplar parallels the figurative logic of the Notre Dame tympanum and seems to inform the figurative economy of the Theophilus story generally.

7. In his *Repentance*, Rutebeuf refers to this kind of ideal as a "fourme chiere" (28). Quotations from the *Repentance* are from the Zink edition (Michael Zink, *Rutebeuf: Oeuvres complètes* [Paris: Bordas, Livre de Poches (Lettres Gothiques), 1989–1990]). *La Repentance Rutebeuf* is also called "La Mort Rutebeuf." All translations of Rutebeuf are my own.

8. Jacques Le Goff, *Pour un autre Moyen Age: Temps, travail et culture en Occident; 18 essais* (Paris: Gallimard, 1977), 367.

9. This image nicely visualizes the trapped feeling that the narrator of Rutebeuf's *Repentance* felt: "L'Anemis qui me veut avoir / Et mettre en sa chartre premiere" (32–33).

10. "The ancient attitude of prayer, with hands outstretched, was replaced by the gesture of the joined hands, borrowed from 'commendation,' and this became throughout Catholic Christendom the characteristic praying posture." Marc Bloch, *Feudal Society: The Growth of Ties of Dependence*, translated by L. A. Manyon (1939; Chicago: University of Chicago Press, 1961), 233.

11. The *Repentance* suggests this power but not its realization. The poet claims that God gives him the intelligence to trick the devil: "Sens me dona de decevoir / L'Anemi" (31–32). But he does not seem able to carry out this "deception." Gautier de Coinci makes this same point a bit more hopefully (393–401), when he has the devil claim that many Christians have received his honors but then deceived him by confessing and repenting (397). This deception makes Gautier de Coinci's devil lose track of them: "ne sai ou vont ne qu'il deviennent" (402). Combarieu and Dumont have compared the (direct) relation between Gautier de Coinci's "Comment Theophilus vint a penitance" and Rutebeuf's *Miracle de Théophile*. (Micheline de Combarieu, "Le Diable dans le 'Comment Theophilus vint a penitence' de Gautier de Coinci et dans le 'Miracle de Théophile' de Rutebeuf," *Senefiance* 6 [1979]: 156–182; Pascale Dumont, "Comment inscrire un parcours existentiel dans le temps et dans l'espace. Comparaison entre le Theophilus narratif de Coinci et le Miracle de Theophile dramatisé de Rutebeuf," in *Memoire en temps advenir: Hommage à Theo Venckeleer*, edited by Theo Venckeleer and Alex Vanneste, 63–83 [Louvain: Peeters, 2003]). Jean Dufournet's introduction to his edition and translation of the text also has an extensive discussion with intertextual references to the Gautier de Coinci version (*Le Miracle de Theophile* [Paris: Garnier Flammarion, 1987]).

12. I think the message of institutional control is very similar here to the one that Meyer Shapiro finds at Souillac—in spite of all the differences between these two versions. Shapiro nicely juxtaposes the issue of control with the issue of individual initiative: "Hence, the church satisfies through this legend the popular demands . . . for an individual, unmediated relation with God. . . . But it encloses them within the physical framework of the organized, orthodox religion." (*Romanesque Art*, 119).

13. Fryer sees the reclining Theophilus in the Souillac relief as an "example of contrition so great that he prostrates himself" ( "Theophilus, the Penitent,"

301). Most other commentators see him as sleeping or dreaming (Shapiro, *Romanesque Art*, 111).

14. F. P. Pickering, *Literature and Art in the Middle Ages* (Coral Gables, Fla.: University of Miami Press, 1970), 111. See also François Garnier, *Le langage de l'image* (Paris: Le Léopard d'Or, 1981), 1:181–184).

15. Pickering, *Literature and Art*, 105. Garnier associates this gesture with another representation of Theophilus. He describes Theophilus as "accablé par le remords après avoir signé son pacte avec le diable" in a thirteenth-century stained glass image at Saint-Julien-du-Sault (*Le langage de l'image*, 184).

16. Cothren, "Iconography of Theophilus Windows," 333–334.

17. Shapiro, *Romanesque Art*, n30, 122.

18. Williamson, *Gothic Sculpture*, 152.

19. For these images, see Cothren, "Iconography of Theophilus Windows," fig. 5b, Beauvais; figs. 9 and 10, Bibles Moralisées. Cothren discusses the larger social context of the image of penitential scourging at some length ("Iconography of Theophilus Windows," 327–331).

20. Michael Davis, "Canonical Views: The Theophilus Story and the Choir Reliefs at Notre-Dame, Paris," in *Reading Medieval Images: The Art Historian and the Object*, edited by Elizabeth Sears and Thelma K. Thomas (Ann Arbor: University of Michigan Press, 2002), 108–109.

21. Davis, "Canonical Views," 111.

22. Michel Zink shows the thematic and manuscript logic of connection between *Le Miracle* and *La Repentance* ("De la repentance Rutebeuf à la repentance Theophile," *Littératures* 15 [1986]: 20). Daniel O'Sullivan also notes the resemblance (*Marian Devotion in Thirteenth-Century Lyric* [Toronto: University of Toronto Press, 2005], 100). David Kuhn notes that the *Repentance* "rappelle exactement . . . l'évêque Théophile" (*La poétique de François Villon* [Paris: Armand Colin, 1967], 478).

23. Quotations from *Le Miracle de Théophile* are from the Dufournet edition.

24. Dufournet, *Le Miracle de Théophile*, 19.

25. See Dumont, "Comment inscrire," 74, 77, and Stéphane Gompertz, "Du dialogue perdu au dialogue retrouvé: Salvation et détour dans le *Miracle de Théophile*, de Rutebeuf," *Romania* 100 (1979): 527. In the context of her fine comparison of Gautier de Coinci and Rutebeuf, Combarieu also concludes that Rutebeuf's Theophilus is, as the title implies, converted by the miracle of the Virgin ("Le diable," 174–175). Dumont likewise underlines the proximity of the divine and facility of access to the Virgin ("Comment inscrire," 68).

26. Mickle's reading of the play as a thematic and linguistic meditation on antithesis also emphasizes a long, constant, and gradual shift from a state of sin to a state of repentance and salvation. Emanuel J. Mickle Jr., "Free Will and Antithesis in the Miracle de Theophile," *Zeitschrift für Romanische Philologie* 99, nos. 3–4 (1983): 304–316.

27. For Zink, the dramatic intensity of the play "est tout entière contenue dans le mouvement intérieur qui pousse Théophile au reniement, puis au repentir et à la conversion. Ce mouvement intérieur s'exprime dans les monologues" ("De la repentance," 19).

28. Nancy Freeman Regalado argues that the play, like the stained glass and sculpted versions of the story, intends only to represent "didactic tableaux," exemplary high points of Theophilus's story, rather than a realistic psychological continuity (*Poetic Patterns in Rutebeuf: A Study in Non-Courtly Poetic*

*Modes of the Thirteenth Century* [New Haven, Conn.: Yale University Press, 1970], 63–65). For her, Rutebeuf's didactic intent aims rather at producing a "convincing realization of sin and repentance" (*Poetic Patterns*, 65) in the audience. I will argue below that Rutebeuf is indeed depicting a psychological journey, but not one that is "realistic" in any modern sense. Rather it is one that corresponds to the psychological economy of the penitential manuals, and, ultimately, it is a more troubled than "convincing" depiction of repentance—for Theophilus and the audience.

29. Zink, "De la repentance," 20.

30. For an overview of the monologues in the *Miracle*, see Roger Dubuis, "Le jeu narratif dans le Miracle de Théophile de Rutebeuf," in *Farai chansoneta novele: Essais sur la liberté créatrice au Moyen Age*, edited by Huguette Legros (Caen: Université de Caen, 1989), 152; also see Jennifer Dueck, "L'art de Rutebeuf: Le texte dramatique et ses fonctions," *Florilegium* 18, no. 2 (2001): 96–97.

31. Hans-Joachim Lope, "Remarques pour l'interprétation de la Repentance Théophile de Rutebeuf (*Miracle de Théophile*, vv 384-431)," *Marche Romane* 19 (1969): 83.

32. Dubuis ("Le jeu narratif," 156) also points out the similarity in these two monologues.

33. Andrew Cowell, *At Play in the Tavern: Signs, Coins, and Bodies in the Middle Ages* (Ann Arbor: University of Michigan Press, 1999), 181.

34. Dufournet mentions the importance of prayer more broadly for Rutebeuf ("L'univers poétique et moral de Rutebeuf," *Revue des langues romanes* 88 [1984]: 47). For Rutebeuf's use of the word in the remainder of the *Miracle*, see verses 431–432 (stage directions) and 500, 532, 545, and 627.

35. Combarieu offers another plausible explanation for the relative failure of Theophilus's repentance in the *Miracle*. She points out that Rutebeuf conforms to the attritionist mentality of thirteenth-century piety. This is in direct contrast with Gautier de Coinci's version of the story, where abundant tears and dramatic conversion gave evidence of a contritionist mentality ("Le diable," 171–172).

36. Shapiro showed clearly how the Souillac relief emphasizes Church control (*Romanesque Art*, 119). The stained-glass images in Cothren give many examples of the presence and impression of Church control. In particular, see images 3a, 4a, 5b ("Iconography of Theophilus Windows"). Image 5b (from the Cathedral of Beauvais, 1245) is a scene of Theophilus's repentance, visualized as a penitential scourging. While all of these images set the Theophilus story visually within the physical context of a church building, this one also visualizes quite literally and distinctly the sacrament of confession and the role of the confessor as the institutional path of salvation. It is almost as if Rutebeuf is seeking, like Souillac and Notre Dame, to promote individual piety, but unlike these two versions of the story, he wants to diminish or even eliminate the physical presence of Church control. See also Plate XI in Fryer, an image of "Theophilus repentant" from the Lambeth Apocalypse (1260), where Theophilus kneels in repentance in front of a massive Gothic cathedral ("Theophilus, the Penitent").

37. Rutebeuf's hostility to the institutional Church is well known. See Richard Spencer, "Sin and Retribution, and the Hope of Salvation, in Rutebeuf's Lyrical Works," in *Rewards and Punishments in the Arthurian Romances and Lyric Poetry of Mediaeval France*, edited by Peter V. Davies and Angus J. Kennedy (Cambridge:

Brewer, 1987), 149–164. For a brief overview of his attitude toward and images of the Church, see Dufournet ("L'univers," 39–40).

38. In the *Repentance* Rutebeuf indirectly juxtaposes writing poetry (and playing games) with praying (Stanza I). Specifically, he refers to saying the psalms ("saumoier," 9). The discourse of prayer and of psalms calls to mind the rise in private devotion in the thirteenth century (see Camille, *Mirror in Parchment*, 140). My reading of the *Miracle* would suggest that Rutebeuf embraces this more private form of devotion.

39. Mickle reads another passage on love (408–409) that gives a similarly encoded message (Mickle, "Free Will and Antithesis," 313). Dufournet suggests that "amer" is a key word, where Rutebeuf likes to embed the contrary conditions of a world where love (amer) has turned bitter (amer) ("L'univers," 49).

40. Regalado also discusses this passage and the annominatio as an important transitional moment. For her the annominatio has the effect of an incantation. It "raise[s] the level of parts of the play from the conversational to the sublime" (*Poetic Patterns*, 237).

41. Mickle, "Free Will and Antithesis," 313, 315.

42. Dufournet also concludes that the *Te Deum* explicitly moves Theophilus beyond the "intermediary" realm of the Virgin to the realm of God.

43. See Combarieu, "Le diable," 162. In the Gautier de Coinci version, the Virgin decides quite on her own to rescue Theophilus when things are going badly for him: "Theophilus est en mal point. / Vers enfer droit son cheval point. . . . Mais ma dame sainte Marie, / Qui ses amis onques n'oblie, / Ne volt souffrir qu'il fust perdus" (621–622; 627–629).

44. Combarieu ("Le diable," 168) and Dumont ("Comment inscrire," 72) find Rutebeuf's version more simplistic than Gautier de Coinci's.

45. This would be a positive fulfillment of the more vain effort to have his poetry count as work, discussed by Miha Pintaric in "Entre le temps de l'église et le temps du marchand," *Acta Neophilologica* 27 (1994): 19.

46. "Le drame du confessionel est le seul moment où la parole profane, dans son désordre et son hasard, devienne une parole sacramentelle" (Kuhn, *La poétique*, 478).

47. For a thorough discussion of the effect of different verse forms, see Dueck, "L'art de Rutebeuf."

# Shielded Subjects and Dreams of Permeability: Fashioning Scudamour in The Faerie Queene

## NATHANIAL B. SMITH

Early modern rhetorical texts repeatedly invoke images of physical pen-etration to describe the effect of words on listeners. I want to suggest that these images of rhetorical incursion were understood in the period to be much more than merely figurative. This essay brings together crit-ical discussions concerning the boundaries of the early modern body and the rhetorical instrumentality of language to query the ethical im-plications of Edmund Spenser's purported project to use the language of his epic romance, *The Faerie Queene*, "to fashion a gentleman or noble person in vertuous and gentle discipline,"[1] a goal about which his poem seems deeply suspicious. As described in his Letter to Ralegh, Spenser's project relies on a paradoxical view of the human subject. On the one hand, readers must be susceptible to influences from language and texts; otherwise, the text will fall on deaf ears. But once influenced, read-ers must be resolute against change and maintain their fixed, virtuous course: They must remain disciplined in the face of temptation to back-slide, lures continually faced by characters in the poem.

These two competing views of the body—malleable or fortified—coexisted in sixteenth-century England. Gail Kern Paster and others, for instance, have suggested that the early modern body was conceived in terms of Galenic humoralism and thus was "a semipermeable, irrigated container," "porous and thus able to be influenced by the immediate en-vironment."[2] Other scholars, though, have discerned the development in the period of what Norbert Elias calls a "*homo clausus*," a closed, im-mured individual with a secretive interior hidden from public view.[3] Spenser, I suggest, works through the implications of these competing

*Medievalia et Humanistica*, New Series, Number 34 (Paul Maurice Clogan, ed.), Rowman & Littlefield Publishers, Inc., 2008.

theories in the paradoxical character of Scudamour. One of Spenser's least-loved knights, Scudamour is both permeable and shielded, a contradiction inscribed in his very name, "shield of love," a combination of the hardness of metal and the softness of loving *caritas*. Spenser uses this character to explore the effects of language on bodies: Scudamour's shield, it turns out, protects him from swords but is useless to defend him against the destructive power of words. Once inside him, these words freeze and fix him in melancholic fascination, a condition judged to be ethically problematic as Scudamour becomes callously closed off to the words and needs of others.

Nowhere is Scudamour's paradoxical subjectivity laid bare more fully than when he experiences a disturbing dream in the house of Care: In this blacksmith foundry in book IV of *The Faerie Queene*, the willful, impervious, hard-hearted knight is revealed to be utterly permeable. Spenser's decision to use a dream at this moment in his poem signals his awareness that the competing theories about the boundaries of the body and self also inform conceptions of dreams from the period. From one perspective, dreams revealed a subject in an interstitial position amidst celestial, psychological, and somatic influences: They recorded influences from the stars, from memories of waking experience, from the humoral imbalances that affected the early modern body, and also environmental influences such as weather, climate, or more immediate noises surrounding a sleeper.[4] In this respect, dreams revealed a porous body open to various external and somatic influences. But other writers, such as Reginald Scot, adopted a view of individuals that stressed their self-enclosed autonomy and largely denied the intersubjective possibilities of dreams.[5] Thomas Nashe's treatise *The Terrors of the Night* similarly voices an almost Freudian skepticism about dreams, holding that they originate merely from within the individual, where thoughts, fears, and wishes from the day re-circulate at night.[6] For those who stress the openness of the self, then, the dream is an inevitable record of the exterior influences shaping the impressionable, *permeable* subject, whereas for adherents of the closed self, the dream replays thought-images on which the subject obsessively *fixates* from the daytime.[7] For Spenser, the dream does both of these at once: Spenser's dreamers at night respond to, re-work, and appropriate in their bodies the formative influences from their waking senses—including, significantly, the stuff of words, books, and poems. The dream-episode in Care's cottage recounts Scudamour's pathological subjectivity by re-enacting his linguistic wound in material form and revealing the noxious effects of self-enclosure.[8] His impenetrability in the poem manifests a profound lack of concern—or Care—for the other, a condition that directly leads to his own anxious, care-filled night of bad dreams. In this episode, then, linguistic permeability, openness, and vulnerability come to be figured not as the inevitable physiological condition of the subject but instead as an ideal, a dream Spenser extends to his own readers.

A dream is the perfect medium for Spenser to explore the penetrative power of words, because both dreams and language-reception—experiences that are today considered "mental" phenomena—were commonly situated in a bodily register in medical texts, moral and natural philosophy, and rhetorical and poetic theory from the period. Notions of the organic soul situated the processes of perception, memory, common sense, imagination, and cognition in the bodily organs of the heart or the brain.[9] Stephen Batman's 1582 modernization of a medieval encyclopedia, for instance, outlines the soul's tripartite "inner vertue," which corresponds to "three small celles . . . in the braine," each of which houses an important mental power or faculty. These inner powers work on products gathered from the outer senses. Representations of sensation move from front to back through the ventricles or cells of the brain, from the *sensus communis*, a kind of storehouse of perceptions, into the *vis imaginativa*, the creative, image-producing faculty, then to the middle cell of the *vis estimativa* or instinctual reason, and finally to the posterior cell, home of the *memoralis* or memory.[10] For Batman and most early modern thinkers, material and somatic sense-perceptions are ultimately communicated to the immaterial, rational soul by a liminal, "quasi-material" substance called *pneuma*, *spiritus*, or animal spirit, a fiery, airy fluid produced from one of the body's four humors, blood.[11] The animal spirit, according to Batman, works in the cells or "hollownesse of the braine," communicating representations that facilitate cognition. The spirit is thus not the equivalent of the "reasonable soule: but more truly the chaire or vpholder therof, and proper instrument. For by meane of such a spirit, the soule is ioyned to the bodie: and without the seruice of such a spirit, no act, the soule may perfectly exercise in the bodie."[12] Playing a role not only in cognition but also in movement, sensation, perception, and emotion, the spirit was usually considered to be a "natural" bodily fluid[13] and was "an agent in all of the body's vital functions, including consciousness, moral disposition, and by implication many of the traits constituting an individual's 'character' . . . virtually everything that constitutes an individual identity."[14]

Every dream-theorist in early modern Europe thought that dreams were formed in the spirits, and registered influences from inside and outside the body. According to Thomas Hill's *A Most Briefe and Pleasant Treatise of the Interpretation of Sundrie Dreames*, the first English vernacular collection of dream theory, dreams are "caused through the spirites lightlye moued."[15] For Hill, dreaming essentially reverses the standard process of sense-perceptions moving from front to back in the brain: "lyke as the motion of wakynge beginneth from the outwarde senses, and endeth at the memoratiue, euen so dothe the motion of sleepe contrarye begynne from this [the memory], and Endeth at the outwarde motions."[16] Dreams, that is, usually emanate from the memory of waking activities and are brought to life by spirits in the imagination, the only faculty capable of reading memory-images. The spirit in this view is an ultra-sensitive medium, easily stirred by a variety of psychological, somatic, celestial, and even daemonic influences. The belief in the spirit's impressionability served as a foundation for the use of dreams to diagnose humoral imbalance: People suffering an abundance of the melancholy humor, notes Timothie Bright, tend to have "fearefull" dreams, "partly by reason of their fancie waking, is most occupied about feares, and terrours, which retayneth the impression in sleepe, and partly through blacke and darke fumes of melancholie, rising vp to the braine, whereof the fantasie forgeth obiectes, and disturbeth the sleep of melancholy persons."[17] Neoplatonists, including Marsilio Ficino, agreed that dreams could serve a role in medical diagnosis and took the receptivity of spirits one step further: Ficino postulated a substance called the *spiritus phantasticus*, an even more highly refined form of animal spirit present in the imagination or "phantasy" that enabled the capture of celestial and daemonic dreams.[18] The fact that the spirit works in and on the body means that dreams were not merely "mental" or psychological phenomena; dreams were thought to affect the body, creating what Hill calls "outwarde motions" that move the spirits and ultimately influence bodies and behaviors. In just the same way, listeners and readers would have felt and experienced language in their bodies and bodily fluids: Words, originating as sounds outside the body, pierce, move, and affect the early modern subject.

The origin of the words that will echo through Scudamour's body in the house of Care originate in a character called Ate, who works wickedness with words. At the start of book IV, Britomart and Scudamour's bride Amoret are traveling together in search of their respective mates; Amoret at first does not know that the cross-dressed knight of chastity, Britomart, is in fact a woman. They come across a pair of ruffian knights and seeming ladies, including Ate, who takes her name from the Greek goddess of Discord and Strife. Not long after, Scudamour and his traveling companion, Britomart's nurse Glauce, encounter Ate and her crew. Ate concocts a story for Scudamour about Britomart and Amoret: "I saw him [that is, Britomart] haue your Amoret at will, / I saw him kisse, I saw him her embrace, / I saw him sleepe with her all night his fill" (IV.i.49.1–3). Haunted by this image, Scudamour continues on and seeks shelter for the night with a blacksmith named Care, at whose "cottage" he passes a troubled night during which he dreams that "those two [Amoret and Britomart] disloyall were" (IV.v.32.9, 43.8).

Just as the words of the Blatant Beast in book VI leave near-lethal bite-wounds on their victims, Ate's words take material form in her listeners' bodies. Ate materializes language in another sense as well: She shares characteristics with the tongue, that language-producing body part that is also the word for language itself. Her description is reminiscent of Desiderius Erasmus's discussion of the tongue in his treatise *Lingua*, where he describes this "Ambivalent Organ." "The tongue," says Erasmus, "is Ate, strife personified, if it lacks a pilot. It is a horn of plenty, if you use it well."[19] Perhaps recalling Erasmus, the Spenserian narrator offers a kind of linguistic blazon of Ate, describing her "double"-speaking mouth, "That naught but gall and venim comprehended, / And wicked wordes that God and man offended"; her "lying tongue," divided "in two parts . . . And both the parts did speake, and both contended"; her "hart" similarly "neuer thoght one thing, but doubly stil was guided"; and even her ears have an "ambivalent" nature (IV.i.28.1, 27.4–5, 27.6–7, 27.8–9):

> Als as she double spake, so heard she double,
> With matchless eares deformed and distort,
> Fild with false rumors and seditious trouble,
> Bred in assemblies of the vulgar sort,
> That still are led with euery light report. (IV.i.28.1–5)

Just as the tongue, in Carla Mazzio's words, "encodes a relation between word and flesh, tenor and vehicle, matter and meaning,"[20] so Spenser's Ate materializes the processes of language, from thought and speech to reception and action, "leading" people's behaviors. Ate's lies are, perhaps predictably, described as an assault on Scudamour's body:

> Which when as *Scudamour* did heare, his heart
> Was thrild with inward griefe, as when in chase
> The Parthian strikes a stag with shiuering dart,
> The beast astonisht stands in middest of his smart. (IV.i.49.6–9)

The knight here is shot with the dart of Ate's rhetoric.

What has not been recognized by Spenserians is the way this assault is re-played in the form of Scudamour's dream, which provides evidence that Ate's words have penetrated his mental faculties and stuck in his spirits. The episode in Care's cottage re-enacts the initial effects of Ate's words on his body and mind by literalizing many common ideas about the impact of rhetoric and sound on the body of listeners. Spenser's choice of a blacksmith's foundry as the site of Scudamour's dream emphasizes the qualities of softness and hardness at issue in the two conceptions of subjectivity described earlier: open permeability and sealed fortification. This play of hardness and softness in the art of blacksmithing serves as the backdrop for one of Spenser's *Amoretti* sonnets: "The paynefull smith with force of fervent heat / the hardest yron soone doth mollify: / that with his heavy sledge he can it beat, / and fashion to what he it list apply."[21] The blacksmith's craft here is revealed to be analogous to Spenser's stated desire to "fashion" his audience "in vertuous and gentle discipline," and Spenser highlights this connection by enacting in Care's foundry many tropes for rhetorical efficacy and the power of words in the period. Wayne Rebhorn, for instance, has argued that Renaissance rhetorical texts often used the physical language of hardness and softness and the figure of words as hammers to describe the orator's control over the will, emotions, and behaviors of listeners. Richard Rainolde's *Foundacion of Rhetorike*, for instance, argues that "the moste stonie and hard hartes, can not but bee incensed, inflamed, and moved" by the power of language.[22] A Spanish rhetorical manual even more aptly discusses "The little flowers of Rhetoric" that "awaken the spirit [*spiritus*] and wound it, and they prepare wills in such a manner as when, by hammering, workmen soften and render hard iron malleable in order to make their objects out of it,"[23] an explicit model of the malleable, permeable self under the influence of powerful language. So when Scudamour "to sleepe did thinke," he is kept awake by "The hammers sound," which "his senses did molest" (IV.v.41.1–2). This hammering explicitly recalls Ate's word-wounds inflicted earlier, still molesting and echoing in Scudamour's "carefull minde," fashioning him physically into a state of sickness and despair.

At a critical point during the Care episode, Scudamour himself becomes the object of the blacksmith's work, and Spenser introduces a new trope for rhetorical efficacy when the knight's armor is literally penetrated—an invasion directly recalling Ate's language. The Spenserian narrator tells us that the knight "in his armour layd him down to rest" (IV.v.39.2). But just as Ate's words have assaulted him, so he is physically attacked in the house of Care: Each time he approaches sleep, for instance, one of the blacksmith's helpers "rap / Vpon his headpeece with his yron mall" or hammer (IV.v.42.3–4). It is left to Care himself finally to penetrate the knight's armor:

> With that, the wicked carle the maister Smith
> A paire of redwhot yron tongs did take
> Out of the burning cinders, and therewith
> Vnder his side him nipt, that forst to wake,
> He felt his hart for very paine to quake,
> And started vp auenged for to be
> On him, the which his quiet slomber brake:
> Yet looking round about him none could see;
> Yet did the smart remaine, though he himselfe did flee. (IV.v.44.1–9)

In these lines of a dreamer wakened by physical pain, Spenser painfully conflates the blacksmith's tools with Ate's invading words: Care's "redwhot tongs" that "nipt" the knight's body here are not merely a tool for grabbing but also a common sixteenth-century spelling of "tongues."[24] Ate's *lingua* has penetrated Scudamour, and the blacksmith's actions re-enact the Ate-Scudamour exchange more visibly—but, I want to stress, just as materially as the initial word-wound.[25]

In the Care episode, Spenser emphasizes Scudamour's shielded exterior in part by depicting the breeching of it. But what happens to words, Spenser wonders in this episode, once they have "gotten into" the subject? It has become axiomatic to link humoral theories of the body's permeability with Paster's influential description of the "leaky" body, and Michael Schoenfeldt has forcefully argued that early modern subjects sought to maintain a perfect osmosis between the body and its environment, a two-way balance between influences and expulsions.[26] My contention about Scudamour, though, is that he lacks precisely this balance. Ate's words penetrate and then harden in his mental faculties, a kind of fixity signaled from the initial moment of linguistic penetration: When Scudamour hears Ate's lies, the narrator tells us, "his heart / Was thrild with inward griefe" (IV.i.49.6–7). Scudamour here is rendered frozen and speechless in his very physical grief. That Scudamour's heart is "thrild" with Ate's words and images shows his somatic permeability, but the word also implies a binding and enslavement that is reflected in the image of the stag "astonisht," paralyzed by the "shiuering dart." In this moment, Scudamour is (to use one of Spenser's favorite words) "astonied"—stone-like, impenetrable, frozen, and obsessed.

There are humoral reasons for this fixity, which resembles a process Ficino called a lover's "fascination" by the love-object, leading to the dangerous illness of melancholy. As Spenser knew, Ficino explains the affect of love in terms of an exchange of spirits between lover and beloved that captures the subject in the productions of the imagination or fantasy.[27] Ficinian "fascination"—or the fixation on the desired love-object—begins with the emission of spirits from the eyes in the form of "rays" or "darts" that travel "into the eyes of the bystander." As he says in *De Amore,*

since [spirit] is shot from the heart of the shooter, it seeks again the heart of the man being shot, as its proper home; it wounds the heart, but in the heart's hard back wall it is blunted and turns back into blood. This foreign blood, being somewhat foreign to the nature of the wounded man, infects his blood.[28]

Ficino takes quite literally the stories of Cupid's wounding arrow, providing a physiological explanation for the workings of eros that describes the "heart's hard back wall" as a kind of love-shield (scud-amore?) that, rather than deflecting the love-arrow, instead transmutes it into an even more contagious form. The lover, in addition to having this foreign blood circulating in the body, also is infected with images, or phantasms, of the beloved so powerful that the lover becomes obsessed and even possessed by them, leading to the condition of "erotic melancholy" or *amor heroes* legible in Spenser's description of his blacksmith,[29] including his "hollow eyes and rawbone cheekes forspent" and his "Full blacke and griesly" appearance (IV.v.34.4, 34.6).[30]

Spenser draws attention to the harmful effects of Scudamour's melancholic fascination by emphasizing the early modern association between blacksmiths and harmonic music, an association Spenser uses to explore the rhetorical might of Orphic music and its perverse double, Ate's slanderous words. As John Steadman points out, classical legend recounts how Pythagoras overhears blacksmiths at work and notices the musical tones produced when their hammers strike anvils. Similarly, when Scudamour and Glauce first approach the house, "they heard the sound / Of many yron hammers beating ranke, / And answering their wearie turnes around" (IV.v.33.6–8). The episode's clearest allusion to the Pythagoras legend, though, comes with the description of Care's "six seruants," who "soused" or banged on an "Andvile" with "heaping stroakes" from "great hammers" (IV.v.36.1–4).[31] These strokes produce a kind of music, the narrator continues, because of the differences in size (and thus sound) of the hammers:

All sixe strong groomes, but one then other more;
For by degrees they all were disagreed;
So likewise did the hammers which they bore,
Like belles in greatnesse orderly succeed,
That he which was the last, the first did farre exceede. (IV.v.36.5–9)

Steadman notes the obvious irony here of the hammers whose music "disagreed," a reversal of the Pythagoras story and an anti-Orphic *exemplum* of the "might" of destructive language such as Ate's. This passage also recalls the narrator's lament immediately following the Ate episode concerning the "wicked discord" that language can cause: Only "a God or godlike man" such as "*Orpheus*" or "that celestiall Psalmist" David can "moderate stiffe minds, disposd to striue" (IV.ii.1.67, 2.1, 2.6). Perhaps in preparation for the Care episode's equation of language with the sound of hammers and bells, here the narrator lays bare the metaphor between music and words: "Such Musicke" as can cure, he says, "is wise words with time concented" (IV.ii.2.5), where the "concent" or harmony between music and words suggests not only the book's emphasis on concord and friendship but also the magical, intersubjective connections between discrete things that explain the rhetorical power of Orphic language.

By the time Scudamour has reached the house of Care, though, he is in no condition to hear such healing words: His melancholic fixation has, quite literally, destroyed his ability to allow words inside his faculties. Britomart's nurse Glauce—certainly no Orpheus, but with the best of intentions—tries to use language ("wise words") "To calme the tempest of [Scudamour's] troubled thought" (IV.ii.3.2), but her words are utterly ineffectual.[32] They fall on deaf ears much like Scudamour's own questions to the smiths, who, fixated on their work, "Ne let his speeches come vnto their eare" (IV.v.38.6). In this condition, images and affects freely circulate within the boundaries of his skin, but he is closed off to anything beyond this boundary. The narrator gestures toward this paradoxical condition in the labors of the blacksmith, who

> neither day nor night, from working spared,
> But to small purpose yron wedges made;
> Those be vnquiet thoughts, that carefull minds inuade. (IV.v.35.7–9)

These Spenserian thought-wedges primarily refer to ingots of gold, silver, or another metals cast in a forge, but the primary sense of *wedge* as a tool placed in a space between things is oddly appropriate here. Care's wedges, just like the "shiuering dart" (IV.ii.49.8) of Ate's words, both invade and then fix or lock the "mind" in place. Rather than being open to other voices, Scudamour is stuck inside his own armor, wedged into a narcissistic concern for no one but himself.

The circumstances surrounding Scudamour's dream, then, explicitly contrast the knight's paradoxical vulnerability and impervious fixity, a distinction that acquires an ethical connotation when Spenser names the blacksmith "Care." The smith's work depicts Scudamour's care (his jealous anxiety, the traditional reading of the episode) but also signals Scudamour's imperviousness to care (or concern). For Spenser, that is, the callousness to language that characterizes the knight's aggressive, predatory sexuality is diagnosed as both physically and ethically dangerous. It turns out that Scudamour's dream rehearses not only Ate's word-wounds but also Scudamour's first heartless encounter with his bride Amoret, described near the end of book IV. Scudamour falls in love with Amoret through a rumor of her beauty, leading him on a single-minded quest of possession. He bursts into the Temple of Venus and, once his "eye was fixt" on Amoret, he "robs" her from the women who raised her, terrifying everyone including Amoret herself (IV.x.56.2, 53.3). As he's leading her out of the temple, he recalls, Amoret

> often prayd, and often me besought,
> Sometime with tender teares to let her goe,
> Sometime with witching smyles: but yet for nought,
> That euer she to me could say or doe,
> Could she her wished freedome fro me wooe. (IV.x.57.1–5)

Abducted utterly against her will, overpowered and mastered by Scudamour, Amoret's beseeching words clang off shielded Scudamour like so many blunted arrows.

Scudamour's callous reaction to Amoret here denotes not a literal invulnerability (Scudamour will reveal his openness to some kinds of language later when he encounters Ate) but a phantasmic one; he experiences a fantasy of autonomy and individuality that belies his continuing vulnerability. It is significant, then, that Scudamour, who never removes his armor in the house of Care, *dreams* of being influenced from outside his body,[33] as if in fulfillment of a wish to escape the tortured feedback loop of being trapped inside the boundaries of his peculiar armor. Scudamour's armor and shield symbolize his own imagined invulnerability and narcissistic entrapment, psychic conditions that work in his body to make him immune to the normal kinds of environmental penetrations associated with dreams but also from the healing power of words like Glauce's. Scudamour's errors—his lack of Care—originate not in his vulnerability to evil language but from his unidirectional fixity, his inability to change, to purge evil words and harmful emotions from the system of his embodied faculties. His careful anxiety renders him immune to more beneficial influences. In this way, Scudamour's dream gestures dialectically toward a more divine notion of *caritas*. It signals Spenser's ethical wish for a sustained vulnerability of the subject, a wish that the narrator exposes in his musings on the subject of reading—another form of linguistic penetration of the subject.

Scudamour's struggles with language and the poem's implied wish for a properly vulnerable subject seem not to have been merely theoretical concerns for Spenser, whose narrator uses the imagery of shields and permeations to describe struggles with actual, historical readers. In the proem to book IV, for instance, the narrator defends his poetic project against an influential reader, probably William Cecil, Lord Burleigh, whose "rugged forhead"—itself a kind of rough shield—"doth sharply wite" or blame the narrator's "looser rimes" in books I through III (IV.proem.1.1, 3).[34] This authority dislikes love stories and considers poetry to be something "By which fraile youth is oft to follie led, / Through false allurement of that pleasing baite" (IV.proem.1.6–7). Such criticisms, which the narrator considers the work of "Stoicke censours" immune to feeling, ignore the power of love, or *caritas*; these readers "cannot loue, / Ne in their frozen hearts feele kindly flame" (IV.proem.3.9, 2.1–2). Physiologically frozen and fixed, such readers experience a Scudamourean immunity to the power of poetry, characterized in the proem as vital, active, in motion, and growing: Poetry at its best, the narrator says, "brings forth glorious flowres of fame" (IV.proem.2.7).

Spenser's purported desire, from the Letter to Ralegh, "to fashion a gentleman or noble person in vertuous and gentle discipline," reappears in these stanzas as well: The Stoic readers would much prefer that audiences "were in vertues disciplined" than that they read love poetry (IV.proem.1.8). Spenser would clearly disagree that poetry and discipline are mutually exclusive. But we might also hear in this line a change in Spenser's thinking about his own project: He questions the ethics of "disciplining" readers and encouraging the sort of fixity and frozenness that cause Scudamour so much trouble in the poem.[35] The narrator instead offers his poems directly to "my soueraigne Queene" (IV.proem.4.2), and he calls on "Venus dearling doue" to

> chase imperious feare,
> And vse of awfull Maiestie remoue:
> In sted thereof with drops of melting loue,
> Deawd with ambrosiall kisses by thee gotten
> From thy sweete smyling mother from aboue,
> Sprinkle her heart, and haughtie courage soften,
> That she may hearke to loue, and reade this lesson often. (IV.proem.5.3–9)

Only with a softened heart is one able to "hearke to" and "reade" not only Cupid's "lesson" but Spenser's own. The opposite of this softness is "imperious feare" and "awfull Maiestie"—those aggressive, frightening qualities of Scudamour in the Temple of Venus here used to describe the powerful, awe-inspiring force of a virgin Queen. This language of

hardness and softness, freezing and melting, situates the ideal act of
reading as a dreamlike penetration and the ideal reader as vulnerable,
wary of a fashioned fixation and open to change.

# Notes

1. All citations from Spenser's *Faerie Queene* are from *The Faerie Queene*, ed. A. C.
   Hamilton (London: Longman, 1977). The present quotation is taken from
   Spenser's "A Letter of the Authors" to Sir Walter Ralegh, 737.
2. Gail Kern Paster, *The Body Embarrassed: Drama and the Disciplines of Shame in
   Early Modern England* (Ithaca, N.Y.: Cornell University Press, 1993), 8–9.
3. Norbert Elias, *The Civilizing Process: Sociogenetic and Psychogenetic Investigations*
   (Oxford: Blackwell, 2000), 470–476. See also David Hillman, *Shakespeare's En-
   trails: Belief, Scepticism, and the Interior of the Body* (Basingstoke: Palgrave
   Macmillan, 2007), 6–7.
4. For a comprehensive discussion of dream theory, see Peter Brown, ed.,
   *Reading Dreams: The Interpretation of Dreams from Chaucer to Shakespeare* (Oxford: Oxford University Press, 1999), and Steven F. Kruger, *Dreaming in the
   Middle Ages* (Cambridge: Cambridge University Press, 1992). The most extensive sixteenth-century dream book is Thomas Hill's *The most pleasuante
   arte of the interpretacion of dreames* (London: Thomas Marsh, 1576). In addition to his commonplace ideas about prophetic dreams and dreams that reflect the sleeper's humoral complexion, Hill describes other environmental
   influences on dreams: "men haue truer dreames in the Sommer and the
   Wynter then in the Springe, and the Harueste, for that in those tymes they
   often alter"; "quiet seasons, dooe cause true dreames, but the wynde, and
   boystrouse weather, dooe worke contrarye, and the more boysterouse, the
   rather falser" (sig. D7r–D8r).
5. Reginald Scot argues that "neither witches, nor anie other, can either by
   words or hearbs, thrust into the mind of a sleeping man, what cogitations or
   dreames they list," a denial of the intersubjective possibilities of dreams and
   magical practices (*The Discoverie of Witchcraft*, ed. Rev. Montague Summers
   [1584; New York: Dover, 1972], book 10, chap. 5, 103). For a discussion of
   Scot's notion of the body's boundaries, see Katharine Eisaman Maus, "Sor-
   cery and Subjectivity in Early Modern Discourses of Witchcraft," in *Histori-
   cism, Psychoanalysis, and Early Modern Culture*, ed. Carla Mazzio and Douglas
   Trevor (New York: Routledge, 2000), 325–348, 336.
6. Thomas Nashe, *The Terrors of the Night, Or, A Discourse of Apparitions*, in *Selected
   Writings*, ed. Stanley Wells (London: Edward Arnold, 1964), 141–175: "All the
   night-time [dreamers] quake and tremble after the terror of their late suffering [during the day], and still continue thinking of the perplexities they have
   endured" (153).
7. In general, psychoanalytic "fixation" is a neurosis caused when a person has
   not fully moved past one (or more) of the developmental stages of sexuality.
   I use the term not only because of its psychoanalytic connotation but also in
   homage to a wonderful dream-image from Nashe: As an arrow sometimes
   overshoots its mark, he muses, "so our thoughts, intentively *fixed* all the daytime upon a mark we are to hit, are now and then overdrawn with such force
   that they fly beyond the mark of the day into the confines of the night" in the

shape of "fragments of idle imaginations." Nashe, *Terrors of the Night*, 153 (my emphasis).

8. Michael Schoenfeldt makes this point about the harmful, unhealthy effects of a closed system in Galenic medicine (*Bodies and Selves in Early Modern England: Physiology and Inwardness in Spenser, Shakespeare, Herbert, and Milton* [Cambridge: Cambridge University Press, 1999]). While I agree with him that the early modern self is a function of controlling the permeable boundaries of the body, the case of Scudamour illustrates that a too-intense policing of these boundaries leads to physical and ethical illness.

9. An excellent introduction to the organic soul is Katharine Park, "The Organic Soul," in *The Cambridge History of Renaissance Philosophy*, ed. Charles B. Schmitt (Cambridge: Cambridge University Press, 1990), 464–484. See also Ruth E. Harvey, *The Inward Wits: Psychological Theory in the Middle Ages and the Renaissance* (London: Warburg Institute, 1975).

10. Stephen Batman's *Batman vppon Bartholome, His Booke De Proprietatibus Rerum* (London: Thomas East, 1582) is a modernization of John Trevisa's fourteenth-century translation of Bartholomaeus Anglicus's *De Proprietatibus Rerum*, book III, chap. 10, sig. D3r. There were many different versions of this same basic trajectory of faculties in the period.

11. One of the best accounts of the animal spirit (from the Latin *anima*, soul) is John Sutton's *Philosophy and Memory Traces: Descartes to Connectionism* (Cambridge: Cambridge University Press, 1998), 25–49.

12. Batman, *Batman vppon Bartholome*, sig. E4r.

13. Thomas Eliot's *Castel of He[a]lth* (London, 1539), an enormously popular text to which Spenser alludes in the Despair episode of *The Faerie Queene* (I.ix.31.1–2), treats the spirit as a "natural" part of the body and defines it as "an ayrie substance, subtyl, stiryng the powers of the bodye, to perfourme theyr operacyons" (1561 edition, sig. C1v).

14. Jon A. Quitslund, *Spenser's Supreme Fiction: Platonic Natural Philosophy and* The Faerie Queene (Toronto: University of Toronto Press, 2001), 176–177.

15. Thomas Hill, *A Most Briefe and Pleasant Treatise of the Interpretation of Sundrie Dreames* (London: Thomas Marsh, 1576), sig. D4v.

16. Hill, *Most Briefe and Pleasant Treatise*, sig. B1r.

17. Timothie Bright, *A Treatise of Melancholie* (London, 1586), 131. Perhaps the most well-known literary discussion of medical, humoral dreams occurs in Geoffrey Chaucer's *Nun's Priest's Tale*, in *The Riverside Chaucer*, ed. Larry Benson (Boston: Houghton Mifflin, 1987): When the rooster Chauntecleer wakes from a dream of a predator, his wife Pertelote responds from a hard-line Galenic perspective: "Swevenes engendren of replecciouns, / And ofte of fume and of complecciouns, / Whan humours been to habundant in a wight. / Certes this dreem, which ye han met to-nyght, / Cometh of the greet superfluytee / Of youre rede colera, pardee" (2923–2928). Dreams, for Pertelote, are caused by bodily processes: overeating ("repleccioun"), the vaporous by-product of digestion ("fume"), and humoral balance ("compleccioun"). For a discussion of what he calls a standard medieval "colour-coded" system for interpreting humoral dreams (where black dream-objects, for example, denote melancholy), see Steven Kruger, "Medical and Moral Authority in the Late Medieval Dream," in Brown, *Reading Dreams*, 58.

18. See Nancy G. Siraisi, *The Clock and the Mirror: Girolamo Cardano and Renaissance Medicine* (Princeton, N.J.: Princeton University Press, 1997), 184.

19. Desiderius Erasmus, *The Tongue*, in *Collected Works of Erasmus*, trans. Elaine Fantham (1974; Toronto: University of Toronto Press, 1989), 250–412, 365.

20. Carla Mazzio, "Sins of the Tongue," in *The Body in Parts: Fantasies of Corporeality in Early Modern Europe*, ed. David Hillman and Carla Mazzio (New York: Routledge, 1997), 52–79, 54.

21. *Amoretti XXXII*, in *The Yale Edition of the Shorter Poems of Edmund Spenser*, ed. William A. Oram, Einar Bjorvand, Ronald Bond, Thomas H. Cain, Alexander Dunlop, and Richard Schell (New Haven, Conn.: Yale University Press, 1989), lines 1–4.

22. Wayne A. Rebhorn, *The Emperor of Men's Minds: Literature and the Renaissance Discourse of Rhetoric* (Ithaca, N.Y.: Cornell University Press, 1995), 92.

23. Rebhorn, *Emperor of Men's Minds*, 43–44.

24. The Oxford English Dictionary entry for "tongue" has this alternate spelling.

25. John M. Steadman, in an important reading of the House of Care, treats the episode symbolically, arguing that "the central image of the episode—the figure of the smithy—was a singularly appropriate symbol for the torments of jealous wrath" (219) because of "a contemporary Italian idiom which described jealousy metaphorically as 'martello' or 'martello d'amore'" (208). I suggest that the blacksmith's hammer does material as well as metaphorical work in the episode. See Steadman, "Spenser's House of Care: A Reinterpretation," *Studies in the Renaissance* 7 (1960): 207–224.

26. Paster, *The Body Embarrassed*, 23, and Schoenfeldt, *Bodies and Selves in Early Modern England*.

27. For a discussion of the way Ficino's ideas inform Spenser's poetry, see Quitslund, *Spenser's Supreme Fiction*.

28. Marsilio Ficino, *Commentary on Plato's Symposium on Love*, 2nd ed. Trans. Sears Jayne (Dallas, Tex.: Spring Publications, 1985), VII.4, 159.

29. The classic study of the *amor heroes* in European medieval literature is John Livingston Lowes, "The Loveres Maladye of Hereos," *Modern Philology* 11, no. 4 (1914): 491–546. Much of the knowledge about erotic melancholy can be traced to Gerald of Berry's thirteenth-century commentary on the *Viaticum*, a small encyclopedia for travelers by Ibn Eddjezzar. See Beecher and Ciavolella's introduction to Jacques Ferrand's *A Treatise on Lovesickness*, trans. and ed. Donald A. Beecher and Massimo Ciavolella (Syracuse, N.Y.: Syracuse University Press, 1990), 67. See also Ioan Couliano, *Eros and Magic in the Renaissance*, trans. Margaret Cook (Chicago: University of Chicago Press, 1987).

30. I cannot help but hear in Spenser's depiction of the melancholy smith a distant echo of a line from Timothie Bright quoted above: In the dreams of melancholics, "the fantasie *forgeth* [terrifying] obiectes," *A Treatise of Melancholie*, 131 (my emphasis). Spenser puns on these various meanings of *forge* earlier in the same canto (IV.v.15).

31. In most stories, there are either four or five blacksmiths with differently-weighted hammers, but Steadman, in "The 'Inharmonious Blacksmith': Spenser and the Pythagoras Legend," *PMLA* 79, no. 5 (1964): 664–665, finds a version of the story with six smiths in Franchino Gafuri's *Theorica Musicae* (1480).

32. Dorothy Stephens notes that the equation of Orpheus and the bumbling nurse Glauce forces us to take the nurse seriously: "Glauce does not succeed in controlling *her* situation, but Spenser's powerful Orpheus simile makes room for at least the wish, if not its fulfillment" (*The Limits of Eroticism in Post-Petrarchan Narrative: Conditional Pleasure from Spenser to Marvell* [Cambridge:

Cambridge University Press, 1998], 72). Stephens sees a connection between Glauce and "a very different old woman" (68), Ate; from the perspective of their influence on Scudamour, however, they play very different roles.

33. That the experience is part of Scudamour's dream is evident in that the pain from the tongs "forst" Scudamour "to wake" (IV.v.44.4).

34. Jonathan Goldberg notices the "imagery of melting and softening" in the proem to book IV: Burleigh "is 'rugged' whereas the text is 'looser,' he is a welder and closer when the text is loose, dilating, and 'magnifying'" (*Endlesse Worke: Spenser and the Structures of Discourse* [Baltimore: Johns Hopkins University Press, 1981], 125).

35. For another critic who finds discrepancies between the Letter to Ralegh and *The Faerie Queene*, see Paul Suttie, "Exemplary Behaviour in *The Faerie Queene*," *Journal of English and Germanic Philology* 99 (2000): 313–333.

# Erotic Symbolism, Laughter, and Hermeneutics at Work in Late-Medieval mæren: The Case of Das Häslein

ALBRECHT CLASSEN

The hare (*Lepus europaeus or Lepus cuniculus*) is one of those animals that have been used all over the world in many different cultures to symbolize a range of meanings. As early as in antiquity, scholars such as Claudius Aelianus (*De natura animalium* 13, 11–15) and Pliny the Elder *(Naturalis historia* 8, 81), then also their successors in the Middle Ages, such as Isidore of Seville (*Etymologiae* 12, 1, 2359) and Bartholomaeus Anglicus (*De proprietatibus rerum* 18, 68), critically dealt with the hare because it seemed to represent so many human characteristics. They noticed its high speed, its particular ability to run up steep hills and to switch course rapidly, allowing it to escape hunting dogs and other dangerous animals—but then they also underscored the hare's excessively timid nature and, probably most important, its extraordinary fertility. Similarly, the cooked meat of a hare proves to be, according to popular, sometimes even learned, opinion, an aphrodisiac, sometimes even a wonder drug, returning fertility to sterile women. Medieval Arabic composers of medical tracts recommended hair, brain, skull, meat, stomach, and so on, of a hare as highly useful to combat pain, to fend off poison, and to serve in many other medical matters.[1] Medieval European writers, such as the anonymous author of the eleventh-century *Physiologus* and the late-medieval preacher Geiler von Kaysersberg (d. 1510), referred to the hare's ability to race up a steep hill as an allegory of man's great need to turn to God as quickly as possible, outrunning the devil down in the valley and escaping from its countless snares.[2]

The dominant features, however, that have always been attributed to the hare pertain both to its fearfulness/nervousness and its sexual

*Medievalia et Humanistica*, New Series, Number 34 (Paul Maurice Clogan, ed.), Rowman & Littlefield Publishers, Inc., 2008.

promiscuity, as reflected on the one hand by Plinius's comment that women generally demonstrate a great preference for these animals in many respects and on the other by the fact that the hare has long been a central icon for men's erotic fantasies (see, e.g., the magazine *Playboy*—the image of woman as a bunny). At the same time, since early Christianity the hare, because of its extraordinary fertility, has been intimately connected with Easter, the time of Christ's resurrection and triumphal ascension to heaven; hence this animal has become, through spiritual allegorization, a most important religious symbol in the Western world.[3] Although best known for its fearfulness and anxiety, these characteristics have been regularly associated with peacefulness and absolute trust in God. Concomitantly, as Albert the Great (1193/ 1206–1280), one of the great doctors of the Church, emphasizes, if a woman "inserts the rennet into her vagina after the mensis, it will always assist her conceiving." By contrast, as he observes, "Some say if a woman drinks the rennet of a hare for three consecutive days after the end of her menstrual period, she will not conceive; on the other hand, Avicenna says this sometimes aids conception" (154).[4] To be sure, animals and human culture have long been intimately intertwined both in the Middle Ages and today, since many of the former provide food, entertainment, and protection for the latter.

Popular folk mythology, religious concepts, and medieval scientific discussions all had a certain impact on the symbolic and allegorical interpretation of the hare. In one literary example from the late thirteenth century, in the anonymous verse narrative (*mære*) *Das Häslein*, many of these elements come to the fore and prove to be most effective in creating one of the most erotic, but also hermeneutically fascinating, late-medieval German narratives. In fact, we might call it a masterpiece, though scholarship has paid only little attention to this tale, perhaps because it seems to be predicated primarily on the play with erotic allusions and does not fit into the traditional courtly context. Nevertheless, both its intrinsic value and the enormously exciting response from modern student audiences invite a more careful and critical investigation.

Whereas I have previously investigated this tale regarding its level of morality and ethics within the context of sexuality and the subsequent transgressions as a basis for humorous entertainment that can easily accept minor infractions and displays considerable tolerance in sexual matters, here I will argue that the anonymous author probed how to overcome critical challenges of self-perception and self-analysis by way of erotic discourse and a plethora of sexual allusions, whether understood prima facie or not. By focusing on the highly symbolic animal, the little hare, this *mære* demonstrates how much the treatment of human desires makes possible the analysis of fundamental epistemological issues within society concerning the principles of understanding and comprehension on a psychological level, because only the appearance and reappearance of this animal in various and changing contexts shed light on the protagonists' true feelings and desires and allows the male hero to see through a web of deception regarding his planned wedding. These feelings are indirectly revealed through laughter about the symbolic function of the hare in a variety of significant contexts.

The basic facts concerning this short and delightful narrative are well known, though the tale itself has not been examined by many German medievalists,[5] with the notable exception of Stephen Wailes, whose findings have been very helpful but with whose interpretation I differ considerably. There are numerous elements directly related with the experience of sexuality, but it is not sexuality itself, the catalyst for other developments here, that assumes center position. As so often the case with Middle High German *mæren*, here the narrative impetus rests on gender relationships, and those in turn hinge upon basic ethical and moral values, and these are finally deeply informed by questions of human epistemology concerning understanding reality, then identity, and love.[6]

My discussion will focus almost exclusively on *Das Häslein* because this tale all by itself contains a wealth of intriguing topics, themes, motifs, symbols, and issues. Moreover, the careful analysis will allow us to investigate some of the critical concerns dealt with by the plethora of similar tales of this popular late-medieval genre.[7] The purpose hence will be to present a case study of this one narrative as an illustration of the extraordinary literary wealth and complexity of this large corpus of comparable *mæren* that easily could stand the comparison with contemporary collections of similar tales, whether we think of Boccaccio's *Decameron*, Chaucer's *Canterbury Tales*, Franco Sacchetti's *Novelle*, or, further down the line in history, Marguerite de Navarre's *Heptaméron*.[8]

*Das Häslein* easily emerges as an extraordinary representative of latemedieval literature, although it has survived in only one manuscript, S (the St. John's Manuscript A 94 of the former Strasbourg City Library), which unfortunately was lost when the library burned down in 1870.[9] The author is unknown, but we can surmise that he or she composed the text at the end of the thirteenth century (from now on only "he" as the more likely option).[10] There are several parallel narratives in German (*Der Sperber, Dulceflorie*) and also in French literature (*La Grue* and *Le Héron*), though we cannot say with any certainty where exactly our author drew his material from and whether he influenced any other writers.[11] As is commonly the case in this genre, this *mære* aims for public entertainment, and couples this with didactic purposes of moral, ethical, and then also with hermeneutical intentions according to the Horatian principle of *delectare et prodesse*.[12] A synopsis of *Das Häslein* can be found in several previous studies on the genre itself,[13] but it deserves to be repeated here briefly.

A young knight catches a young hare and intends to take it with him as a gift for his ladylove who so far has been only lukewarm in her responses to his wooing. In a village he comes across a young woman who immediately wants to purchase the hare, but he specifies as price only her *minne*. Not knowing anything about it, she soon allows him to carry out this barter, and later she proudly displays the hare to her mother, believing that she has made a good deal. Of course, her mother reacts most angrily and punishes her harshly. Three days later—which might be a symbolical allusion as well—the girl sees the knight again. Now she demands that their barter agreement be rescinded, to which he happily agrees because it allows him to have sex with her one more time. Later he is supposed to get married to a noble lady, but mindful of the delightful tryst with the village girl, he invites her and the mother to his wedding. When he notices them arriving at court with the hare, he laughs so hard that his fiancée requires from him the truth about it. Once having learned everything about the secret deal with the hare, she scoffs at the other young woman, pointing out that she herself had done the same thing a hundred times with the village priest, and yet her mother never found out about it. Horrified about this realization, the young man quickly changes his mind, relates everything to his friends at the wedding party, and following their advice, he dismisses his fiancée and takes the peasant girl as his wife.

*       *       *

Although scholarship has touched upon this narrative from time to time within the wider context of the genre, it deserves further examination.[14] Among many other aspects, the narrative highlights a complex of different questions concerning human sexuality, eroticism, human language and communication, the significance of laughter, and gender relationships.[15] Ultimately, as I want to demonstrate here, a critical reading will reveal numerous levels of meaning that point in the direction of a hermeneutic discourse that is predicated on the basic experiences in human life, love, and sex. Multiple levels of innuendoes and satire, the use of iconic language, and the ambivalent meaning of animal metaphors within human society all strongly contribute to the literary accomplishment of this tale, which concludes with the protagonist's hearty and most revealing laughter in which we as the audience are allowed to join as a sign of mutual agreement concerning the symbolism of the hare.

Significantly, transgression seems to be the name of the game throughout the entire tale. Despite the traditional symbolic function assumed by the young hare representing sexuality and fertility[16] or the drive toward God, we normally do not hear of knights in the Middle Ages who would bother hunting these little animals because it is beneath their honor. Siegfried in the *Nibelungenlied*, for instance, though not a normal knight, hunts a lion, an elk, a boar, and so forth, all mighty and dangerous animals, but he never shows any interest in such small animals as hares (*Nibelungenlied* 936–939). Tristan in Gottfried von Strasbourg's romance proves to be an expert at cutting up the carcass of a deer when he comes across King Marke's huntsmen during his youth, and later, while spending time in the love cave, he and Isolde go hunting deer as well. The famous medieval expert on hunting, Gaston Phébus, also mentions hares as some of the many quarries in his *Livre de la chasse* (1387–1389), but he stresses the use of snares and a group of hunters in this context, which has no bearing on the situation in *Das Häslein*.[17] The illustration of the poet Herr Geltar in the *Manessische Liederhandschrift* (no. 110) exceptionally depicts a hunting scene with one greyhound having caught a fox, whereas another is in hot pursuit of a hare.[18]

By contrast, in our *mære*, the male protagonist does not really go on a hunt and does not even have any equipment with him to kill a hare from a distance; instead, he is leisurely spending his time without pursuing a specific goal, although he is accompanied by two dogs and his sparrowhawk (26–28), the typical trappings of a courtly knight and a lover. However, as Stephen L. Wailes has argued, the entire set-up seems to be wrong for a traditional courtly context because the knight has only ordinary dogs with him—that is, no greyhounds, the only ones that would be capable of catching a fast-running hare. On the other hand, we might assume that the little animal is still very young and inexperienced, which makes it possible for the harvester to catch it. This would also explain why the hare proves to be a most fitting anticipatory symbol of and parallel to the youth and ignorance of the village maid. It is the time of harvest, again a rather unusual season for a courtly narrative or for the account of courtly love, and the little animal runs away from him into the field where one of the workers catches it for his lord.[19]

Significantly, the hare is not killed because the knight figures that he could use it well as a gift for the lady who has rejected him so far. The narrator's comment, however, signals that the protagonist is not really interested in the ideal of any type of love because he mocks young women in general who cannot understand the true value of important objects and easily accept an egg in return for a whole country (55). Of course, this does not imply that the protagonist knight is much better prepared to evaluate realistically the relevance of his own goals and actions, especially since we will never hear again of that elusive maid for whom his heart, at least at this point, is burning with love (47–49).

When the young man and the village maid meet, another remarkable discrepancy emerges because despite her low social status the narrator describes her with the standard terms of courtly love, identifying her as a "juncfröuwelîn" (61; "young noble maid") who is "edel, schœne unde fin" (62; "noble, beautiful, and attractive"). The audience is invited to share voyeuristically in the encounter between both people through multiple perspectives involving their individual gazes. Since he is greeting her first (70), he has obviously espied her from the distance and turned his horse toward her. At the same time she does not even really notice him as a person; instead her attention is entirely focused on the hare that distracts her even from the knight: "daz ersach diu junge magt" (69; "the young maid noticed it"). He himself has already displayed considerable enjoyment in this untamed animal (67), which he is holding with one hand and softly stroking with the other, a most curious gesture that might have further implications of a sexual kind, although the narrative is not specific enough here to venture further interpretations.

The maid is entirely obsessed with the young animal and desires to purchase it right away (72–73), completely oblivious to the dogs, the sparrow-hawk, and perhaps even to the man: "vil gerne het ich daz heselîn" (78; "I really would like to own the hare"). Ultimately, she will achieve her goal, first by "selling" her love, or rather the use of her sexual body, to the knight; then she is allowed to keep it after all, three days later once he has, upon her demand, given back this *minne*, that is, her virginity through a second sexual act. Finally when she attends the wedding ceremony and brings the hare along with her, by now almost as her very own attribute, she triggers deeper feelings in the knight who suddenly realizes that she would be a much worthier bride for him. And we must assume that the hare stays in her possession during their marriage, probably as a symbol of her fertility. Wailes summarizes this phenomenon as follows: "From her first experience of sexual pleasure she and the hare are inseparable" (96). Although she claims utter ignorance and innocence when asked for her *minne* as the price for the hare, using an almost classical formulation in her retort— "'minne, herre, waz ist daz"(85; "love, my lord, what is that?")[20]— further probing reveals something else. She offers at first most symbolic objects as payment for the little animal: many rings, dice, and, above all, a silken belt, interwoven with gold threads and adorned with pearls (89–100).

The belt seems to be the most costly object among her little treasures and would suffice, as she believes, in exchange for the hare, particularly because her mother had made it for her, putting all her skills to work (96–97), obviously in preparation of her daughter's future wedding.[21]

The young man rejects all her offers, disregarding their material and also symbolic value; instead he requests her "minne reine" (104; "pure love") as price for the animal, which could mean, however, many different things, such as love, sex, affection, and so forth. Although she is of lower social status, the knight treats her as an equal and applies his best courtly language to seduce her. Wailes places too much emphasis on their social class difference, erroneously detecting here the "spirit of Neidhart" that allegedly permeates the subsequent scene when the young woman reports everything to her mother and presents the hare to her. Further, Wailes claims that the union of knight and maid amounts to a travesty at the cost of the simple peasant girl, as if the erotic dimension were predicated upon the clash of social classes: "For a landed knight to marry a village girl because her lechery was naïve made no more sense to a mediaeval audience than trying to run down a hare with spaniels."[22]

This seems to be an overly narrow reading that disregards the symbolic meaning of the various objects and the hare, and so also the hermeneutic function of the sexual theme, as we will see later. To put this curious relationship between knight and maid into the proper perspective, we only need to remember that Hartmann von Aue had already presented a similar case in his *Der arme Heinrich* (c. 1200), with the young but deadly sick nobleman suffering from leprosy marrying the young and beautiful farmer's daughter who had been willing to die for him but whose sacrifice he had rejected at the last moment. Significantly, Hartmann's verse narrative was also contained in the same manuscript S (no. 17) as *Das Häslein* (no. 25),[23] and despite the concrete rural setting, at the end the young nobleman happily marries the maid upon all of his friends' specific recommendations (483–497). Their words are revealing and confirm our reading that the focus does not rest on the social class difference: "daz er die junge fîne / mit dem heselîne / ze rehte wîben solte, / ob er gedenken wolte, / waz billich wære und êre" (493–497; "to take the young fine lady, the one with the hare, as his rightful wife, if he were to consider what would be proper and honorable").

As Wailes and others have pointed out, the anonymous author was obviously familiar with Gottfried von Strasbourg's *Tristan*, since he quoted a line from his prologue and borrowed his "manner and complex of ideas." But despite his best attempts subsequently to paint a picture of grotesque satire of the traditional hunt within the courtly context, Wailes's claims do not find adequate support in the text: "To such a tutored passion the bizarre first scene in the *Häslein* must have been uproarious, for the hare-hunt early became the paradigm of the form and procedure of venery."[24] The young knight does not go out to hunt a little hare; instead he happens to come across one and then pursues it just for fun. But he succeeds in capturing it only with the help of a harvester, and subsequently intends to employs it as an erotic object to win long-desired love from a noble lady.

By the same token, the village maid does not view the little hare as foodstuff or as a simple animal. For her it is nothing like a pet or a toy, as she reveals by her ardent desire to gain possession of it at all costs (rings, belt, and then her own body). It would be difficult to estimate her age, but we can be certain that she is nubile according to the narrative framework, which includes the subsequent marriage with the knight and also, rather significantly, her prior passionate longing for the animal, not to speak of the sexual trysts with the knight. We might even speculate that her mother has already prepared her daughter for marriage by creating the symbolic belt for her, though it proves to be unnecessary since she grants the knight free access to her body anyway. Possibly the implied meaning could also rest in her gesture of offering the belt to him, which can only be read as a highly erotic signal in that he is invited, so to speak, to open the belt and take possession of her.[25]

The narrator invites his audience to take a good look at this young woman, at least virtually, when he describes her as "daz linde turteltiubelîn" (115; "the sweet little dove"), and" ir wonten wîbes site bî" (129; "she displayed a woman's manners"). The erotic gaze finds additional support through the subsequent allusions to their sexual union, though the author abstains from any graphic terms and images, and only incites the (male?) imagination, concluding with the revealing remark: "und nôz ir jungen süezen lîp, / biz daz diu maget wart ein wîp" (155-56; "and enjoyed her young sweet body until the maid became a woman"). Once she has tasted the pleasures of sexual intercourse, she demands ever more and expresses her disappointment with him when he leaves her without having slept with her a third time (180–185)—a typical male projection of female sexual needs (nymphomania) perpetuated since the time of the Church Fathers and influential even today.[26]

The irony consists, of course, in her continued lack of understanding of the true meaning of what has happened to her, not to speak of the term *minne*, which ultimately proves to be the crucial linguistic aspect that determines the development of the entire narrative, although its meaning cannot be easily defined since the word embraces a wide range of aspects, both erotic and ethical, social and emotional. The immediate point addressed by the poet is the free and pleasurable experience of sexuality, but the audience can partake in those only vicariously. Nevertheless, the humor is predicated on the conflict between knowledge and ignorance, the perception of truth and the misunderstanding of the meaning of words. After all, the young woman naïvely presents the hare to her mother once she has returned home, herself delighted with the seemingly advantageous purchase that she has made, pointing out the beauty of the small animal (193). At this point we would expect the mother to teach her daughter finally the basic lesson regarding sexuality to prevent further accidents, but she only resorts to violence, which makes her daughter commit basically the same mistake—if we can call it that—once again when the knight happens to pass by their house three days later.

But would we be justified in identifying her behavior as foolish and wrong, perhaps even sinful, and his request as lustful, abusive, and mean-spirited? After all, he had requested her *minne*, a heavily charged word that cannot simply be equated with "sexuality," and she had freely granted it to him in exchange for the hare, representative of fertility on a symbolic level.

The young man fully grasps her low level of intelligence and cunningly, though without great effort, sleeps with her a second time. Remarkably, now she does not seem to experience particular sexual pleasure and is apparently only concerned with recovering her former virginity. She does not demand from him that he return her *minne* twice, if not three times, in order to complete the transaction precisely and thus to reconstitute her innocence; instead she submits to him quietly without voicing any opinion or discussing her feelings. One small comment by the narrator, however, forces us to consider another aspect, reconnecting our analysis with the initial cultural-historical and ethnological reflections. The little hare represents a most meaningful erotic symbol, if it is not a representative of fertility itself. In the more or less contemporary Old French *fabliau Trubert*, for instance, the trickster protagonist refers to his penis using the metaphor "hare" that wants to live in the princess's vagina.[27]

While the knight "returns" the love to her, she only gazes attentively at the little animal: "diu juncvrouwe dicke blicket ie / an ir vil liebez heselin" (272–273; "the young woman often [intently?] looked at her much beloved little hare"), obviously regretting already that she will lose it. She is truly obsessed with the animal, and when he finally grants it to her as a gift, she feels great satisfaction and actually regards the young knight as a fool for giving up such a valuable object (280).[28]

Although at first sight the erotic and sexual do not seem to be of true importance for her, especially since a male voyeuristic perspective dominates, the outcome of the narrative demonstrates that she was right after all. The primary goal of the narrative rests on the hare, which in turn represents fertility, and since the two young people will eventually marry, we can assume that they will be blessed with progeny. And when we pay close attention to the narrator's commentary, we also discover the subtle budding of true love between these two people: "wer zwîvelt an dem mære, / dem guoten ritter wære / mit ir reiner minne wol? / nieman daz unbilden sol / noch waz der âventiure geschiht, / als uns daz mære hie vergiht. / der minnen übergulde, / nu wer behup ir hulde?" (259–266; "Who would doubt that the good knight was deeply pleased with her pure love? No one should object to what happened here as the story tells us. The crown of love—who deserves to receive its grace?").

Significantly, at the end the village girl arrives at his wedding festival to which he has invited her and the mother as his guests, carrying the hare with her as he had bid her, though, as the narrator emphasizes, "ân arge liste" (393; "without any evil thought"). Nevertheless, it is the hare itself that makes the knight burst out in loud laughter because the little animal reminds him of how he had at first "cheated" the young woman out of her virginity and how much she herself subsequently had enjoyed the sexual experience with him, demanding triple payment for the animal in the form of love-making (168–175).

Laughter, as we know from numerous older and recent studies on this phenomenon, also characterizes courtly life and plays an integrative function, ostracizing outsiders, especially those from another social class.[29] Nevertheless, laughter implies epistemological ambivalence and ambiguity, opening a hermeneutical gap that invites unexpected, often transgressive responses and sheds light on underlying truth. When Wailes argues that the "story's comedy is at the girl's expense, and there is no warmth in the apparently conciliatory ending,"[30] he takes a very one-sided view, disregarding several important factors: The young peasant woman experiences double happiness insofar as she can marry into the higher class and because she can rely on her own fertility, since she holds the hare as her possession, which, at the end, intimately links her with the knight who was equally intrigued by this furry animal. Of course, the narrative focus rests mostly on his decision, strongly supported by his friends' advice to consider what would be the most honorable and appropriate decision in this situation. Nevertheless, the narrator concludes with these significant comments: "daz sîn sol, daz muoz geschehen" (504; "whatever has to be will happen").

In other words, everyone fully approves the joining of hands of the two people who truly fit together, and we might argue that his laughter at the arrival of the two women with the hare indicates a deep, if not involuntary, realization that all the wedding plans are for naught because his true bride has arrived only now, unbeknownst to the entire company except for himself. No wonder, we may conclude, that his fiancée gets so upset, because she senses a deep rupture between them resulting from a secret that he does not want to divulge to her. After all, his laughter is not mean-spirited or aggressive; instead, it is the result of him remembering a delightful sexual tryst that had been possible for him because the maid had displayed such innocence and naïveté.

Significantly, a most remarkable second laughter erupts, though outside of the narrative. Once the bride-to-be has learned the truth about the knight and the girl, she suddenly reveals her own secret that she has slept with the chaplain, who is doing his service at their estate, about a hundred times without her mother ever having found out. The audience both then and today would regard this confession as quite facetious because it has such shock value and entirely robs the young woman of all her good reputation and honor, while it reveals her vicious intentions to ridicule the other woman whom she regards as a contemptible competitor. Because we laugh about her, the other, rather innocent claimant on the knight's heart and hand suddenly rises to a much higher level where the social class distinction hardly plays a role anymore, whereas honor, honesty, sincere love, and chastity determine an individual's true character. The knight had laughed out of sympathy and perhaps a budding love, whereas the audience laughs out of contempt for the sycophant fiancée who falsely claims the rank of nobility but has deliberately and deceptively betrayed her own honor and that of her family.

Of course, the village maid had also given up her virginity to a man she was not married to, but she had obviously no idea what his request had meant, probably because her mother failed to instruct her about the meaning of sex, and that at a time when she had already entered the nubile stage. By contrast, we laugh about the fiancée because she knew what sex really meant, and yet, although she was aware of having transgressed, she still reveals her secret openly to her bridegroom because she wants to ridicule the other woman.[31] This would not necessarily allow us to determine the narrative framework as a parody of courtly values or courtly love because the experience of sexual love ultimately reaches a point where an honorable couple joins hands in marriage.[32] Otherwise both the knight's laughter when he sees the maid arrive with her mother and the hare, and the audience's laughter indirectly implied through the shock revelation by the noble lady would not make much sense.

Without the appearance of the hare and the knight's subsequent laughter the hypocrisy of the wedding would not have been uncovered—which underscores, once again, the hermeneutic function of the hare as the catalyst for the protagonist's learning process. Particularly because of the fiancée's immediate contempt for the other young woman who had enjoyed sexual contact with her future husband first, she talks about her own skills in hiding the affair with the priest, not grasping how much she is hurting herself with this careless confession.[33]

Why would we as the audience laugh about the outcome of the narrative (and we certainly do)? There are more dimensions in the tale than those outlined above. When the mother learns that she and her daughter are invited to the wedding, she considers it with a heavy heart because the bridegroom has slept with her daughter first and should therefore marry her and not the other woman: "sît er des hoves solte / billîch, ob er wolte, / pflegen mit der tohter dîn" (371–373; "since he should celebrate the wedding, as would be proper, if he were to agree, with your daughter"). She thinks that without even considering the social class distinction, which further weakens Wailes's arguments discussed above. Then she accepts the invitation, as if she were happy about it (379) because it would be an honor for them (378). This makes the knight rather happy (383), and we might wonder about his motivation and emotional response in this situation.

After all, when he had seen the maid the first time, her beauty had struck him deeply, and he obviously enjoyed their subsequent tryst both times. But he invites the mother and daughter later because he feels obligated to do so out of a sense of honor: "sîn edel herze niht enlie, / sie müeste dâ ze hove sîn" (348–349; "his noble heart did not rest, they had to come to the court festival"). Nevertheless, when they arrive at his court he immediately focuses on the hare and on the young woman's childish appearance, which is both innocent and highly erotic at the same time (389–406).

When we pay close attention to the narrator's explanation, we discover the reason for his uncontrollable laughter: "der wirt, der dâ wol wiste, / wie der hase wart gekouft, / und wie diu tohter wart zerrouft, / und wie der wehselkouf geschach, / der lachet unt tet einen kach" (394–398; "the host, who knew well how the hare was bought and how the daughter was abused and how the trade took place, laughed and made a big noise"). Hence, his laughter reveals a most complex process of an innocent, certainly also abusive, then, however, consensual sexual relationship. Although the maid did not understand what he meant by *minne*, she fully appreciated it and soon enough demanded more, and later when she has entered the court he realizes that she is his true bride-to-be, whether we read this as the expression of male sexual fantasy or as a comment about the value of true love that reaches beyond all class distinctions. So we might say that his laughter destroys the illusion concerning the noble fiancée's claim to honor and respect and uncovers his actual love relationship with the maid.

He laughs because he has suddenly discovered his own self, his true desire, and his longing for a woman who loves him back and does not hesitate to give him what he needs. After all, at the beginning we heard about a lady who had rejected all his wooing; and at the end, during the wedding ceremony, his new fiancée threatens to make his life miserable if he does not obey her order. No wonder that his choice for the village maid proves to be the right one, and that everyone agrees that she is his ideal marriage partner.

\* \* \*

Ultimately, as the title of this *mære* indicates, it is the hare itself that carries the whole hermeneutic weight insofar as it symbolizes at the beginning the knight's sexual desires, then the maid's erotic obsession, and finally proves to be the catalyst for his realization of the true goal, or objective, of his love. The protagonists constantly gaze on this furry animal, touch it, and carry it, so they slowly but surely begin to grasp their deep-seated feelings and longing for a happy marriage, predicated both on the sharing of emotions and fulfilled sexuality irrespective of their social backgrounds. Sexual deception determines much of the plot, but the regular reappearance of the hare transcends this challenge to true love and makes possible the marriage of the knight and the village maid, which amounts to explicit criticism of arranged marriages, class arrogance, and lack of honesty in the realm of love and sexuality. Whenever the protagonist laughs, he is getting closer to his own self and more free from the social constraints imposed on him by his noble background. More to the point, however, this is not a tale about the failings of feudal society and the traditionally strict separation of the classes. The purpose specifically rests in the powerful function of the hare as a symbolic animal of great erotic significance that allows the revelation of hidden desires and dreams about marriage and fecundity. Long before the young knight and the maid marry, the exchange of the hare for her virginity has already bonded them strongly. Once the young woman appears at his wedding ceremony, carrying the animal with her, he laughs out loud because he suddenly realizes what his true destiny will be and that he has deceived himself so thoroughly with the other woman. We laugh with him because the hare easily reminds us of the fundamental bond between people of the opposing gender, both love and sex.

# Notes

1. Rudolf Schenda, "Hase," in *Enzyklopädie des Märchens*, ed. Rolf Wilhelm Brednich, 6:542–555 (Berlin: de Gruyter, 1990); Riegler, "Hase," in *Handwörterbuch des deutschen Aberglaubens*, ed. Hanns Bächthold-Stäubli, vol. 3, *Handwörterbucher zur deutschen Volkskunde*, 1504–1526. Abt. I: Aberglaube (Berlin: de Gruyter, 1930–1931); jetzt auch Bernhard Dietrich Haage and Wolfgang Wegner, *Deutsche Fachliteratur der Artes in Mittelalter und Früher Neuzeit* (Berlin: Erich Schmidt, 2007), 177–246.
2. Hans Biedermann, *Knaurs Lexikon der Symbole* (Munich: Droemersche Verlagsanstalt Th. Knaur Nachfl., 1989), 181–183.
3. See, for example, Albrecht Dürer's famous painting "Der Feldhase" from 1502.
4. Peter Dinzelbacher, "Mittelalter," in *Mensch und Tier in der Geschichte Europas*, 181–292 (Stuttgart: Kröner, 2000); see also the other contributions to Dinzelbacher's volume; cf. the monograph by Salisbury.
5. Stephen Wailes's analysis from 1969 continues to be one of the very few indepth investigations dedicated exclusively to our narrative ("The Hunt of the Hare in 'Das Haslein,'" *Seminar* 5, no. 2 [1969]: 92–101). W. M. Sprague concerns himself mostly with intertextual references ("Down the Rabbit-Hole," *Jahrbuch der Oswald von Wolkenstein Gesellschaft* 15 [2005]: 315–348). Elsewhere I examine moral and ethical issues ("The Fourteenth-Century Verse Novella *Dis ist von dem Heselin*: Eroticism, Social Discourse, and Ethical Criticism," *Orbis Litterarum* 60, no. 4 [2005]: 260–277). Rather speculatively, Walter Haug tries to deconstruct the genre itself and suggests that the *mæren* authors as a whole renounce all search for meaning and protest against any kind of narrative epistemology ("Entwurf zu einer Theorie der mittelalterlichen Kurzerzählung," in *Kleinere Erzählformen des 15. und 16. Jahrhunderts*, ed. Walter Haug and Burghart Wachinger [Tübingen: Niemeyer, 1993], 7).

6. Klaus Grubmüller, *Die Ordnung, der Witz, und das Chaos: Eine Geschichte der europäischen Novellistik im Mittelalter: Fabliau—Märe—Novelle* (Tübingen: Niemeyer, 2006), 194–201.

7. See the following studies, among others: Hanns Fischer, *Studien zur deutschen Märendichtung*, 2nd. ed. Ed. Johannes Janota (Tübingen: Niemeyer, 1983); Ingrid Strasser, *Vornovellistisches Erzählen: Mittelhochdeutsche Mären bis zur Mitte des 14. Jahrhunderts und altfranzösische Fabliaux* (Vienna: Fassbaender, 1989); Hans-Joachim Ziegeler, *Erzählen im Spätmittelalter: Mären im Kontext von Minnereden, Bispeln und Romanen* (Munich: Artemis Verlag, 1985); and Grubmüller, *Die Ordnung.*

8. Wolfgang Spiewok, trans., *Altdeutsches Decamerone*, 2nd ed. (Berlin: Ruettenn & Loening, 1984); see also Robert J. Clements and Joseph Gibaldi, *Anatomy of the Novella: The European Tale Collection from Boccaccio and Chaucer to Cervantes* (New York: New York University Press, 1977); and Albrecht Classen, *Erotic Tales of Medieval Germany* (Tempe: Arizona Center for Medieval and Renaissance Studies, 2007).

9. Sprague, "Down the Rabbit-Hole," offers a detailed discussion of the manuscript and its content, as far as we can still figure this out today.

10. Because of the emphasis on male fantasy, it seems most unlikely that a female author composed this tale.

11. Grubmüller, *Die Ordnung*, 1221–1223; Sprague in "Down the Rabbit-Hole" investigates possible connections with earlier Middle High German texts, treating *Das Häslein* as a repository of intertextual allusions on the basis of parody.

12. See the introduction in Classen, *Erotic Tales*, along with Grubmüller, *Die Ordnung.*

13. Strasser, *Vornovellistisches Erzählen*, 219–220; see also Fischer, *Studien*, 194–195, and Sprague's extensive comparative analysis ("Down the Rabbit-Hole").

14. Strasser, *Vornovellistisches Erzählen*, 220, note 741, summarizes some of the older research. For more extensive commentary, see Klaus Grubmüller, ed., *Novellistik des Mittelalters: Märendichtung*, Bibliothek des Mittelalters, 23 (Frankfurt a. M.: Deutscher Klassiker Verlag, 1996), 1221–1227. See also Grubmüller's general remarks in his monograph *Die Ordnung*, 141–142.

15. Similar observations can be made with respect to the genre as a whole. See Albrecht Classen, "Gender Conflicts, Miscommunication, and Communicative Communities in the Late Middle Ages: The Evidence of Fifteenth-Century German Verse Narratives," in *Speaking in the Medieval World*, ed. Jean Godsall-Myers, 65–92 (Leiden: Brill, 2003).

16. Peter G. Beidler, "Chaucer's French Accent: Gardens and Sex-Talk in the *Shipman's Tale*," in *Comic Provocations: Exposing the Corpus of Old French Fabliaux*, ed. Holly A. Crocker (New York: Palgrave Macmillan, 2006), 155–159.

17. *The Hunting Book of Gaston Phébus: Manuscrit français 616 Paris, Bibliothèque nationale* (London: Harvey Miller, 1998), chap. 80–85; for a summary and translation, see 72–75. Hares as quarry are mentioned numerous times in Middle High German literature, see the database www.mhdbdb.sbg.ac.at :8000/mhdbdb/App?action=TextQueryModule&string=hase&texts=%21 &startButton=Start+search&contextSize=1&contextUnit=1&vertical Detail=3&maxTableSize=100&horizontalDetail=3&nrTextLines=3. But the hare as an erotic object or symbol finds no parallels in medieval German literature, as far as I can tell.

18. See www.tempora-nostra.de/tempora-nostra/manesse.php?id=203&tfl=111; again, there is no erotic symbolism contained in this scene. The parallels to

the illustration of the poet von Suonegge (no. 67) are striking, but there the hunted animal is a stag. See Ingo Walter, ed., *Codex Manesse: Die Miniaturen der Großen Heidelberger Liederhandschrift*, 4th ed. (Frankfurt a. M.: Insel, 1988), 138–139; 224–225.

19. Wailes comments: "How remarkable that the little animal famed for evasiveness should be taken by a peasant on foot and barehanded" ("Hunt of the Hare," 95). But then he continues, entirely missing the symbolism contained in this scene, hence its significance for the overall interpretation: "Both in the details of equipment and action, and in the manner of the hunt's conclusion, the introductory scene is a ludicrous distortion of reality, more entertaining, no doubt, for an audience familiar from immediate experience with hunting procedure and the relations between noblemen and peasants than for modern students of the text."

20. Sigûne in Wolfram von Eschenbach's *Titurel* uses basically the same question, expanding on the complexities of the term: "Minne, ist daz ein êre? maht du minne mir tiuten? / ist daz ein sit? kumet mir minne, wie sol ih minne getriuten? / muoz ich si behalten bî den tocken? / oder fliuget minne ungerne ûf hant durh die wilde/ ich kan minne wol locken?'" (Hg., übersetzt und mit einem Stellenkommentar sowie einer Einführung versehen von Helmut Brackert und Stephan Fuchs-Jolie [Berlin: de Gruyter, 2003], 64). See also Albrecht Classen, "Wolframs von Eschenbach *Titurel*-Fragmente und Johanns von Würzburg *Wilhelm von Österreich*: Höhepunkte der höfischen Minnereden," *Amsterdamer Beiträge zur älteren Germanistik* 37 (1993): 75–102.

21. Albrecht Classen, "Der Gürtel als Objekt und Symbol in der Literatur des Mittelalters: Marie de France, *Nibelungenlied*, *Sir Gawain and the Green Knight* und Dietrich von der Glezze," *Mediaevistik*, forthcoming. See also the gifts Poor Henry brings to the peasant girl in Hartmann von Aue's *Der arme Heinrich*, which carry strongly erotic symbolism: "gürtel unde vingerlîn. / Mit dienste brâhte er sî ûf die vart, / daz si im alsô heimlich wart / daz er si sîn gemahel hiez" (Hartmann von Aue, *Der arme Heinrich*, ed. Hermann Paul, 16., neu bearb. Aufl. besorgt von Kurt Gärtner [Tübingen: Niemeyer, 1996], 338–341). See also Sprague, "Down the Rabbit-Hole," 325–329.

22. Wailes, "Hunt of the Hare," 98–99, 100. His evidence, however, proves to be ambivalent since the harvesting does not necessarily separate the knight from his workers; instead he pursues the hare into the field and receives it from one of the men as his own property. Moreover, his approach to the maid and ultimately his marrying her make the specific markers of class distinction disappear, or at least become blurry.

23. W. M. Sprague, *The Order of Saint John's Manuscript A94 of the Strasbourg Commandery* (Göppingen: 2005). That manuscript also contained *Der Sperber* (no. 5), very similar to *Das Häslein*, and a range of other verse narratives of mixed content, none of them specifically idealizing courtly life and nobility. The girl in Hartmann's tale does not have to be read literally as a farmer's daughter. According to medieval hermeneutics, everything, and so people, could be interpreted morally, allegorically, and then even anagogically; see Albrecht Classen, "Herz und Seele in Hartmanns von Aue 'Der arme Heinrich.' Der mittelalterliche Dichter als Psychologe?" *Mediaevistik* 14 (2003): 7–30.

24. Wailes, "Hunt of the Hare," 100; Sprague, "Down the Rabbit-Hole." Sprague pushes the interpretation of *Das Häslein* as a reception, parody, or travesty of

previous courtly narratives almost to the breaking point. The degree to which the tale is predicated on satire (341) seems rather debatable.

25. See the specific meaning of Brunhilde's belt that Siegfried takes away from her and which Kriemhild later displays to her in triumph, thereby demonstrating publicly that her husband had slept with Brunhilde first, as far as she can tell (849); see also Classen, "Der Gürtel."

26. For the tradition beginning in late antiquity, see Alcuin Blamires, ed., with Karen Pratt and C. W. Marx, *Woman Defamed and Woman Defended: An Anthology of Medieval Texts* (Oxford: Clarendon Press, 1992), 25ff. For the late Middle Ages and early modern age, see Lyndal Roper, *Oedipus and the Devil: Witchcraft, Sexuality, and Religion in Early Modern Europe* (New York: Routledge, 1994).

27. Norris J. Lacy, "Trickery, Trubertage, and the Limits of Laughter." In *The Old French Fabliaux: Essays on Comedy and Context*, ed. Kristin L. Burr, John F. Moran, and Norris J. Lacy (Jefferson, N.C.: McFarland, 2007), 88.

28. This is the same conflict discussed in Dietrich von der Gletze's more or less contemporary *mære The Belt*, where the stranger knight hands over all his magical animals and his fantastic belt that guarantees its bearer to win honor in return for the lady's love. Afterward she scoffs at him for having done a bad deal, but he corrects her misunderstanding since he has experienced the happiest hour of his life. Not surprisingly, she willingly grants him a kiss when he departs, as if she had suddenly realized the true nature of love (Classen, *Erotic Tales*, 23).

29. See Cunneware's laughter at the sight of the foolishly looking Parzival in Wolfram's romance, 151, 19, for which she is immediately punished severely by the court seneschal Keye. She laughs because she thinks Parzival is a boorish but highly presumptions person, but in reality, as the narrative development indicates, her laughter anticipates the truth about the young protagonist, the savior both of the Arthurian and the Grail world. The same seems to apply to our case: The knight laughs about the girl and the hare, not knowing that his future wife has arrived. See Thomas Zotz, "Urbanitas. Zur Bedeutung und Funktion einer antiken Wertvorstellung innerhalb der höfischen Kultur des hohen Mittelalters," in *Curialitas: Studien zu Grundfragen der höfisch-ritterlichen Kultur*, ed. Josef Fleckenstein (Göttingen: Vandenhoeck & Ruprecht, 1990), 402–403. Coxon demonstrates that the semantic function of laughter depends very much on the specific social-historical context, class orientation, and cultural framework (Sebastian Coxon, "*do lachete die gote.* Zur literarischen Inszenierung des Lachens in der höfischen Epik," in *Wolfram-Studien* XVIII: *Erzähltechnik und Erzählstrategien in der deutschen Literatur des Mittelalters. Saarbrücker Kolloquium 2002*, ed. Wolfgang Haubrichs, Eckart Conrad Lutz, and Klaus Ridder. [Berlin: Erich Schmidt, 2004].) See also the contributions to Werner Röcke and Helga Neumann, eds., *Komische Gegenwelten: Lachen und Literatur in Mittelalter und Früher Neuzeit* (Paderborn: Schöningh, 1999).

30. Wailes, "Hunt of the Hare," 100. He concludes: "The 'Häslein' is an excellent example of literary amusement for the courts which depends on a depreciative involvement of the lower classes." He mistakes, however, the sarcastic undermining of the traditional courtly values by the noble fiancée and by the foolish agreement to wed the young knight with this rather dubious woman. She would have turned into a wife-dragon for the rest of his life if he had not revealed the secret behind his laughter (vv. 404–405), but at the

end, as in the earlier *lai* by Marie de France, *Bisclavret*, her insistence on being informed about everything in his private life leads to her downfall and utter loss of happiness.

31. Henri Berson, *Le rire: essai sur la signification du comique* (Paris: F. Alcan, 1928), 13, points out: "Un personnage comique est généralement comique dans l'exacte mesure où il s'ignore lui-même. Le comique est *inconscient.*" He also comments on laughter resulting from speaking ignorantly and revealing involuntarily something about oneself: "Se lassier aller, par un effet de raideur ou de vitesse acquise, à dire ce qu'on ne voulait pas dire ou à fair ce qu'on ne voulait pas fair, voilà, nous le savons, une des grandes sources du comique" (85). After all, the audience is invited to laugh about the fiancée, although the poor knight turns pale and is shocked about her revelation, knowing only too well that she would never display any hesitation to cuckold him once they were married.

32. Heribert Hoven, *Studien zur Erotik in der deutschen Märendichtung* (Göppingen: Kümmerle, 1978), 91; Sprague, "Down the Rabbit-Hole," 323.

33. Bergson, 65, fittingly for our case, emphasizes: "Nous rions de quelque chose que cette disproportion peut, dans certains cas, manifester, je veux dire de l'arrangement mécanique spécial qu'elle nous laisse apercevoir par transparence derrière la série des effets et des causes."

# The Romance Epic Hero, the Mercenary, and the Ottoman Turk Seen through the Lens of Valentin et Orson (1489)

## SHIRA SCHWAM-BAIRD

The classic French epic has often been seen as an expression of the crusading ethic of the late eleventh and twelfth centuries.[1] Thus when Roland declares that "Paien unt tort e chrestïens unt dreit" (1015; "The pagans are wrong and the Christians are right"),[2] he is speaking not (or not only) in terms of the conflicts of Charlemagne's time, but is (also) expressing the ethos of the great movement of men and arms that wrested the holy places of Jerusalem from the hands of the infidels. But history and politics are not static, and the enduring popularity of the Carolingian epic, particularly as it evolved through the *mises en prose* into the fifteenth century, suggests that, beyond the recycling of motifs, it was filtered through the lens of a later period. In the late Middle Ages, the Latin West was in fact fighting a new type of "Saracen," the Ottoman Turk, and crusading had taken on an entirely new aspect. The goal of recovering the holy places (lost at the end of the thirteenth century with the defeat of the last crusader stronghold in the East in 1291) was only nominally important in crusade preaching; instead, the focus, when any Western power could focus on it, was on shoring up the beleaguered stronghold of Constantinople, or, after its defeat in 1453, recovering it, and halting the Ottoman push into Europe. The question is further complicated by the fact that the Ottomans became involved in European politics in a way that the Muslims of Outremer never had. At the same time, any literary text stands linked to its literary forbears. Thus, it is in the context of contemporary politics and conflicts, Christian-Turkish relations, and changing perceptions of "the Saracen," as well as in the literary context of the Christian knight serving as a mercenary in Muslim

*Medievalia et Humanistica*, New Series, Number 34 (Paul Maurice Clogan, ed.), Rowman & Littlefield Publishers, Inc., 2008.

courts, that this chapter proposes to look at a particular romance epic,[3] *Valentin et Orson*, from 1489.

This little-known text is typically prolix in fifteenth-century fashion, and the following summary does it little justice; but for the purposes of this writing it shall be brief. The eponymous heroes are twins, born to King Pepin's sister and the emperor of Greece. Having been banished owing to a false accusation of adultery, their exiled mother gives birth in a forest, where accident then separates the three. Orson grows up wild among bears while Valentin is raised as a foundling at court by his own uncle, King Pepin. Once he becomes a knight, Valentin vanquishes his wild-man brother and brings him to Pepin's court, where the deafeated brother undergoes the process of civilizing. Supernatural intervention soon reveals the secret of the brothers' noble birth, and, about halfway through the text, they are reunited with their mother and father. The rest of the narrative follows the numerous adventures of Pepin, the brothers, and their companions, while drawing on a wide variety of romance and epic narrative motifs, including the search for the lost beloved, many battles with Saracens, and a little hagiography thrown in for good measure.[4]

A particularly puzzling passage from *Valentin et Orson* is the focal point of this chapter, for, without placing this literary passage in the context of the web of political, social, and perceptual realities of its time, it is difficult to fathom.[5] Valentin, the twin raised at Pepin's court, becomes embroiled in a series of adventures in Saracen lands while seeking his kidnapped beloved—a common enough literary motif. At first involved only in internecine Saracen wars, Valentin is asked to take on *and accepts* the responsibility of leading a Saracen army in battle against a Frankish army led by his uncle, King Pepin, and his own brother Orson. This turn of events is an unusual and perhaps unique situation in romance-epic literature. Valentin is no prisoner under constraints;[6] he has freely chosen the role of mercenary as part of his quest to recover his lost beloved. However, the actual confrontation with his king and kin is prevented through the machinations and magic of the sorcerer Pacolet, whose schemes and spells keep Valentin out of the subsequent battle in which the besieging Christian army defeats and slaughters the Saracens. Then, to maintain a show of fidelity (albeit superficial), Valentin honors his promise to return to Brandiffer, the Saracen lord who had sent him to relieve Pepin's siege against his land.

To be clear, it is the circumstance of Valentin, engaged in no quarrel with his kin and certainly no renegade, yet prepared knowingly to lead an infidel army against his own side, that surprises and disturbs here, not the idea that he is a mercenary fighting on behalf of a Saracen lord, for that motif occurs with some frequency in romance epic, as will be discussed below. The explanation for this narrative anomaly is, I believe, twofold. First of all, the singular nature of the relationship that the Ottomans had with Europe (which shifted not infrequently from conqueror or opponent to ally) opened a narrative space for Valentin's "cross-confessional" military role. Secondly, the enduring nature of the romance of chivalry, not capable of abiding betrayal of the chivalric ideal, closed off that space before any harm could be done.

Cross-confessional relations between Christians and Muslims were long part of the political landscape in the Middle Ages, both in the Iberian peninsula and in the various crusader states of the Middle East. Frankish mercenaries were prized for hundreds of years throughout much of the Muslim and Byzantine worlds, known for the warrior virtues of "leadership and ingenuity, as well as courage,"[7] and, "to Byzantine eyes, *the* model of superb military horsemanship."[8] Mercenaries such as the Cid[9] and Reverter,[10] serving Muslims in the eleventh and twelfth centuries respectively, illustrate the mutability of loyalties in medieval Spain. In the twelfth-century crusader East, the new crusader states became active players in the hurly-burly of regional politics, allying themselves with one emir against another in the constant political jockeying of the region.[11] And in the twelfth and thirteenth centuries, the Almohads recruited Christian mercenaries, the latter of whom had no less than the authorization of the pope, who apparently saw this as part of the larger mission to convert Muslims to Christianity.[12]

Sharon Kinoshita makes the point that "amid crusades and polemics there was an almost continuous history of political accommodation, commercial exchange, and cultural negotiation across the Muslim-Christian divide."[13] Kinoshita has focused on this "thematics of cultural interaction," as she terms it, in early French literary production, interpreting, for example the opening scene of the *Chanson de Roland* (in which Marsile considers offering Charlemagne a promise of money, service, and conversion to Christianity) as, in fact, a recognizable offer of *parias*, "the tribute money the politically weak *ta'ifa* kings of Muslim Iberia paid to their Christian neighbors."[14] She says that it would have been recognized as such at the time,[15] and that Roland's behavior throughout the text is, in fact, a call to a "politics of intransigence" to protest this "lax accommodationism" current in Iberia.[16]

This example comes from a world that conceived crusade primarily as the quest to win and control the Holy Land. But by the end of the thirteenth century, Christendom had lost Jerusalem and its primary Middle Eastern holdings to "the infidel," and, in real terms, there was a shift in crusade thinking.[17] According to Norman Housley, however much the idea of a recovery crusade may have "continued to exercise the imagination," such planning in any meaningful way was over by 1370.[18] Attention turned to the struggle against the Ottoman Turks and the need to aid or liberate beleaguered Constantinople, leaving the traditional goal of retaking the holy places as part of the crusade rhetoric against the Turks but not its realistic focus.[19] The shift seems to have occurred between 1365 and 1396, the former date being the year that the crusaders targeted Mamluk Egypt, which controlled Jerusalem, and sacked Alexandria, and the latter being the disastrous year that the crusaders set their sights (although they failed miserably) on Nicopolis, with the goal of relieving the Ottoman pressure on Constantinople and Hungary.

The Ottomans presented a different political problem than had the Saracens of Outremer. For one, Outremer was precisely that—across the sea. The issue there was finding a way to rouse sufficient fervor and raise enough funds to transport men and arms to a faraway place in order to take possession of what they deemed to be theirs by God-given right. However, there was little real concern that the infidel horde would spread to the West. The most serious incursion of Islam into Europe had been contained in Iberia after the eighth-century Frankish victories over the Umayyad forces pushing up from Spain into France. Moreover, Iberia itself was slowly being reconquered by the forces of Christianity. But the Ottomans were different in their steady push into Europe. As James Hankins points out, they presented a physical threat to the Christian West, particularly after the psychological blow of the fall of Constantinople, as well as an economic threat to trading interests.[20]

And yet, cross-confessional relations were common. One reason was the relatively tolerant way in which the Ottomans dealt with their conquered subjects. In the fifteenth century, the usual practice in the Balkans was to allow the local Christian aristocracy to hold their land as fiefs from the sultan. With no constraints on worship or the maintenance of clergy, and only a special tax to pay, the policy created many loyal subjects and prevented the kind of discontent that might have fostered rebellion and crusade.[21] So successful indeed was the policy that one loyal Christian vassal, Stephen Lazarevic, the despot of Serbia, fought on the Turkish side at Nicopolis and is credited with turning the tide of battle in the Ottomans' favor.[22]

As Housley states, "It is possible that the shrill denunciation of the Turks which we encounter in the writings of Bessarion and Pius II [a cardinal and a pope who urged the Western powers on to crusade] derived from the unpalatable fact that Turkish conquest was actually not that painful an experience. This may be deduced from the way in which the rule of some Christian princes came to be unfavourably contrasted with that of the sultan."[23]

Both individuals and states had reasons to find themselves in cooperation with the Ottoman forces. Renegades were attracted by good pay, and fugitives from justice by relative safety.[24] Italian trading cities in particular found that their commercial interests often outweighed confessional loyalty. The disastrous Crusade of Varna was preached by Cardinal Cesarini, who persuaded several Eastern rulers who had concluded a ten-year truce with the Ottomans to break the truce and attack. When the Sultan Murad needed quickly to cross the Dardanelles to counter the offensive, it was the Genoese who ferried his army across, according to a contemporary Burgundian account. As John Vine explains, "It was in Genoa's interests to aid the Turks and thereby preserve its Black Sea monopoly."[25] When Cardinal Bessarion preached crusade in Venice in August 1463, after the fall of Constantinople in 1453, he included warnings of excommunication against those who impeded the crusade or "defrauded the funds collected for the crusade, *transported arms to the Turks or their allies*, or placed obstacles in the path of crusaders seeking to fulfill their vows" (my emphasis).[26] Obviously the Venetians often put commercial interests ahead of religious duties against the infidel.

Thus, as the Ottomans established themselves in Europe, they came to play a more and more significant role in political conflicts within Europe, much in the way the crusader states had formed alliances and involved themselves in the conflicts of the Middle East among various Muslim players in the twelfth century and beyond. Complicated relations between Venice and Genoa as well as among various Greek territories led to scenarios in which the Turks were called in as allies to one group or another against fellow Christians.[27]

Also of significance was the Ottoman practice of taking non-Muslims into their armies from the lands they conquered. As Turkish scholar I. Metin Kunt explains it, "The Ottomans viewed the communities they conquered, like their own, to be composed of military men and subjects; the military of conquered societies could, if they were judged to be trustworthy, join the Ottoman *askerî* [military officials] without converting to Islam."[28] This Ottoman penchant in the early days of its empire for incorporating non-Muslims into its fighting forces is one more factor in the historical context of political, commercial, and military interaction between Europe and the Ottoman Turks that helps explain the unusual turn taken by Valentin's stint as a mercenary in a Saracen land.

However, to make the case that the way in which the hero interacts with Saracens in *Valentin et Orson* is shaped by contemporary relations with the Ottoman Turk, one should establish what knowledge the anonymous composer of *Valentin et Orson* might have had of the politics of East-West relations in his time. We know only the date and location of publication—Lyon, 1489.[29] Throughout the fifteenth century Lyon was a major European commercial city with trading fairs sanctioned by the French crown that linked it to Italy and the East. France was certainly called upon for crusade projects in the late Middle Ages, although the intermittent war with England took up much of the kingdom's attention and energy. According to Clarence Rouillard, after Louis IX's crusade in 1270, the French were largely uninterested until there was a lull in the Hundred Years' War at the end of the fourteenth century and the need for a defensive crusade "for self-preservation from the advancing Turk" was acknowledged.[30] Fourteen hundred knights from France, Burgundy, and Flanders followed Jean sans Peur and the Maréchal Boucicaut to the Crusade of Nicopolis in 1396, and many of them died there. Those who did not were ransomed and returned to France, carrying back with them accounts of the sultan's power, magnificence, and courtesy.[31] Subsequently, many French knights fought with the armies of the Hungarian John Hunyadi and the Polish King Ladislaus when they were having some success against the Turks in 1442 and 1443, and they were also caught up in the terrible defeat at Varna in 1444.[32]

Philippe le Bon of Burgundy, long fascinated by the romantic ideals of crusading, sent ships for the Varna campaign. Indeed, according to Housley, Philippe was the only Western power to show any real interest in crusade in these last years leading up to the final defeat of Constantinople.[33] He asked one of his bishops, Jean Germain, to exhort Charles VII to go on crusade with him.[34] It is precisely to the "more warlike and spirited virtues, as depicted in the epics of the early Crusades," that Germain urged the case (in vain, as it turned out) on Charles and his men.[35] Nevertheless, after the fall of Constantinople, the threat seemed much more real to the West, particularly to Italy. The story was that "Mehmed II wanted to conquer 'Old Rome' just as he had 'New Rome.'"[36]

Philippe le Bon continued to plan to go on crusade, mounting the famous Feast of the Pheasant (la Fête du faisan) in Lille in 1454 at which 200 nobles made their vow ("le voeu du faisan") along with Philippe to go fight the Turk.[37] The French were also involved in Pope Pius II's plans for crusade,[38] when it seemed that Philippe le Bon might finally go himself, but, according to Housley, Philippe backed out when "Louis XI persuaded his Burgundian vassal that his departure on crusade would expose France to the threat of an attack by the English, 'who have done more harm here than the Turks have in the lands they have conquered.'" In his stead, he sent his son Anthony with three thousand men; they only got as far as Marseilles when they received word that the aged and ailing pope, who had been planning to lead the crusade himself, had died in Ancona, and the crusade died with him.[39]

Such is the historical context of spotty crusading and cross-confessional interaction of which the composer could reasonably have been aware and in which Valentin's behavior must fit. Christians did ally with the Turks against other Christians, and Christians did fight with the Turks against other Christians—it was part of the political landscape. The very name of the city Valentin goes to defend against Pepin, Angory, is a link to the Turks, as it is the Old French version of the name of the city today called Ankara.[40]

But when Valentin accepts his role to lead the army of the Saracen King Brandiffer to relieve the siege of Angory, Brandiffer's city, he stands not only in the nexus of a long military history of Christian-Muslim interaction, he also belongs to a line of literary knights errant serving in Saracen courts.

Christian knights of romance epic come to serve Saracens for various reasons. When it is a way to free oneself from captivity, it is regarded not as "treason, but rather a chivalrous adventure."[41] Yvonne Friedman highlights several passages in *Les Chétifs* in which carrying a message or performing chivalric feats earns not only freedom but also riches and women.[42] Similarly, in *Lion de Bourges*, Lion's father Herpin, a prisoner of the emir of Toledo, is let out of prison to take up the challenge of a giant who demands the hand of the emir's daughter; he succeeds with divine aid in defeating a Saracen force.[43]

In other cases a spell as a mercenary offers escape from persecution at the hands of an unjust lord, as in the surviving fragment of *Mainet* in which young Charles (the future Charlemagne) must flee after his illegitimate half-brothers kill his parents. He takes the name Mainet, and distinguishes himself in service to Galafre, the Saracen King of Toledo, so impressing a troop of Syrians whom he has led that they choose conversion to Christianity.[44]

Often, as in Valentin's case, the entry into Saracen lands and Saracen service occurs in the course of the search for a lost comrade or loved one. In *L'Entrée en Espagne*, Roland, in service to the King of Persia, battles Hugues de Floriville, a French knight who has temporarily taken service with the Saracen ruler Malcuidant while searching for Roland himself. Hugues fights "the duel of his life" until he recognizes Roland, at which point he turns on Malcuidant, battling and defeating him.[45] Similarly, in *Lion de Bourges*, Lion, while searching for his parents, takes up arms for the Saracen King of Cyprus against the latter's enemies, the rulers of Damascus and Palermo. His success, due to the miraculous intervention of the White Knight, convinces the king of Cyprus to convert to Christianity.[46]

*Aye d'Avignon* presents a variation on the motif of service to the Saracen while searching for a lost loved one.[47] The eponymous heroine is kidnapped by her husband's enemy, Berenger, a Christian, and ends up in the court of the Saracen ruler Ganor. In the search for his wife, Aye's disguised husband, Garnier, enters Ganor's service to help him in his war against another Saracen ruler, Marsilion, who is being aided in turn by Berenger. Unlike Valentin, Berenger, the son of Ganelon, is a renegade Christian knight who has clearly crossed sides and desires the death of the Frankish knights he fights. Thus, when Garnier fights and kills Berenger in the course of the war between the two Saracen kings, it is no evil action or betrayal of the Christian side but rather a good action, both for the Saracen King Ganor (a "good" Saracen who will later convert and marry the widowed Aye), and for the Christian cause, which has rid itself of a true traitor.

The thirteenth-century *Estoires d'Outremer* presents us with the case of a prisoner who serves a Saracen lord under duress with no promise of freedom. Here the Christian knight, Reynaut of Brittany, serves Saladin, the greatest of all Saracens. Saladin, who loves Reynaut for being "si preudom et si loiaus," places him in his advance guard in his battle against King Elxelin, and allows him to keep his religion ("k'il li laissoit entour lui tenir sa loy").[48] But when Saladin faces the Franks in battle outside Damascus, Reynaut is killed by one of his countrymen. This is seen as a great shame by his compatriots, for he had been considered a good knight and his actions were somewhat excused by the fact that as a prisoner he had been obligated to do what was demanded of him. Moreover, the text reports that Reynaut himself was sorry to have to fight against fellow Christians.[49] The interest of this particular example is contrastive, for Valentin is not in a similar situation. He is not a prisoner under constraint, nor does he express regret for the situation in which he finds himself.

The closest analogue to the situation in *Valentin et Orson* may be seen in *Tristan de Nanteuil*, in which numerous Christian mercenaries fight professionally in Saracen armies. In one particular battle episode a certain knight, Richer, refuses to give up the fight even after most of the Saracens he has been leading have fled, for he has been paid by the sultan and sworn his service to him.[50] This suggests a formal loyalty resembling Valentin's respect for his promise to return to his provisional Saracen lord. Of course, unlike Valentin, Richer is engaged in battle against other Saracens, not Christians, so this passage mainly serves to demonstrate the general superiority of Christian warriors in comparison to the Saracens whom they are engaged to lead. Nevertheless, the remarkable fact about *Tristan de Nanteuil* is the way in which, as Jean-Louis Picherit points out, Christian knights, depending on their own circumstances and needs for movement, circulate quite freely in Saracen lands, serving one Saracen lord after another.[51]

We have seen the truth of Paul Bancourt's observation that "Christian heroes [in epic texts] have no scruples about serving Muslims against other Muslims"[52] in the actions of Valentin, Lion de Bourges, Charles/Mainet, Richer and others in the texts considered just above, but the motivations are usually of a noble nature (seeking the lost beloved, etc.) and never pecuniary. However, Bancourt also points to a passage in *Aye d'Avignon* in which an old pilgrim taken prisoner by the Saracen King Ganor has been released in order to go into Frankish territory ("en France") to seek mercenaries ("soudoiers") who will be able to make good money in the deal ("Qui la vodroit aler bien porroit gaengnier" [vv. 1817–19]).[53] Indeed, the passage reveals with unadorned and uncharacteristic frankness the normalcy of Christian mercenaries serving Saracen lords for pay. One might call it a bit of historical reality breaking through the romantic veil of chivalry that enshrouded the literary text and usually filtered out harsher interpretations of warrior behavior. Valentin's conduct is arguably another such incursion of historical reality.

Valentin's career as a mercenary begins when he presents himself at the court of King Lucar in the hope of hearing something of his beloved Esclarmonde's fate.[54] Lucar is the son of King Trompart who had carried off Esclarmonde, but due to his ineptitude in flying the wooden horse stolen from the magician Pacolet, he had landed in the enemy territory of India and been executed by its king. Lucar is now engaged in a war with the King of India to avenge his father's death, which explains his immediate need for mercenaries.[55]

Valentin engages in a kind of service to Lucar which proves at times to be only superficially loyal, delivering for example double messages to the King of India's court (one for Lucar, another for Rozemonde, Lucar's queen, who is, for her part, attempting to flee her husband and make her way to the King of India, a husband more to her liking).[56] He foils Rozemonde's first escape attempt,[57] which action elevates his worth in the eyes of his provisional Saracen lord, Lucar,[58] but the lady manages to escape on her second attempt.[59] In a second mission to the King of India to demand the return of Rozemonde in exchange for an end to the war, Valentin plays another double game, agreeing to the task with words of loyal service: "'Sire,' dit Valentin, 'pour vous je vouldroye mon corps aventurer, et plus que pour nul aultre'" (chapter 43, 101r; "Sire," said Valentin, "I would be willing to risk myself in service to you above all others");[60] indeed, he communicates Lucar's demands faithfully, but then adds a second message of his own that precisely contradicts what Lucar had bid him to say, namely, that Rozemonde must be returned:

Mais nonpourtant que je soye chargé de vous faire tel message, mais se croire me voulez jamais ne vous y consentirez, mais garderez la dame que tant a de beaulté et que si chier vous aime. Et sachez que jamais jour de ma vie ne seray en lieu ne en place ou je seuffre son blasme et ne deshonneur a vous faire pour l'amour de la dame. Tout le temps de ma vie je luy vouldray honneur porter et a vous faire service.

[chapter 43, 101r; "However, despite my charge to deliver this message, believe me when I say you should not consent to his demands; rather you should keep the lady who is not only beautiful but loves you dearly. And know that wherever I go throughout all the days of my life I will never allow her to be blamed nor you to suffer dishonor for love of the lady. For the rest of my life I wish only to bring her honor and do you service."]

Should such remarks compromise our perception of Valentin's uprightness as a knight? The King of India and his new consort may respond admiringly to Valentin's lofty speech (while of course dismissing Lucar's demand), but any sincerity on his part is immediately undermined for the reader by the narrator's comment: "Ainsi a prins congé moult fort joyeulx d'estre hors d'Inde et eschappé du roy" (chapter 43, 101v; "Thus he took his leave from them, absolutely filled with joy to be away from India and escaped from its king")—the implication being that Valentin probably remembers too well the King of India's reputation for killing Lucar's messengers and feels little compunction in using feigned sentiments to play the Saracen kings off one another to stay alive.

This is not to say that Valentin is a coward. We see him exhibit exceptional bravery too many times in the text to think that the narrator intends such an insinuation, but one of the recurring aspects of Christian knights serving in Saracen lands in romance epics is that disloyalty against a Saracen lord is not necessarily regarded as such by the narrator or audience. As Paul Bancourt puts it, "They don't hesitate to betray their master when he is a Saracen."[61] Bancourt offers the example of

Huon de Bordeaux (in the epic of the same name), who is to fight a judicial duel as champion of Yvorin, a Saracen. When he discovers that he is fighting against his companion, the Christian Gériaume, neither he nor Gériaume entertains any scruples about betraying the Saracen master for whom he has pledged to fight. As Bancourt says, "Such offenses committed at the expense of infidels do not seem to be considered as such by the composers of the *chansons de geste.*"[62]

Huon de Bordeaux had arrived at a Saracen court while searching for his beloved, much like Valentin. Gériaume, the companion from whom he had become separated, had come to another Saracen court while searching for Huon (another example of the search as the motive for service to Saracens). Thus both Christians fight for provisional lords out of expediency, rendering their commitment superficial and easily overridden by tribal loyalty (reinforced, of course, by loyalty to a beloved companion). Yet the parallel of circumstances between *Huon de Bordeaux* (and indeed that of all the previous examples) and *Valentin et Orson* fails in Valentin's next stage of service to Lucar when service means battle against a Christian force. Valentin appears ready to honor formal loyalty above tribal, that is, faithful service to Lucar at the risk of fighting his own uncle and brother.

Both Lucar and Brandiffer, expressing complete confidence in Valentin "sur tous aultres vaillant et hardy et couraigeux" (chapter 44, 102r; "above all others valiant, bold, and courageous"), decide to send him with Murgalent, Brandiffer's uncle, to relieve the siege of Angory by the French army "car en toutes choses je l'ay trouvé vray et en ses fais loyal" (chapter 44, 102r; "for in all things I have found him true and loyal in his actions"). Upon seeing the impressive Christian host, Murgalent asks for Valentin's advice, which, as commander, he gives—in short, that a messenger should be sent into the besieged city to announce this arrival of reinforcements and urge the men of the city to sally forth the next day against the Christians at the same moment the new arrivals attack from the seaward side.[63] Murgalent agrees and Pacolet immediately volunteers for the job of messenger based on his knowledge of all the requisite languages. But Pacolet, always "subtil et cautelleux" (chapter 44, 102v; "sly and crafty"), goes first to the Christian camp to inform Orson of Valentin's presence in the enemy camp and of the need to effect a defeat of the Saracens without letting the blame fall on Valentin. His plan is to keep Valentin from accompanying the night guard, then to cast a sleeping spell over the guard, allowing the French forces easily to attack and massacre the Saracen army.[64] Orson and Pepin embrace the plan, while it is clear that Valentin knows nothing of it.

Pacolet then crosses over to the Saracens besieged in Angory to deliver the official message with the strategy for the following day. Returning to Valentin, Pacolet informs him that he has seen Orson and Pepin to apprise them of the next day's attack so that they will not be taken by surprise, for, as he puts it, "grant pitié et dommaige seroit" (chapter 45, 103v; "that would be a great pity").[65] Valentin approves of his actions, but Pacolet tells him no more, for, according to the narrator, he knows that Valentin would never commit or consent to treachery, a clear admission on the part of the narrator that such would be the name to apply to Pacolet's plan.[66]

Valentin wants to take charge of that night's guard, but Pacolet, knowing what is to come, persuades him not to do so. Once the army under Valentin's command succumbs to the sleeping charm (all of whom are put to sleep, not only the night guard, as had been the original plan outlined to Pepin and Orson), Pepin's army attacks, setting fire to the camp and massacring the Saracen force. When Pacolet wakens Valentin to pull him out of harm's way, Valentin immediately guesses what Pacolet has done:

"Helas, Pacolet," dist Valentin, "je cognoy bien que tu as icy ouvré, et que les payens as enchanté et deceu. Si ne sçay comment je doy faire pour mon honneur sauver, car au partir de Brandiffer je luy promis et juray que se vif povoie eschapper je retourneroye devers luy. Or suis je seur que s'il a nouvelles de ceste chose, il me fera mourir."

[chapter 45, 104r; "Alas, Pacolet," said Valentin, "I recognize your hand in this— you have bewitched and deceived the pagans. And now I don't know what I can do to save my honor, for when I took leave of Brandiffer I promised him and swore that if I came out of this alive I would return to him. Once he knows of this he will have me killed."]

Pacolet's response is to promise always to come to Valentin's rescue, no matter the situation, even if Brandiffer's rope is around his neck. Valentin replies that one must cherish such a servant.

With the army he had led to relieve the siege now wiped out, Valentin apparently feels exempt from any further duty and abstains completely from the next day's battle. The Saracens besieged in Angory, ignorant of any change in circumstances, sally forth from the city into a full-scale massacre at the hands of Pepin's army, which subsequently occupies the town.

Valentin brings Murgalent's body back to Brandiffer in honorable fashion to make it look more convincing that they had actually fought together (which of course they had not), and tells a tale that blames the night guard for falling asleep and opening the way to the Christian attack. Brandiffer, furious, accuses Valentin of treachery, but the more credulous Lucar points out that if Valentin had been guilty of treachery, he would not have returned, thus allowing Valentin's ruse to work. Soon after, in the renewed war against the King of India, Valentin fights bravely on behalf of Brandiffer and Lucar, even capturing their enemy, Rozemonde's new husband, the King of India, which restores his reputation completely, even in Brandiffer's eyes.[67]

The passage recounting the battle of Angory is interesting in that it ratifies Paul Bancourt's thesis that treachery against a Saracen in epic texts is not regarded as such. Valentin's sense of honor, once satisfied on a technical level, relaxes to allow him to tell a doctored version of events, even declaring his willingness to undergo a judicial battle to prove his story. Pacolet himself functions outside the chivalric code, but the fact that he reveals nothing of his plan to Valentin implies his recognition of Valentin's commitment to do his best to fight for the side for which he has signed up, much like hero knights of romance who choose sides in a tourney. But while accepting Valentin's strong sense of chivalric duty in this case, Pacolet feels sanctioned nevertheless to conduct his part in the war outside the rules of chivalry to the advantage of the Christian side.[68] Although he has used magic previously to put enemies to sleep in order to help one or another of the heroes escape from prison, this is the only time he employs it with the sole purpose of rendering an enemy army easier to defeat.[69] Moreover, Orson and Pepin are fully complicit, for when informed of Pacolet's planned tactics, they exhibit no scruples whatever about taking advantage of them.

What is truly remarkable then about this passage is Valentin's initial apparent intention to maintain his commitment to lead the Saracen troops in the battle against Pepin's army. With no modern edition of the French text, there has been little scholarship written, and virtually none that addresses this particular situation. Only Arthur Dickson, who wrote a thorough source study of the Valentin and Orson story, notes that Valentin had no plan for what he would have done had proper battle taken place: "The author is careful to make it plain that Valentin is innocent of any complicity; but he does not explain how Valentin regarded his own position as leader of an army against his own people, or what he proposed to do about it if Pacolet had not so neatly solved the problem."[70]

The fact of the matter is that the narrative presents him as ready to go forward with the battle, while no commentary on the part of the narrator attempts to explain or judge his action. I would argue that the complicated reality of alliances and common causes with the Ottoman

Turks raised the level of normalcy perceivable in Valentin's entry into mercenary service in Saracen courts and opened a narrative space in which Valentin (who exhibits irreproachable behavior in every other adventure in the text[71]) acts more in accordance with the realpolitik of his time than with the chivalric norms of literature. But, in effect, the composer of this tale wrote himself into a narrative bind, for it is not so readily acceptable to betray one's Christian kin as it might be to turn against one's provisional Saracen lord (the pattern identified by Bancourt[72]). I would also argue that fifteenth-century readers probably received this work differently from the way we do and were not shocked when Valentin took on the leadership of Brandiffer's army, for they trusted that that narrative space would be closed for the sake of preserving the chivalric ideal, and that Valentin would not in the end actually fight against Pepin and Orson. Then the question becomes how the text will resolve the dilemma. The deus ex machina here is Pacolet and his brand of magic. When he persuades Valentin not to accompany the watch on the night before the planned attack to lift the siege, Valentin's honor as a Christian knight is safe, and with a little finagling of the truth, so is his chivalric honor toward his provisional Saracen lord, at least on the surface. But it is also possible that not all readers were satisfied with that solution, which still seems to taint Valentin's otherwise consistent uprightness as a knight. Some readers may have reacted to Valentin's actions the way the count of Tripoli reacted to John Gale in an incident that took place just before the battle of Hattin in 1187, which raises some of the same issues as those in Valentin's situation.

It is historian Jean Richard who has identified John Gale, Knight of Tyre, as the knight called upon to give advice before the battle of Hattin because of his experience of having served with the Turks.[73] John Gale had sought refuge in Muslim territory after having killed his lord, whom he had found with his wife.[74] He was also apparently sufficiently trusted by Saladin to be given the responsibility of the military education of one of Saladin's nephews, a trust he subsequently betrayed by handing the young man over to the Franks to be ransomed (his way of buying his way back into the Frankish fold).[75] It is this action that Richard posits to be the reason for which the count of Tripoli warns against trusting John or his advice given in the council taken before Hattin, saying that "he should not be believed since, when he had disowned our side by swearing fidelity to the Turks, he had broken his oath."[76] As Richard points out, the count's main reproach is not that John served with the Turks,[77] even though that might be seen as a bit disreputable,[78] but rather that "he had broken the oath of fidelity pledged to the Muslim prince, thus revealing himself to be lacking in loyalty, one of the essential knightly virtues. A man who has shown himself to be disloyal cannot be trusted,"[79] despite the fact that it is to a Saracen that he has been disloyal. In fact, the count's position stands in contradiction to Bancourt's observation, cited above, that, in the epic texts, disloyalty to a Saracen is not considered treachery. The count's position, extrapolated to Valentin's situation, would critique the sleight of hand that the composer employs to solve the narrative dilemma.

John Gale, a pragmatist, acted most likely according to his immediate needs and expediency—he first needed to escape the wrath of his murdered lord's family and later wished to reinstate himself with his compatriots. And it is not likely that Raymond of Tripoli would have preferred John to serve Saladin so faithfully as to have fought on his side against the Franks at Hattin. He was using the criterion of consistent loyalty to judge the trustworthiness of John's advice (and judged wrongly, as it turned out). Valentin, like John, is "serving with the Turks," but that, in and of itself, is not the real problem, as the brief review of literary antecedents of Christian knights serving in Saracen courts demonstrated. The difficulty was created when the composer conceived a narrative turn of events that reflected the reality of complex relationships with the Ottoman Turks and led to a serious inconsistency of character in the text's hero.

As Paul Bancourt has rightly pointed out, "the epic poems give an image that has been embellished, romanticized and simplified."[80] Because it is a fiction, Pacolet's magic neatly solves the narrative problem of how Valentin can serve with the Turks without breaking his promises to them nor fighting against his own side. But however much magic has finessed the situation with a fine pretense of chivalric duty on Valentin's part to the Saracen lord to whom he had promised service, it cannot erase the inconsistency it introduces into Valentin's character. The narrator, as pointed out above, never judges him, but if the count of Tripoli's objections to John of Gale are any indication, it may be that at least a minority of opinion was uncomfortable with this representation of realpolitik that was allowed to bleed into literature.

In conclusion, for those Christian knights who had direct or indirect experience of the Turks, it was primarily through crusade. Either they actually fought the new Saracen at Nicopolis (1396), or in Hungary (1443), or at Varna (1444),[81] or they planned to go on crusade, making their vows alongside of Philippe le Bon at the Feast of the Pheasant, or preparing to join Pius II's crusade, stillborn at Ancona.[82] They conceived of war and crusade as great chivalric enterprises, a kind of thinking that also shaped the way Froissart described events in his *Chroniques*.[83] It is that chivalric conception of war and crusade that sets the pattern for most of Valentin's military adventures in the text. He battles Saracens numerous times (chapters 10, 28, 32, 58, 62, and 66), always with exemplary bravery, but when he becomes a mercenary (chapters 33–47), he breaks with the usual literary patterns of the Christian knight in a Saracen court (examples of which were given above). Stories of those who fought or allied with the Turkish side, aided the Turks with transport or arms, or turned renegade must have circulated along with nobler tales of military adventure, and gave the composer of *Valentin et Orson* the idea for an unusual dilemma into which to place his upright hero. As Dickson said, the text's author "was extremely well informed as to the contents of all the narrative literature of the day, and he hit the taste of his time, and of later times as well, by producing what is in some sort a compendium of many of the favorite stories and situations."[84] But even Dickson, who untangled and found the sources of the many narrative threads, did not know what to make of this passage.[85] I have argued that it can only be understood as an intrusion of the realpolitik of contemporary Ottoman-European relations, which then created a narrative problem solved through the machinations and magic of someone who operated outside the chivalric code. This may be a unique case, but perhaps a closer look at other texts in the corpus of late romance epic is warranted in order to see in what other ways the political realities of the Ottoman push into Europe might have been filtered through the lens of the long popular Carolingian epic.

# Notes

1. A modern critical edition and translation of *Valentin et Orson* by the author of this article is forthcoming but not yet published, thus I make reference in parenthesis to the chapter numbers, original to the 1489 edition, and the folios according to my own numbering. All translations of the text into English are my own. This early printed book survives in three known copies, found today at the J. Pierpont Morgan Library in New York, the Bibliothèque Nationale de France in Paris, and the British Library in London.

    Although there are no extant manuscripts of this text, and the 1489 incunabulum by Jacques Maillet is the first surviving version of the tale in French, scholars believe it to have been the extensive expansion of a lost rhymed narrative in French, owing to the existence of several surviving verse redactions (some fragmentary) in German, Dutch, and Swedish. As the Middle Low German translation is entitled *Valentin und Namelos*, the lost French original is normally referred to as *Valentin et Sansnom*. The existence of this original was first posited in 1846 by Gustaf Edvard Klemming. See his *Namnlös och Valentin: En Medeltids-roman* (Stockholm: Norstedt, 1846). A. Dickson includes a valuable episode-by-episode comparison of the relatively short

*Valentin und Namelos* to the much expanded *Valentin et Orson;* see Arthur Dickson, *Valentine and Orson: A Study in Late Medieval Romance* (New York: Columbia University Press, 1929), 159–164.

2. For original French, see Gerard J. Brault, ed., *The Song of Roland: An Analytical Edition*, vol. 2 (University Park: Pennsylvania State University Press, 1978), 64; for English translation, see Glyn Burgess, trans., *The Song of Roland* (London: Penguin, 1990), 61.

3. "Romance epic" is the term of choice for the Société Rencesvals for medieval epic literature in Romance languages, and equally is used for late-medieval *mises en prose* of earlier rhymed epic narratives. The term is also often used to express the mixing of elements more typical of romance into the genre of epic, although some scholars have challenged that concept. See in particular Sarah Kay, *The Chanson de Geste in the Age of Romance* (Oxford: Oxford University Press, 1995). *Valentin et Orson* is usually considered a late *mise en prose*, part of the genealogical expansion of the Carolingian romance epic.

4. Valentin's final years bear many parallels to those of St. Alexis. See chapters 69 to 74 of the original text, and Dickson's comparison in Dickson, *Study*, 251–264.

5. This incident occurs only in the expanded prose version of 1489. It has no analogue in *Valentin et Sansnom*.

6. A text in which that is the case, the *Estoires d'Outremer*, will be discussed below.

7. Jonathan Shepard, "The Uses of the Franks in Eleventh-Century Byzantium," *Anglo-Norman Studies* 15 (1993): 275–305, 290.

8. Shepard, "Uses of the Franks," 278. Shepard notes on the same page that Anna Comnena praises the horseback skills of her brother-in-law by comparing them to those of a Norman. See *The Alexiad of Anna Comnena*, trans. E. R. A. Sewter (London: Penguin, 1969), 301.

9. The famous Cid, Rodrigo Diaz de Vivar, demonstrates well the mutability of loyalties in medieval Spain in the late eleventh century. Although portrayed by legend (and the French classical dramaturge Corneille) as a great slayer of Moors and defender of Christian Spain, historians are well aware, as Charles-André Julien points out, that he "placed his sword sometimes at the service of the King of Castile, more often at that of the Hudid dynasty of Saragossa, and above all at the service of his personal ambition." Such a career represents better the reality of mercenary activity than any literary text, which has practically a duty to finesse the harsh truths of politics. Charles-André Julien, *History of North Africa: Tunisia, Algeria, Morocco*, trans. John Petrie (London: Routledge, 1970), 85.

10. Reverter, the twelfth-century Catalan noble, "served the Muslims as commander of all Christian mercenaries and eventually became a general in the army of the sultan, Ali ibn Yusuf." When Reverter perished in 1144 during one of the battles between the old Almoravid empire that he served with his Christian militia against the conquering Almohads, it is said that the latter had "the pleasure of crucifying his corpse," a gruesome tribute to the faithful service he had rendered his Muslim Almoravid masters. Julien, *History of North Africa*, 105.

11. See Hadia Dajani-Shakeel, "Diplomatic Relations between Muslim and Frankish Rulers 1097–1153 AD," in *Crusaders and Muslims in Twelfth-Century Syria*, ed. Maya Shatzmiller (Leiden: Brill, 1993), 190–215, for details of the various treaties agreed to during this first Crusader period, including Mu'in al-Din's agreement with King Fulk of Anjou for help against Imad al-Din Zengi on 207–208. The Damascus Chronicle reports that in

1140, as Zengi (Imad al-Din Atabek) approached Damascus in conquering mode, the Damascene rulers came to an agreement with the Franks for a certain unnamed sum "to take common action and support one another, and to unite and join forces in driving off the Atabek and preventing the achievements of his aims." See Ibn al-Qalanisi, *The Damascus Chronicle of the Crusades*, trans. H. A. R. Gibb (London: Luzac, 1967), 259. A few years later, in 1146–1147, the Franks sided with Altuntash, the rebellious ruler of Sarkhad and Bosra, against Mu'in al-Din, only to be defeated (Ibn al-Qalanisi, *Damascus Chronicle*, 276–279). Then again, in the early 1150s, as Nur al-Din made his move on Damascus, its ruler, Mujir al-Din, called upon the Franks to help him. The Damascus Chronicle, in its enthusiasm for Nur al-Din's greatness, lauds his restraint and reluctance to spill Muslim blood as the reason for which he signed a treaty with Mujir al-Din (Ibn al-Qalanisi, *Damascus Chronicle*, 296–312), although noted French historian Jean Richard explains it as the Franks forcing him to retreat. See Jean Richard, *The Crusades c. 1071–c. 1291*, trans. Jean Birrell (Cambridge: Cambridge University Press, 1999), 173.

12. Youssef Courbage and Philippe Fargues, *Chrétiens et juifs dans l'Islam arabe et turc* (Paris: Fayard, 1992), 78.

13. Sharon Kinoshita, *Medieval Boundaries: Rethinking Difference in Old French Literature.* The Middle Ages Series (Philadelphia: University of Pennsylvania Press, 2006), 7.

14. Kinoshita, *Medieval Boundaries*, 18.

15. Kinoshita, *Medieval Boundaries*, 21.

16. Kinoshita, *Medieval Boundaries*, 32.

17. Jerusalem was lost for the second time in 1244 (it had been regained by treaty under Frederick II), and the rest of the Latin holdings were lost to the Egyptian Mamluks in 1291.

18. Norman Housley, *The Later Crusades: From Lyons to Alcazar, 1274–1580* (Oxford: Oxford University Press, 1992), 45.

19. Housley, *Later Crusades*, 46. Also James Hankins, "Renaissance Crusaders: Humanist Crusade Literature in the Age of Mehmed II," *Dumbarton Oaks Papers* 49 (1995): 111–207, 113.

20. Hankins, "Renaissance Crusaders," 113.

21. Housley, *Later Crusades*, 71.

22. Aziz S. Atiya, *The Crusade in the Later Middle Ages* (1938; New York: Kraus, 1965), 455.

23. Norman Housley, "Introduction," *Crusading in the Fifteenth Century: Message and Impact* (New York: Palgrave Macmillan, 2004), 1–12, 8–9.

24. Dorothy Vaughan recounts the incident in Venice's intermittent war with the Turks when Venice won a battle in 1416, capturing or sinking the entire Turkish fleet, and taking prisoners, many of whom were Christian renegades, whom they "hanged without mercy as a warning to others willing to serve the Turk for pay and not as slaves." Dorothy M. Vaughan, *Europe and the Turk: A Pattern of Alliances, 1350–1700* (1954; New York: AMS, 1976), 44.

25. John V. A. Fine Jr., *The Late Medieval Balkans: A Critical Survey from the Late Twelfth Century to the Ottoman Conquest* (Ann Arbor: University of Michigan Press, 1994), 550. Fine points out that other sources do not make the accusation, but whether or not it was true, the perception current at the time was that Christians were willing to ally themselves with the Turks or aid them if it served their own interests. And the fact that it was a Burgundian report

that made the accusation demonstrates that what went on further east was discussed and known in that part of Western Europe.

26. Housley, "Introduction," 2.

27. Vaughan, *Europe and the Turk*, 48–51. Speaking of a sixteenth-century French-Turkish alliance between François I and Barbarossa, M. A. Screech reminds us that "for many centuries—not least since the establishment of French-speaking states in Outremer during the Crusades—alliances of Christians with Moslems against other Christians and Moslems were a fact of diplomatic and military life. With the fall of Byzantium to the Turks, such alliances became both more urgent and more attractive." François I needed Barbarossa to attack his Christian enemy, the Emperor Charles Quint. Michael A. Screech, *Rabelais* (Ithaca, N.Y.: Cornell University Press, 1979), 167.

28. I. Metin Kunt, "Transformation of *Zimmi* into *Askerî*," in *Christians and Jews in the Ottoman Empire: The Functioning of a Plural Society*, ed. Benjamin Braude and Bernard Lewis (New York: Holmes & Meier, 1982), 55–67, 59.

29. We also have the name of the publisher, Jacques Maillet, but there is no evidence or reason to believe that he is the composer of the text.

30. Clarence Dana Rouillard, *The Turk in French History, Thought, and Literature (1520–1660)* (Paris: Boivin, 1938), 15. Also from Rouillard, "The tragic stories and warnings of Hugh of Lusignan, King of Cyprus, awakened a stir of generous sentiments in men's minds. The Pope leagued with France and Venice and ordered a crusade preached, which, according to Froissart, caused great delight in France, 'et espécialement à ceux qui vouloisent le temps employer en armes, et qui adonc ne le savoient bien raisonnablement où l'employer.' Clearly the spirit of chivalry and adventure had to a certain extent supplanted religion as the chief motive power of a crusading expedition" (15–16).

31. Rouillard, *Turk in French History*, 17–18.

32. Rouillard, *Turk in French History*, 20–21.

33. Housley, *Later Crusades*, 91–93. As Housley sees it, this might have been based partly on his desire to avenge his father's defeat at Nicopolis, and partly because of "the perception that an active part as organizer and sponsor of a major crusading effort would assist his political pretensions in Western Europe." One can also make a case that it was his love for the romantic idea of chivalric performance. The idea of crusading as a chivalric enterprise had never died. Just as it survived as a literary phenomenon in the multiple romance epics that saw extended life in prose versions, like *Fierabras* (see Hans-Erich Keller, ed., *Jehan Bagnyon: L'Histoire de Charlemagne [parfois dite Roman de Fierabras]* [Geneva: Droz, 1992]), it framed Philippe's pageantry at the Feast of the Pheasant, allowing the knights who made their ostentatious oaths at the event a kind of performance of chivalry, a chance to emulate the heroes of epic. See also Jacques Paviot, "Burgundy and the Crusade," in *Crusading in the Fifteenth Century: Message and Impact*, ed. Norman Housley (New York: Palgrave Macmillan, 2004), 70–80.

34. Summarized in Atiya, *Crusade*, 204–208. Germain lays out the situation, how Christians were beset by the Turks everywhere—in the Holy Land, Syria, Cyprus, Rhodes, Egypt, Ethiopia, Greece, and in the territories of Constantinople (this was before the fall of the city in 1453). Several Eastern European nobles in Bosnia, Wallachia, and Serbia had become tributaries of the sultan, though they should owe their allegiance to the King of Hungary. He believes that Charles and Philippe could ally themselves with the Greeks and

other Balkan nations who would rise up against the Turk, and so on. Nothing came of these efforts.

35. R. W. Southern, *Western Views of Islam in the Middle Ages* (Cambridge: Harvard University Press, 1962), 95.

36. Housley, *Later Crusades*, 99. On the same page, Housley quotes from Lionello Chieregato, the papal legate sent to the French court in 1488 to plead with the argument that "the holy apostolic see has not sent us here to argue the cause of Jerusalem, Asia or Greece, as in the days of your ancestors, but to beseech you on behalf of Italy, the towns, cities and peoples subject to the holy Roman church."

37. Housley, *Later Crusades*, 101.

38. Housley, *Later Crusades*, 106.

39. Housley, *Later Crusades*, 108–109.

40. André Moisan, *Répertoire des noms propres de personnes et de lieux cités dans les chansons de geste françaises et les oeuvres étrangères dérivées* (Geneva: Droz, 1986), 650, 1013.

41. See Yvonne Friedman, *Encounter between Enemies: Captivity and Ransom in the Latin Kingdom of Jerusalem* (Leiden: Brill, 2002), 235–236. Friedman argues that although death and ransom were the most common outcomes of real captivity, "poetry transmuted the harsh consequences of captivity into a dreamland" (236).

42. Friedman, *Encounter*, 236.

43. William W. Kibler et al., eds., *Lion de Bourges: Poème épique du XIVe siècle*, 2 vols. (Geneva: Droz, 1980). See vv. 16,799–18,134.

44. Gaston Paris, "*Mainet*: Fragments d'une chanson de geste du XIIe siècle," *Romania* 4 (1875), 303–337.

45. Léon Gautier, *Les Epopées françaises*, vol. 3 (Paris: Palmé, 1880), 444–447. The phrase is Gautier's: "un duel qui sera l'honneur de sa vie," 447.

46. *Lion de Bourges*, vv. 16,799–18,134. The motif of the fine deed that convinces Saracens to convert to Christianity also occurs in *Valentin et Orson*. Antioch was the first Saracen court in which Valentin served and where he dispatched a dragon plaguing the city, thereby winning the conversion of the king and his people to Christianity (chapters 35–36, 87r–90r).

47. S. J. Borg, ed., *Aye d'Avignon* (Geneva: Droz, 1967).

48. Margaret A. Jubb, *A Critical Edition of the Estoires d'Outremer et de la Naissance Salehadin* (London: Westfield Publications, 1990), 159.

49. *Estoires d'Outremer*, 162. "Si jousta Bauduins de Rames a lui et l'occist, dont mout fu grans damages, car preudom estoit et boins chevaliers et mout estoit dolans quant il li couvenoit aler contre crestiiens, mais il estoit prisons Salehadin se li couvenoit faire sa volenté." Saladin was usually afforded a certain grudging respect in view of his reportedly chivalrous behavior and supposed descent from the Franks through the daughter of the Count of Ponthieu (*Estoires d'Outremer*, 293–294).

50. See Jean-Louis Picherit, "Les Sarrasins dans *Tristan de Nanteuil*," in *Au carrefour des routes d'Europe: La Chanson de geste*, vol. 2 (Aix-en-Provence: Université de Provence, 1987), 941–957, 949. See also vv. 14,035–14,041 in K. V. Sinclair, ed., *Tristan de Nanteuil: Chanson de geste inédite* (Assen: Van Gorcum, 1971).

51. Picherit, "Les Sarrasins," 950.

52. Paul Bancourt, *Les Musulmans dans les chansons de geste du cycle du roi* (Aix-en-Provence: Université de Provence, 1982), 903 ("Les héros chrétiens n'ont aucun scrupule à servir des musulmans contre d'autres musulmans").

53. Bancourt, *Les Musulmans*, 903.
54. Chapter 38, 93r–93v. Valentin is acquainted with Lucar's queen, Rozemonde, from his service in the course of his quest at her previous husband's
   court, Antioch.
55. Esclarmonde's beauty naturally inflames the King of India, but she manages
   to obtain a year's reprieve from a forced marriage on the basis of a fabri-
   cated vow of chastity for such a time period. When the year is up and
   Valentin has still failed to appear, she feigns madness to avoid fulfilling the
   king's desire, a tactic that keeps her safe until her eventual, though long delayed, rescue (chapter 30, 73r–75r; chapter 38, 92v–93r).
56. He is engaged to deliver a message insulting to the King of India and thus
   dangerous for the messenger. But his former admirer, Rozemonde, who has
   given up on winning his affection, directs him to give the king a secret love
   message that in fact spares Valentin the wrath of one known for killing the
   bearers of his enemies' messages. Thus, Valentin, both messages delivered,
   returns safely to Lucar's court to serve him in the ensuing internecine war
   (chapter 39, 95r).
57. Chapter 42, 99r–99v.
58. Chapter 42, 100r. "Grant honneur eust Valentin et de chascun il fust moult
   prisé et loué, de quoy il avoit la dame Rozemonde delivree et recouvree au
   roy d'Inde."
59. Chapter 43, 100v. Pacolet, always ready with his spells and magic, offers to
   help Valentin recover her, but the knight, after some moralizing about Rozemonde's recidivism, decides to wash his hands of her, demonstrating again
   the superficiality of his loyalty to the Saracen he serves. Such moralizing is
   in sync with his refusal of her initial overtures to him back in Antioch when
   he had upbraided her on her desiring someone other than her husband.
   Valentin seems to have a strong stance on the moral duty of wives, and
   Esclarmonde, as his wife later on in the text, never disappoints.
60. All translations are my own.
61. "Ils n'hésitent pas à trahir leur maître lorsque celui-ci est un Sarrasin" (Bancourt, *Les Musulmans*, 295).
62. "Mais ces fautes commises aux dépens des infidèles ne semblent pas être
   considérées comme telles par les trouvères" (Bancourt, *Les Musulmans*,
   295). See also Pierre Ruelle, ed., *Huon de Bordeaux* (Brussels: Presses Universitaires de Bruxelles, 1960), 64–65, and 323–329, vv. 8010–8258.
63. Chapter 44, 102v. "Murgalent," dit Valentin, "je vous diray mon oppinion. Je
   conseille que nous envoyons bien tost ung messaigier dedens la cité d'An-
   gorie. Et mandons a noz gens que nous sommes icy arrivéz et que demain
   ilz ne saillent pour riens que ilz ne saillent sur les crestiens et que par devers la ville fierement les assaillent. Et nous de la part de la mer l'assault leur
   donnerons. Si me semble que par tel moyen ne pourront fuyr ne eschapper
   que tous ne soyent mors ou prins."
64. Chapter 45, 103r–103v. "Sire," dist Pacolet a Orson, "je suis et seray toute ma
   vie subject a Valentin vostre frere et a vous. Mais se jamais je vous fis service
   qui vous deust plaire j'en feray a ceste foys ung. Or escoutez comment il con-
   vient tout premierement que vous soyez sur voz gardez et que ceste nuyt
   vous fachez voz gens armer et mettre en point et affin que nul ne puisse dire
   que Valentin y pense trahyson je le feray demourer dedens les tentes et pavil-
   lons et feray que les payens si iront en moult grant nombre faire le gait. Et
   quant il sera ainsi fait je getteray mon sort en telle maniere que tous ceulx
   du gait je feray sy durement dormir que vous pourrez tout seurement passer

oultre sy viendrez [103verso] tout en leur ost et le feu vous bouterez dedens en tuant et mettant tout a mort ceulx que vous y trouverrez."

65. Chapter 45, 103v. "Puis Pacolet vint vers Valentin et secretement luy a dit, 'Vostre frere Orson et vostre oncle le noble roy Pepin vous saluent ausquelz j'ay fait l'entreprinse sçavoir de vostre venue affin que ilz ne puissent point estre prins en desroy, car grant pitié et dommaige seroit.'"

66. Chapter 45, 103v. "'Amy,' dist Valentin, 'tu as tres bien ouvré.' Or ne luy dit pas Pacolet le fait de son entreprinse, car bien le cognoissoit en tant que jamais en jour de sa vie trahyson ne vouloit faire ne consentir."

67. Chapter 46, 105v. "Sy jure mon dieu Mahommet que jamais jour de ma vie au bon chevalier Valentin je ne fauldray ne de corps ne de biens."

68. See Michelle Szkilnik, "Pacolet ou les infortunes de la magie," *Le Moyen Français* 35–36 (1996): 91–109. Szkilnik considers Pacolet a failure, a "raté" (93), for despite his determination to serve the Christian side, many of his plans turn awry and he himself is murdered by Lucar, one of the victims of his sleeping charm.

69. In fact, the sleeping spell is used no less than nine times in the text (eight times by Pacolet in chapters 25, 26, 29, 31, 32, 45, and 47, and once by Adramain, a rival magician in chapter 30), usually to free Christian prisoners or to kidnap one of the Saracen chiefs and bring him before his Christian enemies whom Pacolet serves. This is the only time it is used exclusively in order to defeat the foe, although such a defeat does subsequently occur in chapter 31 after Pacolet casts the spell in order to kidnap a Saracen enemy.

70. Dickson, *Study*, 233.

71. In chapter 67 Valentin kills his own father, the emperor of Greece, in battle, but this is a tragic error owing to mistaken identity, not a betrayal of chivalric or moral ideals. Nevertheless, it is the motivation for Valentin's decision to withdraw from chivalric practice and, in essence, emulate St. Alexis. See Dickson, *Study*, 251–64.

72. See notes 61 and 62 above.

73. Jean Richard, "An Account of the Battle of Hattin Referring to the Frankish Mercenaries in Oriental Moslem States," *Speculum* 27 (1952): 168–177, 169. It is the Seljuk Turks referred to here.

74. Jean Richard, "The Adventure of John Gale, Knight of Tyre," in *The Experience of Crusading: Defining the Crusader Kingdom*, vol. 2, ed. Peter Edbury and Jonathan Phillips (Cambridge: Cambridge University Press, 2003), 189–95, 189–90. Richard indicates that he derives his information about John Gale from the *Chronique Ernoul et de Bernard le Trésorier*, ed. L. de Mas Latrie (Paris: Société de l'Histoire de France, 1871), 255–256, and from *La Continuation de Guillaume de Tyr*, ed. M. R. Morgan, *Document relatifs à l'histoire des croisades* 14 (Paris: Académie des Inscriptions et Belles-Lettres, 1982), 58–59.

75. Richard, "John Gale," 191–192.

76. Richard, "John Gale," 193. This is Richard's own translation from the text of *Persecutio Saalardini* that he edits and includes as an appendix to Richard, "An Account of the Battle of Hattin," 175.

77. *Le Livre au Roi*, a juridical text of the Latin Crusader kingdom from about 1200, recognizes cases in which a knight might leave his fief to go serve in Saracen lands ("qui estraie son fié et s'en vait en terre de Sarasins, sans recoumander son fié à son seignor"). The problem to be addressed is what happens to those lands, depending on whether he returns before a year is up or not (the king may confiscate his lands for a late return) and what reason he might give for a late return (if he can prove he had been held pris-

oner and had escaped as soon as he could, then his land may be returned). However, the make or break in all cases is whether he renounced his faith, which would render any return of his fief out of the question. Thus the fact of service in a Saracen court is not in and of itself a problem—only apostasy is a crime. See Myriam Greilsammer, ed., *Documents relatifs à l'histoire des croisades*, vol. 17, *Le Livre au roi* (Paris: Académie des Inscriptions et Belles-Lettres, 1995), 200–202.

78. Richard, "An Account of the Battle of Hattin," 175.
79. Richard, "John Gale," 193.
80. Bancourt, *Les Musulmans*, 904. "Les chansons de geste donnent une image embellie, romanesque, simplifiée."
81. Rouillard, *Turk in French History*, 16–18, 20–21.
82. Housley, *Later Crusades*, 101, 108–109.
83. Steven G. Nichols Jr., "Discourse in Froissart's *Chroniques*," *Speculum* 39 (1964): 279–287, 279–80. As Nichols points out, the divide between the writing of history and imaginative literature was not as wide in the Middle Ages as modern historiographers insist it be now. For Froissart, the value of the event recounted in the text is in its being exemplary rather than objectively true in modern terms.
84. Dickson, *Study*, 158.
85. Dickson, *Study*, 233.

# Schoolmasters, Seduction, and Slavery: Polyglot Dictionaries in Pre-Modern England

## SUSAN E. PHILLIPS

In 1639, Michael Sparke Jr. printed a problematic little dictionary. His *New Dialogves or Colloqvies, and, A little Dictionary of eight Languages* (figure 1) is not troublesome in the ways that typically interest textual critics: The book was not censored by early modern authorities, it was not pirated from a fellow printer, and its text does not depart radically from an authoritative critical edition. Rather, Sparke's *New Dialogues* is problematic because it refuses the structuring categories and ideologies that have become, for critics, the defining features of the early modern dictionary. *New Dialogues* fails to install for its readers a clear political, moral, social, or even linguistic, order. Rather than privileging one national language, advancing one particular national cause, or celebrating one national character to the detriment of the others, this little dictionary is an equal-opportunity offender, telling a series of jokes that criticize all the nations represented in its pages. Instead of modeling polite and courteous exchanges or inspiring virtue through moral treatises, the *New Dialogues* schools readers in all manner of inappropriate behavior, scripting sleazy seductions for amorous travelers, staging drunken and disastrous dinner parties, and imagining insult-ridden mercantile negotiations between foreign travelers, local merchants, and their black servants. By abjuring these conventional structuring logics, the disorderly conversations of *New Dialogues* complicate prevailing scholarly narratives about the cultural work performed by early English language instruction manuals. At the same time, the *New Dialogues* troubles our assumptions about the cultural discourses these texts inscribe and circulate—chief among them, I argue, the discourse of race in pre-modern England.

Sparke's "new" colloquies were in fact the old *Colloqvia et Dictionariolvm octo Linguarum, Latinæ, Gallicæ, Belgicæ, Teutonicæ, Hispanicæ, Italicæ, Anglicæ, et Portugallicæ* of Antwerp language teacher Noel van Berlaimont.

*Medievalia et Humanistica*, New Series, Number 34 (Paul Maurice Clogan, ed.), Rowman & Littlefield Publishers, Inc., 2008.

Figure 1. English and polyglot title pages from *New or Colloqvies, and, A little Dictionary of Eight Languages Dialogves* (London: Michael Sparke Junior, 1639), ff. ¶1v-¶2r. Reproduced with permission of The Rare Book & Manuscript Library of the University of Illinois, Urbana-Champaign.

First published in 1530, the *Colloquia* was easily one of early modern Europe's best sellers and certainly its best-selling dictionary, appearing in at least 149 editions from Lisbon to Warsaw during its 278 years in the early modern marketplace.[1] Between 1550 and 1650, an average of one edition of this dictionary appeared each year in one or another European city. As the *Colloquia*'s market share expanded, so did its contents. What began as a short Flemish-French vocabulary with three dialogues and a selection of texts for spiritual edification (the paternoster, the Ave Maria, the Articles of the Faith, the Ten Commandments, and two prayers) quadrupled in size. In its "final" form, as Sparke printed it, the *Colloquia* included eight languages—Latin, French, Dutch, German, Spanish, Italian, English, and Portuguese—and contained seven dialogues, a guide to practical letter writing, a treatise on pronunciation and conjugation, and a little dictionary. An international best seller, it was adapted for a range of local markets: A six-language version contained Czech when it was published in Leipzig (1602) and Polish when it was published in Warsaw (1646).[2] Despite the *Colloquia*'s incredible popularity in the early modern marketplace, it now languishes in relative scholarly obscurity when compared to "canonical" dictionaries and language instruction manuals such as Hollyband's *French Littleton*, Palsgrave's *Lesclarcissment*, Florio's first and second *Fruits*, Eliot's *Ortho-epia Gallica*, Cotgrave's *A Dictionarie of the French and English Tongues*, and Percival and Minsheu's *A Dictionarie in Spanish and English*.[3] Yet this little dictionary has important lessons to teach about both early modern language instruction and the culture that produced and was produced by it.

In this essay, I explore the wider cultural and historical implications of the *Colloquia*'s disorderly conversations. I begin by establishing the presence of this text in the English marketplace, exploring the peculiarities of its evolution and circulation among London schoolmasters. For as I will suggest, not only was this Flemish dictionary incredibly popular in early modern England, but also some of its most disorderly dialogues seem to have originated there. Turning from circulation to content in the essay's second section, I situate this problematic little dictionary in the broader context of early modern language instruction, investigating the seeming paradoxes and peculiarities that characterize the *Colloquia* text and that, in turn, complicate critical paradigms for the early dictionary. The *Colloquia* purports to be a handy guide to practical language instruction ideally suited to "Travellers, young Merchants, and Sea-men," as the title page of Sparke's edition advertises, yet it also traffics in the impractical and the domestic: It teaches English wives how to quarrel with their husbands in Latin, trains German fathers to chastise their sons in Portuguese, and instructs Dutch chambermaids in the art of spurning the unwanted advances of Italian travelers. In its opening remarks to its consumers ("Liber ad emptores"), this little book acknowledges that readers expect to learn decorous gestures and manners through conversation, yet instead of teaching readers how deftly to negotiate social situations with courteous turns of phrase, it offers lessons on how to insult neighbors, spouses, dinner companions, clients, and servants alike.[4] In this chapter's final section, I investigate a larger cultural history traced in the pages of this problematic little dictionary—a history of early modern racial discourse—for what accompanies the *Colloquia*'s refusal to install conventional forms of order is an unconventional representation of black laborers in the English marketplace. That is, while the *Colloquia* offers its early modern audience mischievous language lessons, it invites twenty-first-century readers into a new conversation about the language and representation of race and racial others in early modern England.

## London Schoolmasters and the Text of the *Colloquia*

My claim that the *Colloquia* reflects and shapes English pedagogical and cultural practice rests not on the appearance in London of a unique edition of a best-selling European text, but on the fact that the *Colloquia*'s contents circulated widely in England long before Sparke's publication of the *New Dialogues* in 1639. Consequently, before exploring the peculiarities of the *Colloquia*'s conversations, I want first to consider briefly their origins and evolution. Although Sparke's *New Dialogues* is the first English text explicitly to market itself as the *Colloquia et Dictionariolum*, at least five other language-instruction manuals printed in London have a clear connection to the text. During the first forty-nine years of its circulation, the *Colloquia,* then entitled the *Vocabulare,* contained three dialogues: "a dinner of ten persons [which] conteineth many common speeches that are used at the table," "for to buye and sell," and "for to demand ones debts" (B2v-B3r). Two London manuals—*A Very Profitable Book to Lerne English and Spanish* (1554) and *The English, French, Latine, Dutch, Schole-master* (1637)—constitute English editions of this *Vocabulare*: One is a bilingual edition drawn from a 1551 Louvain imprint, the other is Sparke's four-language precursor to the *New Dialogues*.[5] And although no English imprint survives from the period between these two texts, it seems clear from both Stationers' Company records and prefatory material in late sixteenth-century Continental editions of the *Colloquia* that several editions were published in London during this time.[6]

According to the prevailing scholarly narrative, the contents of the *Colloquia* were expanded in 1579, when an unknown Flemish writer provided Antwerp printer H. Hendrickx with two new dialogues—"for to aske the way with other familiar communications" and "commen talke being in the Inne" (B3v–4r)—for the debut edition of the newly titled *Colloquia cum dictionariolo.* Four years later, the narrative continues, Hendrickx published two additional dialogues—"co(m)munication at the oprysing" and "proposes of marchandise" (B3v–4r)—penned by another (or perhaps the same) unknown author.[7] Two English manuals, which might be termed dual-language derivates, reflect this evolution of the *Colloquia* text. Marten le Mayre copies only the seventh dialogue, retitling it "To buy and to sell," when he compiles his *Dvtch Schoole-master* (1606). The much bolder William Stepney, professor of Spanish in London, pilfers all seven of the *Colloquia* dialogues, adapting and expanding them in his *Spanish Schoole-master* (1591). A timely publication, appearing when memories of the defeat of the Spanish Armada were still vivid and daily threats of Spanish invasion still current, this dictionary was reprinted twice by Nicholas Okes in 1619 and 1620, when the Spanish Match was the inappropriate talk of London.[8]

The standard narrative about the evolution of the *Colloquia* text becomes untenable, however, when we consider the manuals produced by another London schoolmaster, Claudius Hollyband, French-born language instructor to the early modern elite.[9] Hollyband cannot possibly have borrowed for his *French Schoole-maister* (1573) the more accurate (that is, grammatically correct) versions of the four new dialogues provided by the anonymous Flemish writer, not simply because he has integrated them into a single continuous narrative that makes better sense than the manner in which they appear in the *Colloquia,* but more importantly, because his conflated dialogue predates Hendrickx's supposedly original publication by at least six years.[10] It is possible that Hollyband was drawing on a lost Flemish source; that is, he may have encountered variant copies of the later dialogues that were in circulation earlier than previously thought. But it seems improbable that a language teacher living in London would have access to a Flemish text that Flemish printers could not locate themselves in the ten years and six editions printed between Hollyband's *French Schoole-maister* and the "final" version of the *Colloquia*.[11]

It seems even less likely that Hollyband would be so audacious as to borrow his dialogues from a Flemish language teacher after mocking his foreign rivals so mercilessly in his letter to the reader:

> I wil say nothyng of a new booke which came out of Anworpe, and now of late printed at London: because . . . whilste that hee vseth his Rhetoricke in his chirpyng, hee sheweth of what soyle hee is spronge out: for if our Carters of Orleans, Bourges, or of Bloys, had heard the authour chirpe, they woulde sende him back to prattell amonge his Iayes, hauyng layde fiftie stripes of their whippe vpon his ridge. . . . Let him teache therefore his faire language vnto the Flemminges. (A5v–A7r)

Although the abused Flemish author is never identified by name nor is his "booke" given a title, it seems quite likely that Hollyband refers to Berlaimont himself, or at least the writer he holds responsible for the linguistic abominations perpetrated in the *Colloquia*.[12] It is, of course, possible that this insult is a diversionary tactic, designed to hide the source of Hollyband's plagiarism, though presumably his ridicule might backfire all too easily by inciting readers to find the maligned text in order to witness firsthand its philological atrocities. What is more, the *Colloquia* has a history of "borrowing" from French language teachers like Hollyband: Meurier's *Breve Instruction Contenante La Maniere De bien prononcer & lire le François, Italien, Espagnol, & Flamen* (Antwerp 1569) had become the *Colloquia*'s unattributed conclusion.[13] Consequently, it is much more likely, first, that Hollyband expanded and perfected rudimentary, choppy dialogues he found in other texts, presenting them as his own,[14] and, second, that Flemish printers borrowed his dialogues for their texts.[15] And whereas the *Colloquia* was not printed in England until 1639, Hollyband's *French Schoole-maister* was immensely popular, appearing in twenty editions between 1573 and 1660. In short, not only did the *Colloquia*'s dialogues have an undeniable presence in the early modern English marketplace, quite outside the circulation of Continentally produced volumes, but also some of those dialogues had their origins in that very same marketplace. These "English" exchanges, moreover, contain those moments that are the most steeped in humor and impropriety—those moments that would seem most unconventional in light of prevailing scholarly arguments about the early dictionary.

## Contextualizing the *Colloquia*

In recent decades, scholars have shown an increasing interest in the cultural work performed by dictionaries and phrasebooks. Rejecting earlier paradigms that treated language instruction manuals as either agents of humanism and early modern erudition[16] or as stages in the evolution of the great English dictionary from Cawdrey to Dr. Johnson to its apotheosis in the *Oxford English Dictionary*,[17] critics have explored the rhetorical strategies deployed by these manuals and the cultural orders those strategies install. Juliet Fleming's landmark essay on *The French Garden* demonstrates the rich potential of such inquiry, revealing the gender politics of early modern language instruction.[18] For Fleming, Peter Erondell's *French Garden* (1605) subverts women's education, mocks female erudition, and reinscribes a patriarchal order in which subservient women are placed on display for the pleasure of male readers, even as it purports to be designed specifically for women's enjoyment and edification. Similarly, her work on "Dictionary English" traces both the rhetorical maneuvers by which dictionary makers establish the masculinity of "standard" English and the cultural stakes of that project: "femininity was rendered unspeakable within 'standard' English as the grounds out of which that standard is produced."[19] Building upon Fleming's work during the last decade, critics have investigated the myriad social, political, and economic agendas espoused by early dictionaries. Exploring the political aims of these manuals, Deanne Williams has demonstrated how language lessons might be "pressed into the service of Tudor ascendancy."[20] Lisa Cooper turns from royal politics to merchant-class ideology, reading Caxton's *Dialogues in French and English* (c. 1480–1483) as a "social and ethical curriculum" for the advancement of an aspiring merchant class.[21] These richly suggestive essays have uncovered for readers the ideologies that serve as structuring logics for early English dictionaries. Yet, as I will demonstrate in the pages that follow, the *Colloquia*'s disorderly dialogues refuse such consistent structuring logics.

Perhaps the most common underlying logic ascribed to the early dictionary is the discourse of courtesy. Whether a manual's rhetoric is designed to train aspiring merchants or silence potentially unruly women, it nonetheless espouses an ideal of courteous behavior thought to unite a pan-European community. The equation between learning to speak and learning to speak politely is established early on in the history of dictionaries. When Wynken de Worde prints his *Litel Treatyse for to Lerne Englysshe and French* (1497), he appends to it a dual-language edition of Caxton's *Book of Courtesy*. Guides to manners go hand in hand with *Manières de langage*, as the early guides to conversation were called. And perhaps no one illustrates this connection better than John Florio, who instructs readers in Italian decorum as well as Italian turns of phrase. As Niels Haastrup has argued, courtesy books and phrasebooks are complementary to one another: Both teach the rhetoric of conversation; both underscore the importance of reputation and good conduct.[22] Phrasebooks, he claims, demonstrate the behavior prescribed in courtesy books but "do not show what the courtesy-books forbid" (69). That is, they provide models for exemplary speech and behavior, rather than giving readers the tools to speak inappropriately.

Although the *Colloquia*'s prefatory material acknowledges precisely this principle in its claim that decorous manners are "imbibed" through conversation (A3v) and in its promise that learning many languages will enable the reader to earn the "frindship of sundry nations" (A7r), its dialogues refuse the logic of courtesy, instead revelling in insults and impropriety. Rather than depicting an idealized banquet in which elegance and eloquence are on display, the *Colloquia*'s opening chapter introduces a less-than-tranquil domestic scene that teaches readers not how to conduct themselves as readers, but what to expect from these disorderly dialogues. After a perfunctory opening in which John, the son, meets and greets his schoolfellow, readers are made privy to a scene of domestic strife. John arrives home to the nagging of his far-from-exemplary mother, Marie, who chides him for being late, asks him to set the table, and berates him for not remembering the proper manner in which to do so: "[C]an you not remember that? y have told you it more then twentie tymes: You learne nothing, yt is a great shame" (B7v–8r ). While not a breach of courtesy—it does in a sense teach children what is expected of them—the mother's speech is somehow discordant. Moreover, her irritability continues throughout the dialogue. Encountering a reticent female dinner guest, she offers this encouragement: "Anne, you make not good cheere: how cometh it that you say nothing?" drawing unwanted attention to Anne's silence. Anne counters with an impertinent response: "What should I say? It is better to say nothing then to speak evil" (D8v–E1r)—a comment that could be taken straight from the pages of a conduct book, which sounds here more menacing than proverbial.[23]

Anne quickly recovers by explaining that she is silent because she cannot speak French well, and the conversation moves on.

Unfortunately, the new topic—the quality of the meal—is no safer, as the *Colloquia*'s lessons in impropriety continue to unfold. Marie turns her attention to a male guest, David, asking him why he is not eating. Tasting the food, she realizes aloud that one part of the meal is "soden too much" while another is "rosted to little" and then asks her guest to confirm her fears: "[I]s it not?" Readers might expect David to reassure her that all is well or at least to deflect her attention to another dish on the table, but instead he simply concurs, "Mee thincke so to" (D8r–E1v). And the meal spirals downward from there. Husband and wife quarrel about whether the younger son's reluctance to carve for himself is endearing or irritating, an argument that ends with the husband refusing to carve for the boy because he is old enough to do it himself. Still angry, the husband, Peter, engages the previously unsociable female guest in what starts as a simple toast (a "pledge") but devolves into a drinking competition. Perturbed and jealous, Marie criticizes Anne for always having to call attention to herself and then complains that they do not drink to *her* health. Finally, after a few more rounds—both verbal and alcoholic—the dinner guests depart, and readers are left wondering what lessons they have learned from a dialogue in which the children are the only figures who comport themselves properly. To mouth the *Colloquia*'s conversations is not to model polite manners but to negotiate and practice its humorous improprieties.

At the same time that the *Colloquia* resists yoking its language lessons to the discourse of courtesy, it rejects the principle that language instruction should offer moral and religious edification. Many early language manuals combine linguistic and ethical instruction, using prayers and moral treatises to teach foreign languages. As Fleming has argued, phrasebooks "do not just offer opinions and information for consideration, but require that they be learned and repeated."[24] In some cases, moral instruction provides not just the content of the dictionary but its structure. The *Colloquia*'s polyglot rival, the *Sex Lingvarvm, Latinae, Gallicae, Hispanicae, Italicae, Anglicae, et Teutonice*, also known as *Introito e Porta*—a bilingual Italian-German dictionary first printed by Adam von Rottweil in 1477—offers the clearest example of this principle. Like the *Colloquia*, this dictionary expanded to include up to eight languages, with six being the most popular format. The *Sex Linguarum* is structured by a series of ordered lists that are themselves organized according to a moral hierarchy, starting with topics divine. Everything has a particular place—from God down to a poor servant, from Our Lady to a whore, from the old grandfather to the bastard daughter, from the head to the foot—as readers learn not only other languages but also the proper order of the world (figure 2). As John Considine argues, the *Sex Linguarum* offers its readers the "pleasure of seeing the world divided up by language, and of being assured that the languages of Europe all divided it up alike."[25] According to the *Sex Linguarum*, while we speak in different tongues, we all speak the same language.

The *Colloquia*, however, does not subscribe to such a harmonizing ideology. In contrast with its predecessors, contemporaries, and successors, which offered religious and moral instruction to their readers, the *Colloquia* does not contain any prayers, popular moral proverbs, or edifying discourses by esteemed authors.[26] Although it did have these elements in its earliest incarnations, market share turned out to be more important than moral instruction, and these tracts were quickly jettisoned in favor of including additional languages and entertaining dialogues. Its pages do not attempt to put the world in order—or at least not an order that

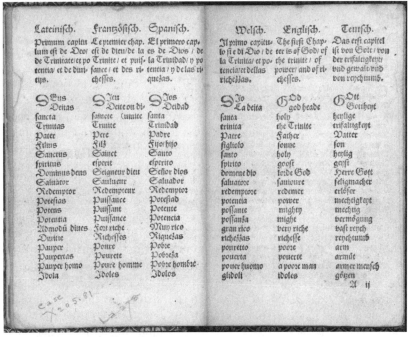

Figure 2. Excerpt from chapter 1, "of God, of the trinitie, of power, and of riches," of *Sex Lingvarvm, Latinae, Gallicae, Hispanicae, Italicae, Anglicae, et Teutonice* (Zurich: Christoph Froeschauer, 1553), ff. A1v-A2r. Reproduced by permission of the Newberry Library, Chicago, Ill.

is immediately obvious—and certainly not one that is universal across languages. This *dictionariolum* (little dictionary) lists its words in alphabetical order according to the Dutch spelling, so that in other languages the order appears to be random (figures 3 and 4): an "egge" comes between an "arsse" and "strawberyes" (V8r), "woman" between "foullie" and "forehead" (Bb5r), "true" between "finger" and "foote." (Bb5r). Quite wisely, Berlaimont left topics divine out of his little word list, lest God appear in inappropriate company. Moreover, this order becomes completely arbitrary in those contemporary dictionaries derived from the *Colloquia* that omit the Dutch entirely. For example, in the bilingual *Colloquia* derivative, *A Very Profitable Book to Lerne English and Spanish* (1554), readers are hard pressed to find any apparent logic to the word list.[27] Although its prefatory remarks celebrate the simplicity of navigating by alphabetical order—"[Y]ou must consider nothyng els, then of what letter the woorde that you seke, dooth begin, whiche afterward you shall easely finde" (E1r)—without the presence of the Dutch language, English readers could not "easely finde" any words in the list.[28]

As the *Colloquia* rejects these conventional ordering principles of morality and courtesy, it abjures even the most basic of structuring logics. As Allon White has argued, "the dictionary embodies an implicit hierarchy of language and produces a linguistic environment that, taken together, powerfully establishes the 'high' language over against all other registers, dialects and sociolects."[29] The languages contained in this little book, however, are not made to succumb to a linguistic hierarchy. Although the *Colloquia*'s *dictionariolum* would appear to privilege Dutch as the organizing language, Dutch does not consistently appear in the first (i.e., leftmost) position.[30] Indeed, the mise-en-page of the *Colloquia*, which places the languages in parallel columns across each opening, would seem to argue for an equality among, rather than a hierarchizing of, national languages. And whereas the *dictionariolum* in part defers to Dutch, the dialogues themselves offer no such privileging of one vernacular over the others. Moreover, the *Colloquia* lacks the scholarly disclaimers about translational difficulties or nationalistic assertions about linguistic superiority that appear in bilingual language instruction manuals. Here, there are no proclamations that "elegant" Italian has been made to follow Dutch syntax or that "effeminate French" will be made to follow English rules.[31] Nor does the text deploy learned Latin as a way to unify and in turn subordinate the vernaculars. Rather it places a quotidian Latin on par with all the tongues of Europe. At the same time, however, this levelling of languages does not translate into an assertion that all nations are equivalent and that through

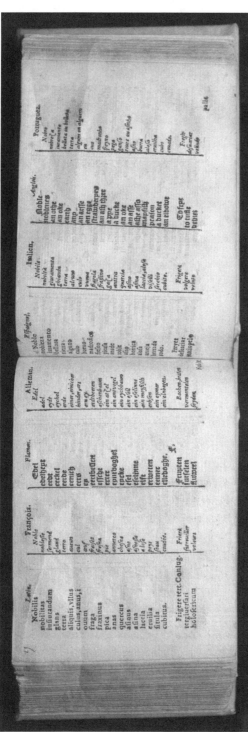

Figure 3. Excerpt from the vocabulary included in *Colloqvia et Dictionariolem Octo Linguarum, Latinæ, Gallicæ, Belgicæ, Teutonicæ, Hispanicæ, Italicæ, Anglicæ, et Portugallicæ* (Amsterdam: Bruno Schinckel, 1598), ff. V7v-V8r. Reproduced with permission of The Rare Book & Manuscript Library of the University of Illinois, Urbana-Champaign.

(*continues*)

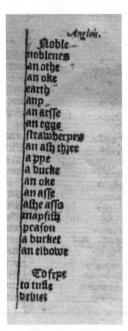

Figure 3. (*continued*) Detail from the vocabulary included in *Colloqvia et Dictionariolvm Octo Linguarum, Latinæ, Gallicæ, Belgicæ, Teutonicæ, Hispanicæ, Italicæ, Anglicæ, et Portugallicæ* (Amsterdam: Bruno Schinckel, 1598), ff. V7v-V8r. Reproduced with permission of The Rare Book & Manuscript Library of the University of Illinois, Urbana-Champaign.

language acquisition one can achieve assimilation.[32] Instead, the *Colloquia* highlights national differences and tells nationalistic jokes: The disputatious French are always at civil war, the overly aggressive Spanish are always defeating their weaker neighbours, shrewd Antwerp merchants are almost unreasonably rigorous about money, and the amorous Italians are bolder if not better lovers.[33] Even typeface is mobilized to highlight national differences (figure 3). In editions that employ three typefaces, Italian and French are always in italics, Latin and Spanish are always in Roman, and Dutch and English are always in Blackletter (or in early modern parlance, "English"); and regardless of the typefaces used, English and Dutch never appear in italics.[34] By contrast, in the *Sex Linguarum*, the polyglot text that promises European similitude, all languages appear in the same type (figure 2). Everard Clopperburg's 1631 Amsterdam edition of the *Colloquia* takes the particularity and peculiarity of nations to an extreme. Its title page (figure 5) depicts eight men, seven of whom are modelling their national attires, including a Dutch

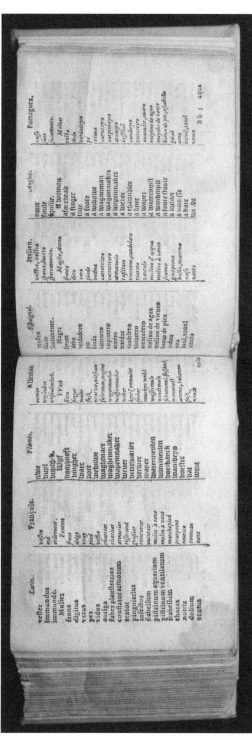

Figure 4. Excerpt from the vocabulary included in *Colloqvia et Dictionariolvm Octo Linguarum, Latinæ, Gallicæ, Belgicæ, Teutonicæ, Hispanicæ, Italicæ, Anglicæ, et Portugallicæ* (Amsterdam: Bruno Schinckel, 1598), f. Bb5r. Reproduced with permission of The Rare Book & Manuscript Library of the University of Illinois, Urbana-Champaign.

(*continues*)

Figure 4. (*continued*) Detail from the vocabulary included in *Colloqvia et Dictionariolvm Octo Linguarum, Latinæ, Gallicæ, Belgicæ, Teutonicæ, Hispanicæ, Italicæ, Anglicæ, et Portugallicæ* (Amsterdam: Bruno Schinckel, 1598), f. Bb5r. Reproduced with permission of The Rare Book & Manuscript Library of the University of Illinois, Urbana-Champaign.

beard, a German hat, a Spanish moustache, an Italian ruff, and generally shoddy English fashion. The eighth does not have an immediate national identity, but, dressed as a scholar holding his book and occupying the first position on the page, he represents Latin, the language that appears in the first column of each opening in this edition. While we might be tempted by humanist logic to see this Latin scholar as a universalizing presence, Clopperburg's title page does not support such a reading. The scholar is the same size as all of his companions, as Latin is levelled—made equal to, rather than being elevated above, the vernacular. The title page bequeaths equal status to each of the languages represented. Yet rather than depicting a European community united in intellectual endeavor, the title page concretely and vividly marks the distinctions among these men and their nations.

Like the prefatory material that introduces them, the *Colloquia*'s dialogues mark the differences in national customs and manners. Adapting and transforming a standard scene from early modern phrasebooks in which readers learn how to obtain food and lodging, the fifth dialogue—"common talke being in the Inne"—combines practical vocabulary with unexpected and indecorous conversations that highlight the differences among nations. Having secured his accommodations for the night, a traveler sits down to a meal and some claret, sharing news with his fellow guests. In the conversation of these men, readers hear once again about the political predilections of particular nations: The French are "c[h]afed the one against t[h]e other" (L8r). The dialogue shifts from the practical to the illicit, however, when our traveler begins to feel unwell and must be shown to his room by Joan, the chambermaid:

B. Ione, make a good fier in his chamber and let him lack nothing.

A. My shee frinde, Is my bede made? Is it good?

F. Iea sir, it is a good fether bed, the scheets be very cleane.

A. Pull of my hosen, and warme my bed, for I am very ill at ease: I shake as a leafe vpon thee tree. Warme my kerchef and bynde my head well. Soft, you bynde it to harde, bryng my pillow, and couer mee well, draw the curtines, and pin them with a pin: where is the chamber pot? Where is the privie?

F. Follow me, and I will shew you the way, go vp straight, you shall fynde it at the right hand, if yow see them not, you shall smell it wel enough. Sir, doth it please you to have no other thing? Are you well?

A. Yes, my shee frinde, put out the candell, and come neerer to mee.

F. I will put it out when I am out of the chamber. What is your pleasure, are you not well enough yet?

A. My head lyeth to lowe, lift vp a little the bolster, I can not lie so lowe. My shee friend, kisse me once: and I shall sleep the better.

F. Sleepe, sleepe, you are not sicke, seeing that you speake of kyssing, I had rather die then to kisse a man in his bed or in any other place. Take your rest in Gods name. God geve you good night, and good rest.

A. I thank you, fayre mayden. (M1v–4r)

Although the exchange certainly instructs readers in the practical vocabulary of nightly ablutions, the center of the scene is the traveler's failed seduction of the savvy Joan. Despite the traveler's rejection, the *Colloquia*'s lessons in seduction are unexpectedly subtle. Teaching readers that seduction has national variations, this little dictionary offers different tactics for different destinations and languages. When seducing a chambermaid in London, the traveler must coyly refer to her as a "she friend" regardless of whether he is inquiring about the quality of his accommodations or asking her for a kiss: "My shee frinde, Is my bed made? . . . My shee friend, kisse me once: and I shall sleep the better."[35] When he is in Lisbon, the chambermaid should be addressed as a sister when she is questioned about bed linen but as a lover when the conversation turns from logistics to romance, as "Irmana" quickly becomes "meus

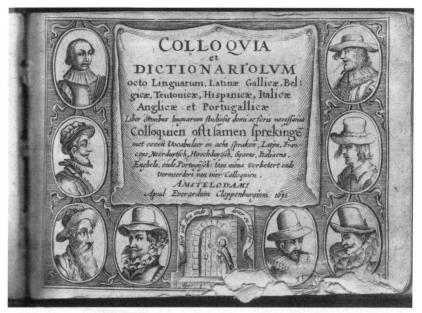

Figure 5. Title page from *Colloqvia et Dictionariolvm Octo Linguarum, Latinæ,
Gallicæ, Belgicæ, Teutonicæ, Hispanicæ, Italicæ, Anglicæ, et Portugallicæ*
(Amsterdam: Everard Clopperburg, 1631), f. A1r. Reproduced by
permission of the University of Iowa Libraries.

amores."[36] But in Venice, our traveler must be bolder and more versatile,
initiating his seduction the moment he meets the chambermaid and
demonstrating his talent for conversational ingenuity: "Amor mia," is
the bed made?; "bella figlia," blow out the candle and come closer to
me; "bene mio," kiss me and I will sleep better.[37]

While the *Colloquia* schools male travelers in the complexities of international seduction, it provides the chambermaid with a way to rebuff the
unwanted advances of a customer who mistakes her for a prostitute. Joan
deftly handles the situation with the ready (and consistent) wit of a
woman who has encountered her fair share of such afflicted travelers:
"[Y]ou are not sick, seeing that you speake of kyssing." Despite the fact
that she is his servant, Joan can call the male traveler's bluff, using his
own words against him to demonstrate her conversational superiority.
She simultaneously asserts her virtue (and behind her the virtue of all
chambermaids and foreign maidens)—"I had rather die than kisse a
man in his bed or in any other place"—and calls attention to his duplic-
ity, making him the butt of her joke. Although the scene is hardly proto-
feminist, it nonetheless departs from the misogynist conventions in

countless other language instruction manuals. Defying stereotypes, Joan is a savvy and virtuous chambermaid, rather than a proper courtly lady or a lower-class strumpet.[38] And we can imagine that male and female readers alike might take pleasure in mouthing Joan's responses. Moreover, the *Colloquia* omits those anti-feminist proverbs and commonplaces that provide the language lessons and dictionary entries for other English manuals, such as Eliot's *Ortho-epia Gallica* and Hollyband's *French Littleton*, offering instead dialogues that depict women who participate in the conventionally all-male spaces of international travel and mercantile exchange.[39] That is, the *Colloquia*'s depiction of women, like its treatment of courtesy, morality, and linguistic hierarchy, refuses the ideological structures that have, for contemporary scholars, defined early modern language instruction manuals.

Troubling current critical paradigms for early dictionaries, the *Colloquia*'s disorderly dialogues not only require twenty-first-century readers to reconsider the cultural work performed by language instruction manuals; they also call into question assumptions about the culture represented in the pages of these texts. And it is to the depiction of one particular aspect of early modern culture that I would like to turn in the final section of this chapter, as I explore the language and representation of race in the *Colloquia*'s concluding dialogue. For at the same time that this problematic phrasebook abjures the charge of mannerly and moral edification, it also complicates and indeed transforms the discourse of race in early modern England. The *Colloquia*'s disorderly conversations, I argue, through their representation of casual but crucial encounters with racial others, provide important, and as yet unexplored, terrain for the analysis of race in the period.

## Knaves, Slaves, and "Negars"

On the surface, the *Colloquia*'s final dialogue appears highly conventional. Its subject, marketplace negotiations ("proposes of marchandise"), is ubiquitous in language instruction manuals from the fifteenth century to the twenty-first. In the details of its scene of international wheeling and dealing, however, readers learn more than simply how to haggle with foreign merchants, for the *Colloquia* provides lessons on the relative value of different kinds of laborers, the most successful tactics for managing and negotiating with them, and most surprisingly, the representation (and perhaps role) of slavery in the European marketplace.

The complexities and complexions of the early modern workforce
come into vivid focus when a tourist surveys the Antwerp marketplace in
search of a piece of rich, black velvet. After several abortive exchanges
with local merchants, this determined customer is drawn to a stall by the
insistent advertising of a diligent apprentice who hawks his master's
wares. Claiming that money is no object, the customer asks to see the
best black velvet in the merchant's inventory, but to prove his mercantile aptitude, he warns the merchant not to tack on any hidden costs:

C. Sir wat lacke you? Doo you seek good saten, damaske, veluet, fustian, wested
buckram, sersenet, or any sort of silke clothe? What will you have? You shall have
good cheape.[40]

B. That prentise hath a good tongue: he waiteth for his maisters profit. Shew
mee a peece of blacke veluet.

C. Well, I will. Beholde, is it not good? Did you neuer see the like?

B. Have you not better?

C. Yes forsooth, but it is of a greater price.

B. I care not what soeuer it costeth if it be good.

C. Here is the best velvuet which you euer did handell.

B. You will make mee beleeue so. I have seen better and worse too. Doo not unfold it all. I have had the sight of it.

C. There is no hurt. He which had unfold it shall fold it againe well. For a knaves
paine is not to bee set by. (O3v–O4r)

The last line of the exchange might easily pass unnoticed. There is after
all nothing remarkable about a merchant who does not consider his apprentice's labor valuable. Moreover, the merchant's use of the epithet,
"knave"—"a boy or lad employed as a servant; hence a male servant or
menial in general: one of low condition" or alternatively, "a base crafty
rogue"[41]—while derogatory, is hardly startling in this context. The lesson on market value that the exchange teaches would thus appear to be
quite simple: The labor of the merchant adds value to the velvet; the labor of an apprentice is insignificant. However, the merchant is not actually referring to his apprentice in this line. It would be difficult to reduce
to silent labor the vocal apprentice, whose quick and diligent tongue is
what initially caught the customer's attention: "That prentise hath a
good tongue: he waiteth [is diligent] for his maisters profit." Indeed, the
merchant has been in verbal cahoots with this apprentice throughout
the dialogue, joking with him at the tourist's expense and boasting to
him about his unrivaled talent for negotiation:

D. They go away, they be gon.

C. Let them go, let them runne: when they have runned their bellie full about
the faire they wil be glad to come againe. (P1r)

Moreover, in all eight languages, the apprentice is specifically identified as a trainee, rather than just a servant: "tyrunculus" ("young beginner"), "apprentis," "leer-jonghen" ("young student/trainee"), "lehriungen" ("young apprentice")," "novicio" ("novice"), "giouane nouitio" ("young novice"), "prentise," and "mancebo nouicio" ("young novice"). In short, nothing about the apprentice suggests that he is a knave. Rather, the merchant in his offhand remark introduces readers to the presence of a fourth, silent character.

In his dismissal of his knave's contribution, the merchant calls attention to the often invisible presence of black laborers in the European marketplace. Looking left and right from the English column to the other seven languages, readers learn that this knave is not just any menial servant:

| | |
|---|---|
| Latin | servilis opera pro nihilo ducitur |
| French | peine de vilain est pour rien contée |
| Dutch | slaven arbeyt en wort niet gherekent |
| German | Iunge(n) arbeit rechnet man vor nichts |
| Spanish | Labour de negro no se cuenta. |
| Italian | Travaglio di schiauo si conta per nulla. |
| English | for a knaues paine is not to bee set by |
| Portuguese | Trabalho de negro naõ se conta.[42] |

The labor that does not count for this Antwerp merchant varies significantly by language, and readers are invited to consider the connections between knaves, slaves, and negroes. While the French, English, and German columns all offer seemingly generic terms for the silent laborer— "villain," "Iungen" and "knave"—the Italian and Dutch exchanges make clear to readers that we are dealing with slavery rather than just menial labor. And most strikingly, the Portuguese and Spanish columns proclaim this inconsequential labor is African.[43]

Given both the existing evidence about slavery in the European marketplace and the *Colloquia*'s penchant for highlighting the differences among nations, we might be tempted to read these linguistic variations as reflections of distinct national practices, determining that while there are African slaves in Spain, there are English knaves in London. However, I would like to suggest that in the imagination of schoolmasters and by extension, their students, English knaves might at times be black servants or, indeed, slaves—a possibility underscored by yet another London language teacher, Richard Huloet. In his *Abecedarium Anglico-Latinum* (1552), a text that predates England's involvement in the slave trade by ten years, readers learn that "Knaueseller" is "he that seleth knaues or slaues."[44] In its parallel columns, the *Colloquia*, I argue, establishes equivalences between negroes and knaves just as it suggests that one might mean "my love" when one says " my shefriend."

In her groundbreaking work on racial discourse in early modern English literature, Kim Hall has argued that in order to establish a complete and accurate picture of race in early modern England, scholars need to consider not only texts, such as *Othello,* that "are 'about' blackness," but also works in which markers of race exist on the margins.[45] As Hall argues, the fact that Africans in England served as menial laborers has contributed to their historical and literary invisibility.[46] The *Colloquia*'s exchange between the Antwerp merchant and his polyglot clientele not only offers a vivid example of precisely this principle in its marginalized and silenced black characters, but also provides a way to rectify this historical invisibility by affording us with invaluable evidence about the language of race as it was both understood and taught in the period.

That the *Colloquia*'s equation of knaves and negros is not merely a linguistic accent—the result of imprecise translation—is evidenced by the fact that one of the English *Colloquia* derivatives, Stepney's *Spanish Schoole-master,* makes the connection explicit. Moreover, Stepney's version of this mercantile exchange does more than instruct its audience how to translate "negroes" into English; more, that is, than provide readers with a new English vocabulary for race. It offers an unexpected depiction of the ways in which black laborers participated in the social and economic life of early modern England, transforming the negro from silent laborer into a spokesperson for the London economy. In the conclusion to the final dialogue, the tourist, having finished his marketplace negotiations and acquired his rich black velvet, returns to his lodgings to settle his accounts. After paying the innkeeper, he summons the stable boy (a "knave" in the *Colloquia* text), whom he tips in order to ensure preferential treatment the next time he is in town. Through their exchange, this little dictionary offers an astonishing lesson, about both the language of race and the way race signified in late sixteenth-century England:

| | |
|---|---|
| Negar, bring hither my horse, haue you dressed him well? | Negro, traed me aca mi caballo, aueys le bien peynado? |
| Yea Sir, he did want nothing. | Si Sr, no le ha faltado cosa ninguna. |
| Hold there is to drinke: this I giue thee, to the end another time thou maysest remember me. | Tomad para tu vino: essso te darè, para que en otro tiempo te accuerdas de mi. |
| I thanke you Sir, you shall finde me at all times readie to do you seruice: passe not this lodging when you come this way, for you shall be as well | Beso las manos de v.m.mi Sr, v.m. me hallara siempre aparejado a su seruiçio: No passa v.m. la casa, quando viendra por este camino, porque serà tambien |

| | |
|---|---|
| vsed and serued, as in any lodging within London. | tratado y seruido, como en qualquier hospedaje que sea en Londres. |
| I haue found it so: I will not change it for another, and so farewell. | Assi lo he hallado: No lo mudarè por otro ninguno, y assi queda os con Dios. |
| God go with you. | Dios vaya con v.m. (L1v–L2r) |

Our stable boy is not a knave but a "negar." Stepney's epithet is one of the earliest occurrences of the word "neger," the somewhat less inflammatory English version of its American cousin. Early uses of the word typically appear not in the context of the London marketplace as in Stepney's textbook but in narratives of New World exploration, such as Robert Leng's account of Sir Francis Drake's final journey (1587)—a text that, like the *Colloquia*, is deeply interested in the connections between slavery, international negotiation, and language acquisition.[47] Over the course of Leng's brief account, English sailors find intelligence about an impending Spanish attack by uncovering (and presumably translating) letters from their Portuguese captives (i.e., galley slaves). These sailors then learn the location of the Spanish king's galleys through intelligence provided by an African slave whom they rescue as he flees from his Spanish captors—information that also must have required some skills in translation on the part of both the sailors and the slave.[48] Finally, the Englishmen defeat several Spanish ships, first seizing, and then presumably selling, their cargo, which turned out to be "400 neegers, whome they [the Spaniards] had taken to make slaves in Spayne and Portugall" (22). The "neegers" in Leng's account are unambiguously involved in the slave trade, but the nature of the connection between these men and the stable boy in Stepney's dialogue remains unclear.

Who, then, is this "Negar," and what is he doing in an English textbook in 1591? The substitution of "negar" for "knave" is original to Stepney—a London schoolmaster who touts his Englishness in his prefatory letters, complaining about all the foreigners who are in his city teaching languages. Thus, the negar's presence in this little dictionary cannot be attributed to a Spanish practice that has been unsuccessfully adapted for an English audience. These are the additions of an English schoolmaster, and thus they offer suggestive evidence about the ways in which racial others were imagined and represented in early modern London, evidence that complicates current scholarly narratives.

As theorists of early modern race have demonstrated, assessing the situation of black people in England is particularly complicated due to the fact that very little information exists testifying to either the presence of black laborers or the social and economic roles they played.[49] Before England's involvement in the slave trade was firmly entrenched in the late seventeenth century, the status of blacks in England was unstable: At times they were slaves, at times domestic servants, and at times property owners.[50] Moreover, the rhetoric used to describe blacks often erases these distinctions. Most of the extant evidence pertains to wealthy landowners and merchants who kept African slaves as domestic servants.[51] That these servants were slaves is suggested by the royal decrees that attempted to treat them as commodities to be exchanged in the political marketplace. Queen Elizabeth twice attempted (in 1596 and 1601) to expel such slaves from England. These "Negars and Blackamoors," Elizabeth complains, "are fostered and relieved here to the great annoyance of her own liege people that want the relief which those people consume."[52] For Elizabeth, these negars were a drain on the domestic economy, providing no tangible contribution and consuming resources needed by hardworking Englishmen. Elizabeth's hyperbolic financial claims, however, are the result of a very specific economic need: She had promised the slaves to a Lubeck merchant, Casper van Senden, as remuneration for rescuing Englishmen from Spanish capture. The Queen's decrees fell on deaf ears, however, as Imtiaz Habib has demonstrated, for merchants and aristocrats refused to relinquish their black servants, privileging household economy over royal debts.[53]

Given the particular bias of the historical evidence, the appearance in Stepney's *Spanish Schoole-master* of a negar working as a stable boy in London is remarkable, not only because of its early date, but also because of the casual way in which he is introduced. This "English" *Colloquia* dialogue suggests that black men may have had a visible presence in the inns and stables of London long before Elizabeth tried to claim that they had "crept into this realm"—or at the very least, that black men were a familiar enough presence that a London schoolmaster could offer this unassuming, even quotidian, representation. Moreover, Stepney's depiction of this "negar" completely lacks the social anxieties that current criticism leads us to expect. Scholars such as Winthrop Jordan and Kim Hall, among others, have convincingly demonstrated the ways in which Elizabethan rhetoric problematized race, as early modern writers propagandized about the physical monstrosity and moral, religious, and sexual depravity of African slaves, while expressing their anxieties about miscegenation.[54] Perhaps the most astonishing aspect of the negar's role in the *Colloquia*'s dialogue, then, is the fact that his appearance is rendered completely unremarkable. In the brief exchange with the foreign tourist, the negar's racial characteristics and associations go unmentioned. Rather than a terrifying other striking fear into the hearts of Englishmen and their foreign guests alike, he serves as representative of the London tourist industry. For a tip, he ensures extra comforts and acts as an ambassador to the city: "[Y]ou shall finde me at all times readie to do you seruice: passe not this lodging when you come this way, for you shall be as well vsed and serued, as in any lodging within London." In fact, it is this racial other who gives the traveler his entrée into London culture. In short, Stepney offers readers a black man who not only has been unproblematically integrated into the London economy but also is invaluable to it.

Although Stepney's representation of a "negar" concierge might seem a startling vehicle for language instruction, the *Colloquia* and its derivatives are not unique in yoking together linguistic and racial discourse. Early modern language instruction manuals both reflect and circulate the discourses of race and racism. Dictionaries offer proscriptive significations, as in the entry for "Caçuéla para pringar" in Minsheu's *A Dictionarie in Spanish and English*: "a pipkin to keepe hot larde to drop vpon Moores or Neagers, and other malefactors."[55] Here, new vocabulary becomes linked to lessons about racial mistrust. By the end of the seventeenth century, as racial slurs acquire the status of proverb and the social and economic position of blacks becomes fixed, racial others and racist humor about them become common features of linguistic textbooks.[56] So intertwined are these two projects that even guides to pronunciation rely upon the discourse of racism. In James Howell's *A New English Grammar* (1662), readers learn to pronounce the letter *n* by means of a gratuitous proverb about the poor hygiene practiced by black women: "*N* in *English* is pronounc'd as in *Spanish*, (and other languages;) but in the *Spanish* toung it hath this singularity, as to have a streight stroke on the top, as for example *ñ*, and then she must be pronounc'd as if *i* immediatly follow'd her, as *Fue la Negra al baño, y tuvo que contár todo el año*, The Negre went to the Bath, and she had news enough for the whole Twelmonth; in this Proverb *baño* and *año* must be pronounc'd as if they were written *banio, anio*."[57] To pronounce the letter *n* properly, it seems, readers must recognize not only the words that contain it (*Negre* as well as *baño*) but also the discourse that attaches to them. That is, proper pronunciation is inextricably linked to the enunciation of racist proverbs.

In the late sixteenth and early seventeenth centuries, when the *Colloquia* acquired its "English" dialogues and achieved the height of its popularity, the discourse of race inscribed in and by language instruction manuals, like the position of blacks in society, was not yet fixed. What the *Colloquia* provides for contemporary critics, then, is a sense of what was possible in the imaginations and, perhaps, in the lives of

English schoolmasters and their audiences. Rather than depicting "negers" as "spectacles of strangeness"—figures of the exotic, the mythic, and the monstrous[58]—these little books represent black laborers as unproblematically assimilated into the London economy. These texts' contemplations of race consist not in the tragic affairs of a high-ranking Moor who leads the Italian forces against the infidels only to be destroyed by his love for Venetian woman, but in the quotidian economic negotiations of a stable boy, a "negar" who lives and works in London, and is more intimately connected to his fellow Londoners than are the European others who visit as tourists. That is, on the pages of dictionaries like this one, we might find some of the more complicated and unexpected ways in which racial others were represented by, and indeed participated in, early modern culture. After all, what better place than a dictionary to reconsider the terms of the debate?

# Notes

1. No other dictionary goes through as many editions or stays on the market for as many years. A close contender, with at least eighty-nine editions published in over 150 years, is the *Sex linguarum*, also known as the *Introita e porta* or *Solenissimo Vochabuolista*, first printed in Venice by Adam von Rottweil in 1477. This text was particularly successful between 1510 and 1570, just before the *Colloquia* achieved the height of its popularity. For a detailed account of most editions of the *Colloquia*, see R. Verdeyen, *Colloquia et Dictionariolum Septem Linguarum*, 3 vols., Vereeninging Derantwerpsche Bibliophilen, Uitgave Nr. 39, 40, 42 (Antwerp: Nederlandsche Boekhandel, 1925–1935), I. xciii–cxv. For additional imprints as well as a helpful summary of Verdeyen in English, see Caroline Bourland, "*The Spanish Schoole-master* and the Polyglot Derivatives of Noel de Berlaimont's *Vocabulare*," *Revue Hispanique* 81, no. 1 (1933): 283–318. In recent years, scholars have continued to find additional imprints; see Margarete Lindemann, *Die französischen Wörterbücher von den Anfängen bis 1600: Entstehung und typologische Beschreibung* (Tübingen: Niemeyer, 1994), esp. 34–57; and Hans-Josef Niederehe, *Bibliografía cronológica de la lingüística, la gramática y lexicografía del español (BICRES)*, vol. 1, *Desde los comienzos hasta el año 1600* (Amsterdam: J. Benjamins Publishing, 1994). The latest extant edition I have located is the 1808 imprint of William Morris, *Dialogues in Six Languages, (viz) Latin, French, German, Spanish, Italian and English* (Shrewsbury: William Morris, 1808).
2. Verdeyen, *Colloquia*, I. cv, cxii. For a seventeenth-century manuscript translation of the *Colloquia* into Ruthenian and Old Church Slavonic, see Daniel Buncic and Helmut Keipert, eds., *Rosmova-Beseda: Das ruthenische und kischenslavische Berlaimont-Gesprächsbuch des Ivan Uzevyc, mit lateinischem und polnischem Paralleltext*, Sagners Slavistische Sammlung, 29 (Munich: Verlag Otto Sagner, 2005).
3. The vast majority of scholarship on the *Colloquia* has been bibliographic and editorial, devoted to the important task of documenting and describing the

large number of imprints of this text, its various stages of development, and the derivatives it inspired, as well as to providing an invaluable critical edition. Verdeyen was the first to trace the textual evolution and dissemination of the *Colloquia*. His facsimile edition has recently been superseded by *Colloquia et dictionariolum octo linguarum Latinae, Gallicae, Belgicae, Teutonicae, Hispanicae, Italicae, Anglicae, Portugallicae*, ed. Ricardo Rizza et al. (Viareggio: Mauro Baroni, 1996). A number of scholars have expanded upon and augmented Verdeyen's findings. Werner Hüllen places the *Colloquia* in the context of the development of English language instruction. Werner Hullen, *English Dictionaries 800–1700: The Topical Tradition* (Oxford: Clarendon Press, 1999), 106–18. Maria Timelli has traced the circulation and popularity of the *Colloquia* as well as that of its rival, *Introito e porta*. Maria Colombo Timelli, "Dictionnaires pour Voyaguers, Dictionnaires pour Marchands ou la Polyglossie au Quotidien aux XVIe et XVIIe Siècles," *Lingvisticæ Investigationes* 16, no. 2 (1992): 395–420.

4. "Simul & gestus, moresque decoros/ Cum lingua imbibere." *Colloquia et Dictionariolum octo linguarum* (Delft 1598), A2v. Unless otherwise noted, all quotations from the *Colloquia* will be taken from this text—the first complete eight-language edition.

5. On the source for *A Very Profitable Book*, see R. C. Alston, *English Linguistics 1500–1800*, no. 292 (Menston, U.K.: Scholar Press, 1971), i. The exact source of Sparke's 1637 text is unknown, but its contents follow the contents of a four-language edition published in Leiden in 1585 (STC 1431.8).

6. According to the letter to the reader ("Benevolo Lectori") added to the *Colloquia* in 1586 and reprinted in editions thereafter, the text had already been published several times in both England and the Low Countries: "prodierintque etiam postea tum in Anglia, tum in Belgia" (A4r). Traces of these no-longer-extant editions of the Berlaimont text might be found in the Stationer's Company records: a four-language version ("a boke intituled Italian, Frynshe, Englesshe and Laten") entered by Edward Sutton in 1566–1567 and a five-language version ("Dictionarie colloques ou dialogues en quattre langues, Fflamen, Ffrançoys, Espaignol et Italien . . . with the Englishe to be added thereto") entered by George Bishop in 1578. Edward Arber, ed., *A Transcript of the Registers of the Company of Stationers of London, 1554–1640 A.D.*, 5 vols. (London: 1875–1877), i.343 and ii.338. On the likelihood that these texts were versions of the *Colloquia*, see Kathleen Lambley, *The Teaching and Cultivation of the French Language in England during Tudor and Stuart Times* (Manchester: Manchester University Press, 1920), 241–242.

7. See Verdeyen, *Colloquia*, esp. I. xxxvi–xlvi; and Bourland, "*The Spanish Schoolemaster*," 298. The imprint that appeared under the final title, *Colloquia et Dictionariolum*, was the 1586 Antwerp edition of J. Trognasesius.

8. Timeliness characterizes most of the *Colloquia*'s English appearances. Along with the three editions of the *Spanish Schoole-master*, *A Very Profitable Book* was published on the eve of the proposed match between Elizabeth I and Phillip II of Spain, and the *Dvtch Schoole-master* appeared on the scene just as Anglo-Dutch tensions were percolating. Indeed, the flourishing of *Colloquia* in the 1580s coincided with the apex of Antwerp's career as *the* center of European commerce. See Fernand Braudel, *The Perspective of the World*, trans. Siân Reynolds (Berkeley: University of California Press, 1992), 138–156.

9. Professor of English, French, and Latin in London, Hollyband (born Claude de Sainliens) instructed the children of the most influential families in early modern England: Robert Sackville, John Smith, and Anne Kelway, mother to

Lucy Countess of Bedford (perhaps even Lucy herself), to name a few. For an account of Hollyband's career and his rivalry with other language teachers, see Muriel St. Clare Byrne, ed., *The French Littleton* (Cambridge: Cambridge University Press, 1953); and Lucy E. Farrer, *La Vie et les Ouvres de Claude de Sainliens alias Claudius Holyband* (Paris: Librarie Ancienne, 1908). For recent work on Hollyband, see Mark Eccles, "Claudius Hollyband and the Earliest French-English Dictionaries," *Studies in Philology* 83, no. 1 (1986): 51–61.

10. Although we might be tempted to read Hollyband's "improvements" as evidence against their priority, the paratextual features of the *French Schoolemaister* mitigate against this. In the 1573 edition, the dialogues appear as one continuous dialogue under the title "For to aske the way, buie & sel; with other familiar communications." Claudius Hollyband, *The French Schoolemaister* (London: William How, 1573), K8v. In subsequent editions, however, printers tried to divide the dialogue into easily negotiable sections, first by means of marginal glosses: "Of news," "of money," and so on, and then by means of headings: "To go to bed," "The rising in the morning," "To buy and sell." Neither the marginal notations nor the headings correspond exactly to the *Colloquia*'s four dialogues.

11. The first extant edition of Hollyband's text precedes the *Colloquia*'s inclusion of dialogues four and five by six years and its inclusion of dialogues six and seven by ten years. Moreover, as Hollyband himself proclaims in the "letter to the reader" of his *French Littleton* (1566), the 1573 imprint of the *French Schoole-maister* was preceded by at least one earlier edition, which must have appeared between 1564, when Hollyband began his career as London language professor, and 1566, when the *Littleton* was published. Although the contents of that edition remain a matter of speculation, it is nonetheless possible that some of the dialogues in question appeared in England almost twenty years before they appeared in the *Colloquia*.

12. For a similar suggestion, see Lambley, *Teaching and Cultivation*, 214; and Farrer, *Le Vie et les Ouvres*, 25: "Serait-ce le vocabulaire en quatre langues, ouvrage de Berlemont, maistre d'école à Anvers?"

13. Bourland, "*The Spanish Schoole-master*," 295–97.

14. Hollyband may have plagiarized some of his material from the dialogues in Peter du Plioche's *A treatise in English and French*, particularly, "To buy and sell," "Another maner to buy and sell," "Other com(m)unications in riding," "To aske the way," and "For to go to bed." Peter du Plioche, *A treatise in English and French* (London: R. Grafton, c. 1550), K2r, K3r, I3v, H2r, and I4v. It is also possible that both Hollyband and Hendrickx's anonymous writer are both drawing from the same as yet unidentified source. Even if this is the case, Hollyband's inclusion of those dialogues demonstrates that they were circulating widely in England before they became popular on the Continent.

15. The delayed printing of dialogues six and seven might be attributed to the necessity of translating the text into five new languages (Dutch, Italian, Spanish, Latin, and German).

16. DeWitt Talmage Starnes and Gertrude E. Noyes, *The English Dictionary from Cawdrey to Johnson, 1605–1755* (Chapel Hill: University of North Carolina Press, 1946).

17. See John Considine's complaint about the "formal and teleological perspective" that has preoccupied early modern dictionary scholarship. John Considine, "Narrative and Persuasion in Early Modern English Dictionaries and Phrasebooks," *Review of English Studies* 52, no. 206 (2001): 195–206, 195.

18. Juliet Fleming, "The French Garden: An Introduction to Women's French," *English Literary History* 56, no. 1 (1989): 19–51.

19. Fleming, "Dictionary English and the Female Tongue," in *Enclosure Acts: Sexuality, Property, and Culture in Early Modern England*, ed. Richard Burt and John Michael Archer (Ithaca, N.Y.: Cornell University Press, 1994), 290–325, 291.

20. Deanne Williams, "Mary Tudor's French Tutors: Renaissance Dictionaries and the Language of Love," *Dictionaries* 21 (2000): 37–50, 38.

21. Lisa H. Cooper, "Urban Utterances: Merchants, Artisans, and the Alphabet in Caxton's *Dialogues in French and English*," *New Medieval Literatures* 7 (2005): 127–161, 132.

22. Niels Haastrup, "The Courtesy-book and the Phrase-book in Modern Europe," in *The Crisis of Courtesy: Studies in the Conduct-Book in Britain, 1600–1900*, ed. Jacques Carré (Leiden: E. J. Brill, 1994), 65–80, esp. 65–70.

23. Technically, Anne remarks that it is better to say nothing than to speak badly (i.e., imperfectly)—"mal parler" rather than "dire du mal," yet the possibility remains that Anne is insulting Marie. And judging by their later interaction, it is likely that Anne intends this ambiguity.

24. Fleming, "*The French Garden*," 26.

25. Considine, "Narrative and Persuasion," 200.

26. See, for example, *Florio, His First Fruits* (1578), *A Very Necessary Book to lerne French and English* (1550), Hollyband's *Italian Schoolmaister* (1575), and Stepney's *Spanish Schoole-master*.

27. The appearance of a vocabulary list that is organized according to an inconsistent or wholly unhelpful alphabetical and/or topical order is not unique to the *Colloquia*'s *dictionariolum*. See for example, the disorderly "a.b.c." of craftsmen in Caxton's *Dialogues in French and English*, which is organized by first name rather than profession; or the eccentric logics that govern the topical word lists found in Hollyband's *French Schoole-maister* and Stepney's *Spanish Schoole-master*.

28. The text repeats without revising the prefatory remarks from an early edition of the *Colloquia* (then entitled *Vocabulare*) printed in Louvain in 1551, declaring that any reader who wants to translate out of German (i.e., Dutch) into French, Latin, or Spanish, should simply follow the Dutch alphabetical order.

29. Allon White, "The Dismal Sacred Word: Academic Language and Social Reproduction of Seriousness," *LTP: Journal of Literature Teaching Politics* 2 (1983): 4–15, 6.

30. On the various orders in which the languages appear in the four-, six-, seven-, and eight-language editions of the *Colloquia*, as well as the principles that might underlie these various, see Hüllen, *English Dictionaries*, 108–111.

31. See, for example, Williams's claim about Palsgrave's political linguistics, which grants English dominance over French, "Mary Tudor's French Tutors," esp. 37–42. Hollyband adopts the opposite strategy, making English obey French sytanx in order to teach his students more perfect French than his competitors: "I doo not prete(n)d to teach thee anie other thing then the French tong, because that if I would keep the English phrase, I should corrupt th'other: the which would turn to thy great hurt: a thing not obserued herebefore" (A4v).

32. Discussing the *Sex Linguarum*, Considine argues that the purpose of such polyglot dictionaries was both ideological and linguistic, proving that "the concepts of one's own language are universal, and that the peoples of the

world can all, potentially join together in conversation or prayer." Considine, "Narrative and Persuasion," 200.

33. While some of these references may have been topical in their first use, because they are repeated without change over the course of nearly 280 years, they become reflections not of specific historical events but of national dispositions. Many of these jokes appear in both the prefatory material and the dialogues. In the "*Liber ad emptores*," the *Colloquia* speaks to its readers about traveling into the realms of the potent Spanish ("*regna potentis Iberi*") and the acrimonious French ("*nunquamue quietos Francigenas*"), and about learning to speak with Italian elegance ("*Italico dabo verba nitore*").

34. The use of the three typefaces (Roman, italics, and Blackletter) varies according to national and local printing conventions. For example, in Venice, printers only use Roman; in Amsterdam and Liége, they use both Roman and italics; and in London, Antwerp, Delft, the Hague, and Leyden, they use all three.

35. The conversation follows the same pattern in Dutch, French, Latin, and English, with "Mijn lief," "M'amie" and "Mea amica" repeated throughout.

36. "Irmana, esta feita à minha cama he boa? . . . Meus amores, beyiayme huna vez, e com isso dormirey melho" (M2r–4r). Spanish and German reflect a similar change in tone and degree of familiarity, shifting from "Hermana" and "Meine freundin" to "Mis amores" and "Mein lieb."

37. "Amor mio, é fatto il mio letto? é egli buono? . . . Si bella figlia, spendete illume & accostateui di me. . . . Bene mio, basciatemi vna volta & io dormiró meglio" (M2r–4r). Amusingly, these nationalistic stereotypes persist in twenty-first-century guides to conversation. The "dating and socializing" section of *The Traveler's Phrasebook*, a four-language polyglot dictionary, offers different pick-up lines for different destinations. The traveler in Germany asks: "Are you free this evening? Would you like to go for walk with me? . . . What is your profession? . . . I thank you for your wonderful hospitality." But in Rome, flirtation must be bold: "Are you free this evening? . . . I'm single. Is your husband here?" Gail Stein, Henry Strutz, Mario Costantino, and Heywood Wald, eds., *The Traveler's Phrasebook*, 2nd ed. (Hong Kong: Barrron's, 2001), 215, 353–354.

38. On this split in the phrasebook tradition, see Fleming, "*The French Garden*," 37.

39. In the *Colloquia*'s dialogues, women host dinner parties, but are also guests at them; they give directions to disoriented male travelers; they sell their wares in the marketplace; and they are hostesses who supervise the economy of the inn as well as chambermaids who allow that economy to function. Although the depictions of these women are not flattering, they are no more critical that the representations of their male counterparts. For the kinds of misogynistic commonplaces that appear in word lists, see Stepney's *Spanish Schoole-master*, where readers find under the heading, "Of the parts of mans bodie," the following phrases: "she hath a skinne as white as snow, and a breast as white as Iuorie: but she painteth herself a little that marreth all the rest" and "she is a proper woman but she hath great buttocks." William Stepney, *The Spanish Schoole-master* (London: Richard Field, 1591), R1v and R4v. See also Fleming's account of women's absence from English phrasebooks ("*The French Garden*," 23–24).

40. Although it is clear from the customer's comments that the diligent apprentice speaks these lines, the speech prefix appears to conflate the apprentice (later identified with the prefix "D") with the Merchant ("C").

41. *Oxford English Dictionary*, s.v. "Knave, *n.*," 2 and 3.

42. O3v-O4r. While I have not been able to consult all extant imprints of the post-1579 *Colloquia*, judging from those imprints I have examined along with all the derivatives circulating in England, the words used in this exchange seem to have been quite consistent over time.

43. Not coincidentally, these are the first two countries both to trade in slaves and to import them as domestic servants: Portugal in 1492 and Spain a few decades later. Braudel, *Perspective of the World*, esp. 392–399.

44. Richard Huloet, *Abecedarium Anglico-Latinum pro Tyrunculis* (London: William Riddle, 1552), R5r. Sir John Hawkins first brought England into the slave trade in 1562 by seizing three hundred slaves from Portuguese galleys and transporting them to the West Indies.

45. Kim F. Hall, *Things of Darkness: Economies of Race and Gender in Early Modern England* (Ithaca, N.Y.: Cornell University Press, 1995), 14.

46. Recently, Imtiaz Habib has both offered archival strategies for addressing this historical invisibility and presented his richly suggestive findings in *Black Lives in the English Archives, 1500–1677: Imprints of the Invisible* (Burlington, Vt.: Ashgate, 2008). Habib's invaluable work catalogues and analyzes the archival traces of black people living in early modern England, collating medical, legal, municipal, and parish records, royal and aristocratic household accounts, government proclamations, and personal correspondence.

47. London, British Library, MS Additional 21620. The text has been edited by Clarence Hopper, *Sir Francis Drake's memorable service done against the Spaniards in 1587*, Camden Society 5 (Westminster, 1863). According to the *Oxford English Dictionary*, Leng's account is the second recorded use of the word "neger," which first appears in Thomas Hacket's *The new found worlde, or Antarctike wherin is contained wonderful and strange things* (1568), a translation of André Thevet's *Singularitez de la France antarctique, autrement nommée Amérique* (1557), in which Hacket renders the French "les Noirs" as "the Neigers" (38). Habib also documents a number of early instances of "negar" being used in parish and county records. Of particular note are the references to "negar" domestic servants prior to the publication of the *Spanish Schoole-master*: Anthony, "negarre" of Nicholas Wichehalse (Devon, 1570); Domingo, "ginny negar" and servant to Sir William Winter (London, 1587); and John Anthony, "a Neyger" buried in Plymouth (1587/88). *Black Lives*, "Chronological Index," items 133, 163, and 168.

48. For a similar instance of an African slave's polyglot translations, see Habib, *Black Lives*, 230–231.

49. See among others, Hall, *Things of Darkness*; Habib, *Black Lives*; Karen Newman, "'And wash the Ethiop white': Femininity and the Monstrous in *Othello*," in *Shakespeare Reproduced: The Text in History and Ideology*, ed. Jean E. Howard and Marion F. O'Connor (New York: Methuen, 1987), 141–162; Margo Hendricks, "Feminist Historiography," in *A Companion to Early Modern Women's Writing*, ed. Anita Pacheco (London: Blackwell Publishing, 2001), 361–376, and "Surveying Race," in *Shakespeare and Race*, ed. Catherine M. S. Alexander and Stanley Wells (New York: Cambridge University Press, 2000), 1–22; and the suggestive essays contained in Margo Hendricks and Patricia Parker, eds., *Women, "Race," and Writing in the Early Modern Period* (London: Routledge, 1994).

50. See Newman, "And wash the Ethiop white," esp. 154–155. For a more pessimistic view, that reads black labor in the period as virtually synonymous with slavery, see Habib, *Black Lives*, esp. 54–60.

51. For a detailed discussion of the domestic and ornamental role that Africans played in aristocratic English households, see Hall, *Things of Darkness*. For the presence of black servants in merchant households, see Habib, *Black Lives*, particularly chapter two.

52. Quoted in Hall, "Guess Who's Coming to Dinner? Colonization and Miscegenation in *The Merchant of Venice*," *Renaissance Drama* 23 (1992): 87–111, 90.

53. According to Habib's findings, the black population in London appears to have increased rather than decreased after Elizabeth's proclamation. *Black Lives*, esp. pp. 112-19.

54. Winthrop Jordan, *White over Black: American Attitudes toward the Negro, 1550–1812* (Chapel Hill: University of North Carolina Press, 1968); Hall, *Things of Darkness*; and Hall, "Guess Who's Coming."

55. John Minsheu, *A Dictionarie in Spanish and English, first published into the English tongue by Ric[hard] Perciuale Gent.* (London: Edmund Bollifant, 1599), E4r.

56. Newman has argued that although the "status of blacks was liminal rather than fixed" in the sixteenth and early seventeenth centuries, by the end of the century, with the slave trade firmly established, that social fluidity was no longer possible ("And wash the Ethiop white," 154). This change in social position is evidenced in language instruction manuals. Like the *Colloquia*, George Fox's *A Battle-door for teachers & professors to learn singular & plural* (1660) uses the social situation of black laborers to teach conversational skills, but here those laborers are made synonymous with slaves: "Ye who through your ambition speak contrary to your own Grammars, Teaching, and Bible; and so are fallen into respect of person, saying to your Negers and Slaves *thou*, but to your better servants *ye* or *you*, or to one another *your worship*; Is not this the Antichrist, who is exalted above all that is called for God? For do you say [*you* or *your worship*] to God or to Christ?" In his hyperbolic lesson about the morally bankrupt use of plural pronouns, Fox instructs readers both about the prevailing social hierarchy and the ways in which that hierarchy is inscribed by popular linguistic practice, to Fox's extreme consternation. George Fox, *A battle-door for teacher & professor to learn singular & plural* (London: Robert Wilson, 1660), B1v.

57. James Howell, *A new English grammar prescribing as certain rules as the languages will bear, for forreners to learn English* (London: T. Williams, 1662), C6v. For the status of this Spanish proverb as well as its later variants, see John Collins, *A Dictionary of Spanish Proverbs, compiled from the best Authorities in the Spanish Language, Translated into English; with Explanatory Illustrations from the Latin, Spanish, and English Authors* (London: S. Brooke, 1823), p. 157.

58. Newman, "'And wash the Ethiop white,'" 154.

# Review Notices

Michael Alexander, *Medievalism: The Middle Ages in Modern England*. New Haven, Conn.: Yale University Press, 2007. Pp. xxviii, 352. 90 b/w, 20 color illustrations.

Michael Alexander's *Medievalism: The Middle Ages in Modern England* is a literary history of the so-called Medieval Revival of the nineteenth century in England that branches off into cultural history and concludes with analyses of some of the ways the Medieval Revival played itself out in the twentieth century. It is the first full-scale history of this literary/cultural movement, and Alexander does much to keep things interesting. The volume is full of pertinent illustrations that help enormously, and Alexander's voice is clever, provocative, and always engaging. There are some rough edges—things with which to take issue and perplexing emphases—but the wide-ranging topic and mass of detail of course make this inevitable. Medievalists who are interested in how their special subject animates surprisingly much of literature from the two centuries just concluded will learn a great deal from this volume while enjoying it as a good read.

Alexander demonstrates that the fashion for things medieval arose in the 1760s with Horace Walpole and James MacPherson, long before modern scholarship began its labors of developing an accurate understanding of the past. The towering figure of Walter Scott, whose early-nineteenth-century novels like *Ivanhoe* made the medieval all the rage in polite society, brought medievalism into the literary mainstream. Tennyson's Arthurian poems, the output and theorizing of the Gothic Revivalist architect and designer A. W. Pugin, and the Church reformers of the medieval-minded Oxford Tractarians supported Scott's influence. The Pre-Raphaelites, for whom visual and literary art were so intertwined, figure prominently in Alexander's book. In particular, Dante Gabriel Rossetti, Edward Burne-Jones, and William Morris made the medieval the center of their creative work. Morris was especially influenced by the ideas of John Ruskin. Gerard Manley Hopkins, the Aesthetes, and the Decadents, all of whom transformed the Pre-Raphaelite agenda in their own quirky ways, brought the first phase of the Medieval Revival to a close, though Alexander demonstrates that the modernists of the

*Medievalia et Humanistica*, New Series, Number 34 (Paul Maurice Clogan, ed.), Rowman & Littlefield Publishers, Inc., 2008.

earlier twentieth century and their immediate followers in the middle
years of that century kept Medieval Revival ideas alive.

Alexander is particularly adept at selling Scott to a reluctant academic audience, whose benign neglect of the novelist Alexander treats
in his second chapter. Though it is not fashionable to read much Scott
today, the esteem in which he was held by his contemporaries and followers from the next generation was formidable. What is especially ap-
pealing about Alexander's treatment of Scott is his reliance on Scott's
poetry as well as novels. His analyses of Hopkins and Auden were for
me quite valuable. After demonstrating Hopkins's affinity with the medieval, Alexander argues that, though Hopkins's meter has long been
ascribed to the influence of Old English verse, it really owes little to
that type of medieval poetry. But in Auden, argues Alexander, that influence is genuine. Alexander's analyses of Pound and Eliot are for me
likewise persuasive.

But his tone can occasionally become dismissive, and his lively style
can sometimes lead him into minor difficulty. His treatment of Morris
offers examples of both. Morris, of course, was a visual artist as well as
a writer, and his reputation as a pattern designer is formidable. In the
latter part of his book, Alexander dismissively mentions "medieval wallpaper"—a clear reference to Morris, who produced designs for both
fabrics and wallpapers. Linking these two words is a clever but inaccu-
rate rhetorical flourish. Morris's wallpaper designs actually have little
to do with his medievalist work, and the major influence on Morris as
a wallpaper designer, besides what he picked up from direct observation of nature, in reality came from seventeenth-century India. Alexander also dismisses Morris's *Earthly Paradise* as unread by people today.
Though certainly long narrative poetry is no longer popular, people
still do read *The Earthly Paradise,* and not only the loyal members of the
William Morris Society. By coincidence I had just finished a complete
reading of it a few days before beginning to go through Alexander's
book for this review.

The perplexing emphases I mentioned earlier reside primarily in the
second half of the book, which treats the twentieth century. Alexander
devotes much space to his insightful and interesting analyses of writers
like Yeats, Pound, Eliot, Waugh, and Auden. I found his work on these
writers convincing and valuable, yet the medieval was not central to their
work in the way it was to Scott, Tennyson, and the Pre-Raphaelites.
Those twentieth-century writers employed the medieval primarily as a
repository of allusions, preferring not to create medievalesque worlds.
They contributed little to the proliferation of the medieval in the twen-

tieth century. What perplexes me is why Alexander devotes little space to writers much more influenced by the medieval, ones who have transmitted the Middle Ages to their contemporary culture much more powerfully and directly than those who most interest Alexander. J. R. R. Tolkien and C. S. Lewis—with whom, admittedly, literary academics are often uncomfortable—have affected the late twentieth century as profoundly as Scott did the nineteenth, but they receive only two and a half pages of direct analysis in Alexander's long book.

Still, *Medievalism: The Middle Ages in Modern England* is a great read— one written in lively, clever, and at times artistic prose. It is full of information and insightful analyses and interesting ideas.

Robert E. Boenig
Texas A&M University

Alexandra Cuffel, *Gendering Disgust in Medieval Religious Polemic.* Notre Dame, Ind.: University of Notre Dame Press, 2007. Pp. xviii, 430. 10 b/w illustrations.

Ms. Cuffel works with sources in Hebrew, Greek, Arabic, Latin, and more than a few of the various medieval vernaculars, which has to be somewhat intimidating to a reviewer whose connection with the medieval is Old Icelandic and Old English and whose connection with Hebrew was via the whip of Bar Mitzvah and who learned all the words needed to vaccinate anally thousands of chickens in the *lul,* the chickenhouse, on a kibbutz way back in 1964. I thus have to take the author at her word except, I suppose, when it comes to knowledge of the revulsion occasioned by fecundity and rot, of the horror of skin gone bad, of the misbehavior of the orifices of human bodies, their discharges—semen, menstrual blood, mucus, saliva, vomit, excrement, afterbirth, and such; and I can also trust to my own knowledge of other unfortunate members of God's creation—pigs, snakes, toads, rats, maggots, even, alas, dogs—who are enlisted as disgusting avatars of humans who have let the side down.

It is hardly surprising that polemical invective should have recourse to the idiom of disgust. Try to let someone know how offensive you think they are without employing images of disgust. Our earliest insults are of the order of "you stink" or "you make me sick." And one suspects the link of the idiom of disgust to certain kinds of deep disapproval is a cross-cultural and transtemporal universal. One particular point about disgust that Cuffel ignores is that it often operates as part of complexly motivated and ambivalent desires that make the disgusting, the prohibited, attractive or at least interesting. Disgust is not wholly aversive. Whole disciplines arise, like anthropology, medieval studies, trauma studies, sex and gender studies, just so the disgusting— "You mean they did (ate) that?"—can be indulged without shame and with no small delight.

That Christians, and to a lesser extent Muslims (back then at least), thought Jews revolting is nothing new; but that Jews thought Christians revolting, and indulged in delightfully blasphemous polemics registering their revulsion, is a refreshing change of pace. Of course they did, but woe to them if the Christians learned Hebrew. Jewish cover was blown by the twelfth century. Jews, as indeed the pagans before them, and Muslims coterminously with them, were horrified by the idea of the Incarnation. God in a stinking womb, lodged so near urine and feces, born in a flush of afterbirth, nourished, as the belief would have it, with menstrual blood in the womb and suckled with milk, itself a transformation wrought on menstrual blood according to standard medical theory?

It was not just that God came from woman, but that he became man, which meant God/Jesus could not escape urination, defecation, or farting. What kind of respectable God, wondered pagan, Jew, and Muslim, would ever do that? One Jewish polemical tract—*Toledot Yesu*—declared Jesus a bastard born of a menstruating Mary. No wonder Jesus challenged the wisdom of his respected elders. That is just what one would expect from a *ben niddah*, a son of menstruation.

Cuffel starts her story with pagan-Christian polemics, in which Christians, because of their own ambivalence about the flesh, anxiously felt the force of attacks by pagan platonists for whom divinity was to be aggressively distinguished from corporality. She takes her account well into the thirteenth century, and though she is careful to document changes in the tone and substance of the polemics, the story remains much the same. Menstrual blood and excrement figure prominently, though the polemic shifts—finding its grounding now in scientific and medical discourse, now in theology, now in just plain name-calling.

But by the eleventh to thirteenth centuries, real Jews were losing their lives because of the more charged meanings that blood had come to take. Blood was now bursting beyond the bounds of female menstruation to encompass a supposed Jewish male menstruation, monthly anal bleeding. Both hemorrhoids and menstruation were caused in the latest medical theory by "corrupt blood," with "corrupt" bearing both moral and medicinal meanings.

Enter the Real Presence. If Jews were revolted by what they imputed to Christians as lack of concern with purity violations, be these with menstruation, ejaculation, skin diseases, or Levitical food prohibitions, Christians repaid the favor by seeing Jews as blood eaters, child murderers, and host desecrators. Trite as it is to observe, it is nonetheless very hard not to see Jews paying the price for Christian anxiety about the incredibility of transubstantiation and, surely, revulsion at the thought of eating Christ and drinking his blood. So Jews excused from drinking Jesus' blood by their stubborn refusal to convert, were, apparently, seen to drink it anyway, by killing Christian children and using their blood as curative alimentation, for that blood had been fed on Jesus' blood: the food chain in a new light.

Eucharistic devotion generated tales of Jews rekilling Jesus by stabbing the communion host, but also tales of Christians being even more blasphemous. Caroline Bynum in her transformational work has, among many other things, focused our attention on the alimentary in devotion, especially female devotion; tales of women seeking to live on the Eucharist alone were not uncommon, but what of the story of a twelfth-century man who decided to do the same in order to prove that he could transmogrify God into shit? He was struck dead fifteen days into his diet. It was claimed that whatever wastes he had discharged in the meantime were formed from his own body consumed from within by its own vileness, not from Christ's (114).

A chapter on impure, sickly bodies shows that, already by the eleventh century, Jews had come to internalize a Christian critique that saw them as ugly and weak, offering early signs that Diasporan Jewish self-hatred predated Jewish emancipation by some seven hundred years. Even the great Rashi accepted Jewish ugliness, referencing the suffering servant of Isaiah 53:3, where he tried to turn physical deformity to Jewish moral advantage.

A final chapter on animal epithets has some surprises, but mostly it is remarkable how durable these kinds of insults are. Jews were thus so many serpents, hyenas, worms, pigs, and ravens. But that they were also owls, hares, stags, and snails might raise an eyebrow—not, however, once it is known that hares and snails were emblems of cowardice, the stag of victimhood, and owls of filth. To this day we still use the pig in standard invective, and the dog—though many of us love them more than we do all but a few humans—still provide common terms of opprobrium.

Cuffel treats us to a wide range of sources, devoting more time to Jewish/Christian hostility than to Muslim/Christian, the former getting down and dirtier as invective at least, because, well, Muslims could fight and thus be engaged in a manly fashion and they, except in Spain and the East, were not present. Jews, however, were very much present and protected, unfortunately, by kings and churchmen. Nor had Jews taken over the Holy Sepulcher. It was all very frustrating for Christians. So they fantasized Jewish violence or presumed it from the impotent hostile wishes Jews gave voice to in their prayers. Then too, as Cuffel notes, because Muslims had more relaxed purity rules than Jews, Muslims were less motivated by disgust for Christians than Jews were. Muslims were mostly just incredulous that anyone could worship a god who felt it necessary to become a man. It seems it was more likely in those days that a Muslim rather than a Jew would complain of a Frank having a "goyische kopf."

Cuffel's footnotes are voluminous, as is her bibliography, both of primary and secondary materials; she is generous in her citations. She knows a lot and presents it well. The notes contain much excellent material and make for good reading themselves, though because they are unfortunately printed as endnotes, they must be enjoyed after the chapter. The book consistently engaged my interest because the primary material from the Jewish and Muslim sides was mostly new to me, and it was riveting.

I have only a couple of minor complaints. One is the cant of "gendering" in the title, since there is very little theory-cant in the book. The other is that though gender is clearly doing considerable work in these polemics, the gendering might just as well be seen as a secondary effect of a more generalized disgust with procreation and death, primarily focused, at least by the eleventh century, on blood—and rather ungendered blood at that. The book is thus more about blood and excrement than about masculine and feminine.

One last note: One item Cuffel mentions from the *Chronicle of Solomon bar Simson* left me sickened; I will never be able to say the grace after meal again—not that I say it very often—without it haunting me. Says the source—though it may not be entirely trustworthy, but that hardly matters, the story being no less horrifying for that—Jews who committed suicide or killed each other to avoid falling into the hands of Crusaders took care to kill each other obeying the laws of *Kashrut*. And those still standing were instructed to say the grace after meals (220). No doubt because it is outside the remit of disgust among people of different creeds, but hardly outside the remit of polemic, Ms. Cuffel does not note, nor does the pious account it is taken from, that the Jews in the story, like more than a few of the psalmists, are perhaps best seen as hurling polemical invective at God, not at their Christian murderers, in order to wake him up, or call him to his duty if he is awake. He has sold them for slaughter like lambs, while they, still faithful, follow his laws to make themselves food that meets all the requirements of the purity rules. In the words of Psalm 44: "Thou hast given us like sheep appointed for meat . . . yet have we not forgotten thee, neither have we dealt falsely in thy covenant." In Christian eyes, however, the Jews' self-likening to slaughtered sheep missed the mark; they were to be butchered as pigs.

W. I. Miller
University of Michigan

Mary Dove, *The First English Bible: The Text and Context of the Wycliffite Versions.* Cambridge: Cambridge University Press, 2007. Pp. xvi, 313. 11 b/w illustrations.

Mary Dove's *The First English Bible: The Text and Context of the Wycliffite Versions* is a timely and informative book. The first book-length treatment of the Wycliffite Bible since Margaret Deanesly's *Lollard Bible and Other Medieval Biblical Versions*, which was originally published in 1920, Dove's book incorporates modern scholarship and pays close attention to many of the approximately 250 manuscripts containing the whole or portions of the late fourteenth-century English Bible. Dove stays close to that Bible, opting neither to write a history of the Lollard movement, to provide biographies of Wyclif and his collaborators, nor to explain proto-Protestant theology. The result is a very useful volume about the origins of the first complete English Bible and the challenges that faced the translators in producing a viable Bible in their vernacular.

Dove offers a full description of what she terms "the Bible debate" (6)—the controversy over whether a translation of the Bible into English should be allowed by the Church. Though valid arguments were made for such a translation and though the Church was more open to it than subsequent Protestant polemic would allow, the Constitutions of 1409, drawn up by a Church council in Oxford under Archbishop Arundel, finally created a religious-political climate severely repressive of the

*Medievalia et Humanistica*, New Series, Number 34 (Paul Maurice Clogan, ed.), Rowman & Littlefield Publishers, Inc., 2008.

English Bible. Before that date a surprisingly large number of people had English Bibles, including many that were not Lollards (though manuscript evidence shows that they were often reluctant to inscribe their names in their English Bibles).

Dove reviews the evidence about the identity of the people behind the translation. She favors retaining John Wyclif himself as an important contributor to the translation. As she explains, "[My] view is that Wyclif integrated the project, that work began in the early 1370s in the Queen's College, Oxford, and that Wyclif, [Nicholas] Hereford and [John] Trevisa all played part in the translation" (2). She explains the thin evidence that John Purvey played a role but reserves most of her analysis for the actual process of translation, preferring to write about the unspecified "translators" rather than assigning names to specific sections. She emphasizes the evolution of the Wycliffite Bible from the "Earlier Version," an overly literal rendition of the Latin text, to the "Later Version," in which the translators developed a style in accord with English idiom and used tools necessary in determining an accurate text from which to translate.

In doing so, Dove demonstrates great ability in handling the sheer mass of her evidence. She adeptly looks at readings from different manuscripts to demonstrate how the translators took great pains to write good English that was nevertheless responsive to the need to provide a faithful rendition of the sacred text. She includes evidence from the general prologue to the work as a whole and the many prologues to individual biblical books. Contrary to Thomas More's later charge that the Wycliffite Bible contains much in the way of spurious readings based on heretical theological ideas, Dove's analysis supports instead (though with some admitted limitations) the translators' desire to be accurate.

One of the benefits of *The First English Bible: The Text and Context of the Wycliffite Versions* is the wealth of ancillary material in its appendices. In appendix 1, Dove lists the contents of the versions of the Wycliffite Bible, including the prologues, and indicating differences between the Earlier and the Later Versions. In appendix 2 she lists selected additions and emendations to the edition done by Victorian scholars Forshall and Madden. She provides in appendix 3 selected variant readings that illuminate points she made in the main portion of her book. The very valuable appendix 4 offers description of major manuscripts of the Wycliffite Bible. She follows these appendices with a select bibliography, an index of the manuscripts of the Wycliffite Bible, and finally a general index to her book. All this back matter comprises 114 pages, making the case for the use of Dove's book as a reference guide as well as a critical study.

Though I find Dove's book admirable in every substantive way, there are two issues that could be addressed in a subsequent edition. First, many Anglo-Saxonists might take issue with the contention that the Wycliffite is "the first English Bible," preferring that the adjective "complete" be inserted into that phrase. Large sections of the Bible were translated into Old English by a number of different people—the Heptateuch, the Psalms, and the Gospels. Some deferential acknowledgment of this accomplishment beyond a couple of passing references to Bede's reputed interest in biblical translation would be appropriate. More important is the matter of Dove's frequent use of Middle English quotations. She relies heavily on them to make her points, and they are, with the exception of sporadic words or phrases included in brackets, untranslated. Specialists in Middle English will have no trouble with them, for they are in fairly easy Middle English, one similar to the language we find in Chaucer, a contemporary of Wyclif and his fellow translators. But Dove's book has two potential audiences that are not served by frequent untranslated quotations in Middle English that employ the daunting "thorn" (þ, with capital Þ) unmodernized into "th"—a practice that gives a very unfamiliar look to the passages. Biblical scholars and historians of the book might not use this fine book to the extent that it deserves, while translations in the footnotes would remedy this problem. We specialists in medieval English might be surprised that we are capable of doing work that can interest others—as Dove's certainly can.

Robert E. Boenig
Texas A&M University

Iain Fenlon, *The Ceremonial City: History, Memory, and Myth in Renaissance Venice.* New Haven, Conn.: Yale University Press, 2007. Pp. 448. 162 illustrations.

This enormous book—in three parts of four chapters each, enclosed by a prologue and epilogue—began life as a much more modest enterprise, as the author reveals in his preface. Initially intended to focus on the cultural reactions to an important milestone in the history of the Venetian Republic, the victory over the Turkish fleet at Lepanto in October 1571, the project grew into a virtual history of Venetian Renaissance culture.

*Medievalia et Humanistica*, New Series, Number 34 (Paul Maurice Clogan, ed.), Rowman & Littlefield Publishers, Inc., 2008.

The first part, which shares its title with that of the book, examines Piazza San Marco as the architectural, social, and religious center of the republic. The second part, A Disquieting Decade, the repository of what must have been the original Lepanto material, treats the four most politically significant events of the 1570s: the negotiations leading up to the formation of the Holy League, the victory itself, the visit to Venice of Henry III in 1574, and the plague of 1576. And the third part, whose title became the book's subtitle, explores the resonance of these events on the subsequent history and mythology of Venice.

Although Fenlon is well known as a musicologist and has published a great deal on music in Venice, this book is a much more ambitious undertaking. Here he sets out to describe the full historical and political contexts in which music participated in Venetian ritual and ceremony, demonstrating just how rich and varied was the soundscape of sixteenth-century Venice. As the author observes in his preface, history is often silent on rituals and ceremonials and their locations. Indeed, what is unique about Fenlon's book, distinguishing it from the plethora of studies of this period in Venetian history, is the extent to which music finds its voice within it.

Very much to his credit, the musical observations are so well integrated within the general discussion that they are not easily extracted. Only one substantial section, twenty-odd pages in chapter 2 on the use of the polychoral style in Venetian ceremony, stands out as musicology. Here, in the course of his description, he clearly summarizes present thinking regarding the origins of the style as a phenomenon that appeared in the Veneto before being adapted by San Marco composers. Music printing, for which Renaissance Venice was especially known, is discussed within the context of printing in general (the subject of chapter 9), and references to secular music occur in connection with the entertainments for the visit of Henry III (chapter 7). Fenlon finds the opportunity to mention the most renowned composers of the period, and he correlates their most characteristically Venetian works with the occasions for which they were intended. While much of this information is available elsewhere, only here does it become so clearly part of the larger picture of Venetian cultural history.

Given the ambitions of Fenlon's study, its intended audience is not easy to identify. Specialists in Venetian history and culture will appreciate the integration of music within the picture they have of Venice, though they may find some of the detailed descriptions and chronologies of certain historical events overly familiar. General readers, on the other hand, may be troubled by a certain redundancy and lack of clarity—left wondering, for instance, until the epilogue, just what is meant by the "Myth of Venice." Indeed, such readers will be confused by Fenlon's equation of the *sensa* with "marriage of the sea" (44), when the term actually derives from the feast of the Ascension of the Virgin, the day on which that marriage ceremony was celebrated, as discussed some ten pages earlier.

Because of the nature of the material and the way the project developed, there is considerable overlap among the various sections. Events are mentioned, even discussed, multiple times, in multiple contexts, often without cross-reference. On a smaller scale, figures are named but not identified until pages later, if at all (e.g., Marin Sanudo), or they are inconsistently identified (as is Giovanni Stringa). Perhaps the most egregious error of this kind, symptomatic rather than crucial, concerns the number of editions of Ariosto's epic *Orlando furioso*, published by the Giolito firm between 1542 and 1560: The number is first given as twenty-eight (235), and, four pages later, as twenty-seven (239). Much of this could have been eliminated by careful copyediting. Such laxity has not done justice to Fenlon's efforts, and it bears some responsibility for making the voyage through this book, with all of its riches, feel like being in a gondola in rough waters: There are too many unsettling bumps.

Ellen Rosand
Yale University

Barnabas Hughes, trans. and ed., *Fibonacci's* De Practica Geometrie Sources and Studies in the History of Mathematics and Physical Sciences. New York: Springer, 2008. Pp. xxxv, 408.

Leonardo da Pisa (Fibonacci) (c. 1170–ca.1240) was the most accomplished mathematician in medieval Europe, credited with introducing Arabic numerals into European calculations. This publication follows new editions of two of Fibonacci's other major works, *Liber quadratorum* and *Liber abaci* by Laurence Sigler. *De Practica Geometrie*, as its title indicates, is a treatise on theoretical geometry, beginning with basic definitions (point, line, units of measure, etc.), and moving to cover two-dimensional matters (measuring and dividing triangles, quadrilaterals, circles, and other more complex figures; calculating square roots) and

*Medievalia et Humanistica*, New Series, Number 34 (Paul Maurice Clogan, ed.), Rowman & Littlefield Publishers, Inc., 2008.

then the equivalent three-dimensional matters. The final sections briefly discuss the measurement of heights from a distance, calculations with figures inscribed in a circle, and a couple of mathematical puzzles. Despite a few remarks about practical applications such as surveying and astrology, the general tone is abstract; the problems are not designed to relate to real life, but to best illustrate complex mathematical relationships or calculations. Readers for whom the Pythagorean theorem is a distant memory will find it a challenging text to follow, a valuable testimony to the technical skill of medieval mathematicians.

Hughes's expert commentary is likewise aimed at the mathematically proficient, specifically in discussing Fibonacci's place in the development of mathematics. He also devotes careful attention to the manuscript history of the text, pointing to problems with the existing copies of the text (the oldest of which dates from more than a century after the text's composition), and making some slight alterations and rearrangements of the text in keeping with what he sees as Fibonacci's original intentions. (The meticulous notation of these alterations in the commentary and footnotes allows the manuscript's original formatting to be easily reconstructed). A section of the commentary is also devoted to discussing confirmed and possible sources for each chapter. Euclid could hardly be avoided; Fibonacci refers to the *Elements* at several points in *De Practica Geometrie*. Most of Fibonacci's mathematics, however—and not just his numerical notation—comes from Arabic sources, which is not surprising given the mathematical strides made by Arabic authors since the classical period and Fibonacci's residence in North Africa as the son of a Pisan mercantile notary (and his claims of travels to other Islamic lands). Hughes cites texts including Abū Bekr's *On Mensuration* and Abū Kāmil's *Algebra* as sources for Fibonacci, and argues that he relied on an Arabic translation of the *Elements* as well.

While for Hughes such comparisons with Arabic sources are critical for the question of Fibonacci's training and originality, for readers interested in the medieval world they are further evidence for deep Mediterranean connections, including the shared heritage of Greek science that provided a common mathematical language. *De Practica Geometrie* also makes clear the practical challenges faced by medieval mathematicians who, lacking decimals and rapid means of calculation, had to resort to approximations and body abacus when the numbers started to get out of hand. Yet despite these still-rudimentary tools, Fibonacci delighted in making problems more complicated and in proving more elaborate relations between geometrical figures. The final mathematical riddles further this impression of virtuosity, serving as the cherry on the sundae.

This translation should find a place in all specialist and research collections. While the technical nature of the text and the commentary does not make it especially accessible for undergraduate instruction, those interested in the exploring the vitality of medieval mathematics will find many areas to explore (and calculate).

Christine R. Johnson
Washington University in St. Louis

John M. Fyler, *Language and the Declining World in Chaucer, Dante, and Jean de Meun.* Cambridge: Cambridge University Press, 2007. Pp. xii, 306.

One of the adjustments we must make when reading pre-nineteenth-century literature is to expect regress where we normally encounter progress. The Industrial Revolution and Darwin have bequeathed to us optimism about where the world is heading. The horse-and-buggy gives way to the automobile as apes morph into humans, leaving us with a faith almost religious that the latest version of Microsoft's Windows is vastly superior to its predecessor. Scattered at the edges of our vision, though, are shards of an earlier, more pessimistic belief that the world is in decline. The angel's flaming sword bars us from Eden, and Ovid's Age of Gold undergoes its metamorphosis into rusty iron. We no longer live to the age of Methuselah, though modern medicine aided by statistical analysis would have us believe that we live on average longer than our grandparents.

Depending on the filter through which we view language, it too either progresses or declines. A dominant modern myth charts language's origin from the simple to the complex: A caveman pointing at a tree just shattered by lightning utters the onomatopoeic "Crack!" signaling a beginning that eventually leads to the inventiveness of Shakespeare and the solemn abstractions of post-modern literary theory. Historical linguists demonstrate, however, how much more complex is Proto-Indo-European grammar than anything we have today, with the loss of things like the optative mood, the dual number, the instrumental case, and the middle voice.

In an informative book graced by insightful literary analysis, John M. Fyler describes how Jean de Meun, Dante, and Chaucer reacted to the

*Medievalia et Humanistica*, New Series, Number 34 (Paul Maurice Clogan, ed.), Rowman & Littlefield Publishers, Inc., 2008.

dominant myth of linguistic decline that they inherited from the Bible and its many commentators. Each of these poets, argues Fyler, has anxiety about language in a declining world—noting the decline before either resolving it (Dante) or accepting it with irony (Jean de Meun and Chaucer). The value of Fyler's book lies in his demonstration of the importance of this issue to these poets, as well as in his persuasive reading of individual passages drawn from their works.

The first eleven chapters of the book of Genesis, which recount the Creation, the Flood, and the Tower of Babel, delineate a Fall of language that is consequent on the Fall of Adam and Eve. On the basis of the spare biblical stories, patristic and medieval commentators constructed a fully developed narrative about the decline of language. Originally there was one language, that of Heaven (Hebrew or proto-Hebrew for most commentators), which was originally spoken in Eden. The most significant characteristic of this language was its essential connection of individual words with what they signified. The word and thing were, in other words, ontologically related. But a consequence of the Fall is the separation of word and referent to the point where words signify only arbitrarily (*ad placitum*, 19–20), opening the door for ambiguity, uncertainty, and lapses in communication.

Fyler argues that there are competing voices in Jean de Meun's portion of *The Romance of the Rose* and asserts that Reason, who is sometimes depicted as possessing the poem's authoritative, pre-lapsarian voice, is "subjected to irony" (71). Fyler notes that Reason claims the ability to name things *ad placitum*, one of the hallmarks of fallen language (93). Jean de Meun thus offers a debate that "is purposively inconclusive" (71). On the other hand, Dante is capable of imagining an unironized, unfallen language, one with which he invests Adam, who shows up in Canto 26 of *Paradiso*. Though language can divide, Dante emphasizes the ability of language, in particular vernacular language, to unify.

Both Jean de Meun and Dante, of course, influenced Chaucer. It is possible thus to read Fyler's book as essentially about the English poet: As ideas about the decline of language influenced his predecessors, so do they influence him. Fyler concentrates on three of Chaucer's works: the early *House of Fame* and two tales from the concluding sequence of *The Canterbury Tales*, those told by the Second Nun and the Canon's Yeoman. Fyler accepts the dominant interpretation of *The House of Fame* as Chaucer's ironic evocation of Dante but one which offers no possibility of unitive language. As Fyler writes, "[Chaucer's] argument that speech, like all other sound, has its home and fitting resting place in the House of Fame, depends on emptying speech of meaning by reducing it to its physical properties; and however terse and pregnant with meaning the Eagle's own speech is (in his opinion, at least), it adds to the cacophony" (147). In the concluding sequence of *The Canterbury Tales* Chaucer emphasizes both language and silence and, for Fyler, he there "celebrates, in a backhanded fashion, the generative powers of fallen language itself, the cacophony that perpetually underlies and undermines human efforts to impose unity, clarity on the evanescent works of human memory and art. This is a language that is itself the very essence of energy and ceaseless flux" (154).

Though one is left wondering how Chaucer's other favored prior authors (Machaut, Boccaccio, and Petrarch) would fit into Fyler's paradigm, his argument is nevertheless effective. This is not the least because of the amount of erudite scholarship Fyler brings to his book, with more than a third devoted to endnotes and bibliography. He successfully explains how an important component of medieval ideology animates the poetry of three of the most significant writers of the age.

Robert E. Boenig
Texas A&M University

D. H. Green, *Women Readers in the Middle Ages.* Cambridge: Cambridge University Press, 2007. Pp. xi, 296. 14 b/w illustrations.

D. H. Green's *Women Readers in the Middle Ages* is a broad survey of its topic that presents examples from the sixth to the early sixteenth centuries and covers three regions of Western Europe—Germany, England, and France. Green is interested in classifying, that is, breaking his topic into various types and carefully listing them. He is successful in what he does, and there is much in the way of useful information that should prove valuable to those interested in women's history and women's literature.

Roughly the first third of his book is devoted to constructing a taxonomy that charts medieval reading in general. Though much of is scheme is discernible by simple common sense alone, I found it nevertheless convenient to see it neatly laid out. One could read aloud to another from a book (*lego librum illi*), the auditor thus reading the book through another (*lego librum ab illo*), or one could simply read for oneself (*lego librum*). This last could be done—contrary to modern practice—aloud or silently. Reading could also be done in Latin or, increasingly as the Middle Ages progressed, in the vernacular. Religious reading, including the specialized mode of *lectio divina* (meditative reading) was one category, while secular reading (chivalric romances in particular) was another. Medieval readers moreover could read on a literal level or on a figurative level, including the allegorical. Scribes also read as part of their craft, and one learned to read pictures as well as texts. Reading for the purpose of memorization was far more prominent than it is today, for the age suffered from a scarcity of books.

The remaining two-thirds of Green's book delineates women's participation in these activities. His method is, again, taxonomic, and the conclusions that he draws are that medieval women participated in all these activities, though in general they had more cultural deterrents than did medieval men, and that in a number of areas women had special influence—particularly in the rise of the vernacular, for their access to Latin was often limited. After describing women's education in general, Green classifies the various types of women who engaged in reading—laywomen, nuns, recluses, semi-recluses (like beguines, who lived in informal religious communities without official Church sanction, and also laywomen with spiritual aspirations like Margery Kempe), and heretics. Green's treatment of this last category is especially interesting. He mentions the fear of male clerics that heretical women would interpret texts on their own authority, since they were not versed in the Church's methods of figural reading. Heretical women or those on the borders of heresy like Margery Kempe and Mechthild of Magdeburg responded by claiming a direct access to God that circumvented the established hermeneutical methods. Orthodox women could do this too, with the prime example perhaps being Hildegard of Bingen. Green emphasizes the centrality of reading books for heretical groups like the Cathars, Waldensians, and Lollards. His concluding chapter broadens his topic by considering women as scribes, as dedicatees, as sponsors (a term he prefers to patrons), and as authors of books. Green's primary examples of women authors are Hildegard of Bingen, Mechthild of Magdeburg, Elizabeth of Schönau, Hrotswitha of Gandersheim, Marie de France, and Christine de Pisan.

Green describes himself as a Germanist, and a consequent strength of his book for the majority of medievalists who are not Germanists is his full treatment of medieval German women readers and writers—not only the famous people listed in the previous paragraph but also quite a few others. That he also does not neglect England and France enables his readers to see beyond borders and realize that the same issues attended women as readers, scribes, and authors throughout a wide range of medieval Western Europe. I would have preferred a greater role in his book for both the art of memory and *lectio divina*, but this does not, I feel, diminish its usefulness and interest.

Robert E. Boenig
Texas A&M University

Gerlinde Huber-Rebenich and Walther Ludwig, eds., *Frühneuzeitliche Bildungsreisen im Spiegel lateinischer Texte.* Weimar and Jena: Hain Verlag, 2007. Pp. 235, 4 b/w illustrations.

In the fifteenth century European intellectuals began to enjoy educational tours to major sites of classical antiquity, and many of them throughout the next centuries composed extensive travelogues, mostly in Latin. Some of these travelers belonged to the highest authorities of their days, and their accounts appealed to their students and colleagues back home. Their travel goals included traditional sites in Italy and Greece, but many times they also extended far into other continents (e.g., E. Kaempfer's journey of 1683–1693).

 During the Third Humanism Symposium in Erfurt, Germany, October 13–15, 2005, a group of early-modern Latinists investigated the genre of these travelogues and introduced significant representatives. The expanded and revised papers make up the present book. Walther Ludwig offers a most welcome survey discussion of the history of educational tours in the Latin travel literature, illustrating how quickly the traditional pilgrimage tours turned into new educational tours that were mostly organized and carried out in light of classical learning. Drawing from the wide range of studies published here, Ludwig successfully summarizes how these travel reports were composed, what they consisted of, and what genres (such as letters, poems, etc.) they included. At times these reports were accompanied by advice literature, but they all aimed to teach understanding of the foreign world, its people and culture, languages, arts, religion, and the economic and political conditions abroad.

*Medievalia et Humanistica*, New Series, Number 34 (Paul Maurice Clogan, ed.), Rowman & Littlefield Publishers, Inc., 2008.

The individual contributions can only be summarily reviewed here, but they indicate the significance and breadth of this fascinating genre as a powerful reflection of early-modern intellectual education and travel experiences all over Europe and beyond. The origins of this approach to educational travel can be found, as Gerlinde Huber-Rebenich suggests, in Magister Gregorius's *Narracio de mirabilibus urbis Rome* (twelfth or thirteenth century), who might have been one of the first to view the ruins of Roman antiquity with a secular, touristic, interest. Folker Reichert focuses, by contrast, on two true humanists and their travelogues, Cristoforo Buondelmonti (c. 1385–c. 1430) and Ciriaco d'Ancona (1391–1452), who both explored the eastern Mediterranean. The former left behind a most popular travel narrative, whereas the latter had a tremendous impact on subsequent artists and architects because of his unique drawings.

Reinhold F. Glei positions the fictional account of Hytholodaeus in Thomas Morus's *Utopia* in the same context, analyzing it concerning its topical and non-topical features. The *Senecan Letter* by Justus Lipsius from 1578 is the topic of Jan Papy's paper in which, among other aspects, the development of a stoic attitude is identified as one important learning experience from traveling. Travelers were often given a most friendly good-bye through poems, a genre also known as *Propemptikon*, as illustrated by Daniel Georg Morhof's prescriptive discussion in his *Polyhistor*, here discussed by Kristi Viiding. Many students who attended universities abroad created so-called *Alba amicorum*, a type of travel companion that contained learned poetry. Chris L. Heesakkers examines a selection of these alba from Dutch students and identifies the names of the contributors from the late-sixteenth and seventeenth centuries.

Other Humanistic travelogues were composed by Johann Heinrich Boecler (1654), here discussed by Justin Stagl; Engelbert Kaempfer (1712), discussed by Karl August Neuhausen; and Johann Caspar Malsch (1719), discussed by Hermann Wiegand.

The volume, which deserves high praise for the outstanding scholarly quality of each contribution, concludes with an extensive name index (an index of location names and subject matter is unfortunately missing). Now we have finally a solidly researched collection of critical articles dedicated to an important topic concerning the early-modern educational tour, or the *Tour d'Europe*.

Albrecht Classen
University of Arizona

Laurence Kanter and Pia Palladino, *Fra Angelico.* Metropolitan Museum of Art. New Haven, Conn.: Yale University Press, 2005. Pp. 348. 312 illustrations (257 in color).

What's the value of reviewing an exhibition that opened and closed more than two years ago? First, it can signal an exceptionally important exhibition catalogue packed with contributions by a team of eminent art historians.[1] Second, it can highlight for non-specialists just why writers on Renaissance society might find that parts of the catalogue will trump any item in the long canon of previously accepted notions about Fra Angelico (d. 1455), who was both a major figure in the history of early-fifteenth-century Florentine painting and a prominent Dominican friar.

No major exhibition of the artist's work had been mounted since 1955. Particularly problematic for would-be organizers is the fact that Fra Angelico's oeuvre is largely non-portable. Among his most important commissions were two groups of frescoes, one at San Marco in Florence and the other in the Vatican Palace, both of which must be studied in situ. And the large panel paintings, some of his greatest masterpieces, cannot be allowed to travel. Nonetheless, a quick browse through the catalogue's excellent bibliography shows that over the past decade or so, having one's say about Fra Angelico and his milieu has become a minor art-historical industry. It must be owned that many of these studies are both repetitive and art-historically conventional. What is more, all present a nearly invariable canon of works reproduced by ever-more-glamorous color photography. By showing small-scale works that could withstand the hazards of transport and temporary relocation, *Fra Angelico* turned this canon on its head

The exhibition gave special emphasis to the early phase of Fra Angelico's career, which began with his training as a manuscript illuminator and continued until his death in 1455 with a characteristic outpouring of smallish pictures executed with the jewel-like sumptuousness of miniatures. That is something we have known since the sixteenth century. What we have not known, or even been able to agree about, is the

1. The earliest biography is Giorgio Vasari's, found in the 1568 edition of his *Lives* (*Le vite . . .* , ed. Gaetano Milanesi [Florence: 1878–1885], 2:505–34). As Kanter shows (3–4), modern scholarship has corrected many of Vasari's inaccuracies. The date of the artist's death, however, is documented.

*Medievalia et Humanistica*, New Series, Number 34 (Paul Maurice Clogan, ed.), Rowman & Littlefield Publishers, Inc., 2008.

identity of Fra Angelico's teacher. For some time various authors have argued unconvincingly that the Camaldolese monk Lorenzo Monaco trained the young Guido di Pietro, as Fra Angelico was known before he entered the Order of Preachers some time around 1420. In addition to being weak, these arguments also rested on the common assumption that Fra Angelico was born in the late 1390s, perhaps as late as 1400, and entered the manuscript industry early in the second decade of the fifteenth century.

However, in a sustained analysis as incisive as it is beautiful, Laurence Kanter, the exhibition organizer, proves that Fra Angelico himself executed major portions of the predella of Lorenzo Monaco's *Coronation of the Virgin* in the Uffizi, securely datable to the years around 1411–1413. This can only mean that Guido di Pietro did, indeed, begin his professional career under the monk's tutelage. Even more remarkable, Kanter also shows that the master had accepted the pupil as a full-fledged assistant and entrusted him with the responsibility of painting parts of the predella without Lorenzo's intervention. That can only mean that Guido di Pietro entered his apprenticeship at least a decade earlier than anyone had previously imagined; in turn we must now assume that the artist was born not in the late 1390s but in the early 1380s. The consequences for the chronology of early-fifteenth-century painting in Florence, surely one of the most vexed of all periods in Italian Renaissance art, are incalculable.

In a short review this lone example can give one an idea of the many comparable revelations of *Fra Angelico*. Fortunately, the exhibition catalogue is as lavishly illustrated as its contents are distinguished. Historians of the period will therefore encounter no serious disadvantage if they did not see the works for themselves. Those who did need to see them are the art historians who specialize in the period. They found that some of Kanter's attributions could seem not only revelatory but even visionary; others, on the other hand, might seem both arbitrary and almost willfully perverse. Nonetheless, they are always stimulating and suggest new ways of studying this all-too-familiar artist. It is a sad fact that few students of Florentine painting have Kanter's courage and audacity, combined with his keen eye and intellect. Otherwise, one can easily imagine that the field would be far more cantankerous, and thus far livelier, than it is at the moment.

William Hood
Columbia University

William Levitan, trans., *Abelard and Heloise: The Letters and Other Writings*. Indianapolis: Hackett Publishing, 2007. Pp. xli, 356. Selected songs and poems translated by Stanley Lombardo and by Barbara Thorburn.

Since 1974 the standard translation of the writings of Peter Abelard and his wife Heloise has been that of Betty Radice in the distinguished Penguin Classics series. With the help of his collaborators Stanley Lombardo and Barbara Thorburn, who translated a selection of Abelard's songs and poems (twenty-two pages placed near the book's end), William Levitan has produced a readable and lively English version of the writings of the twelfth century's most famous star-crossed lovers. Levitan's introduction is helpful, and he includes more works than does Radice. The addition of these pieces makes Levitan's volume valuable, for it brings several important works of Abelard to both scholars and students, thus broadening our view of his work.

Both Radice and Levitan include Abelard's autobiography (the *Historia calamitatum*) and letters 1–4 (accurately termed "Personal Letters" by Radice). These are the writings that give us most of what we know of the tragic love of the two brilliant scholars of the early twelfth century—their secret love affair and marriage, Abelard's castration by the henchmen of Heloise's uncle Fulbert, Heloise's reluctant entry into religion when Abelard became a monk, the subsequent troubles of Abelard, and his founding of a convent for Heloise to rule as abbess, where she still longed for her maimed lover. We hear both sides of the story—Abelard in the *Historia calamitatum* and letters 2 and 4, Heloise in Letters 1 and 3.

Letters 5 through 7, termed "Letters of Direction" by Radice, were written after Abelard silenced the personal content of Heloise's correspondence and redirected her toward monastic and spiritual matters. In letter 5 Heloise requests Abelard's advice on running a convent of nuns, and in letters 6 and 7 he responds by giving lengthy advice. Radice only summarizes letter 6, while Levitan translates it in its entirety. Both volumes offer Abelard's short "Confession of Faith" and the correspondence of Heloise and Peter the Venerable, Abbot of Cluny, who took in the beleaguered Abelard after his condemnation for heresy in 1140 and provided him a home for the last two years of his life. Both Radice and Levitan provide the absolution that Peter the Venerable pronounced for Abelard, Radice in her main text and Levitan in a footnote.

*Medievalia et Humanistica*, New Series, Number 34 (Paul Maurice Clogan, ed.), Rowman & Littlefield Publishers, Inc., 2008.

Abelard produced songs, both writing the words and composing the music. He claims to have written secular love songs in honor of Heloise that were on everyone's lips in the last half of the second decade of the twelfth century. After his entry into religion he wrote in plainchant a number of works for use in church. A handful of these survive, words and music together. (Several are included in the admirable CD *Monastic Song*, performed by the Theatre of Voices directed by Paul Hillier [Harmonia Mundi 907209].) Radice offers her readers two of these religious songs, *Sabbato ad Vesperas* and *In Parasceve Domini: III. Nocturno*. Levitan offers a fuller selection, giving them English titles—"Hymn for Saturday Vespers" (*Sabbat ad Vesperas*), "Hymn for the Feast of the Presentation of Jesus in the Temple," "Hymn for the Night Office and Vespers," "Lament of the Virgins of Israel for the Daughter of Jephtha," "Lament of David for Saul and Jonathan" (all of these translated by Stanley Lombardo). Levitan also includes Lombardo's translation of "Dull Is the Star," a song that survives in the famous Carmina Burana manuscript. It is a secular love song that might be one of those Abelard wrote to Heloise. The song has a possible pun on her name (Heloise/Helius the Sun), and that has led to speculation about Abelard's authorship. Abelard does pun on her name years later in letter 4 (Heloise/Heloim [= "Elohim," one of the Hebrew words for "God"]), possibly strengthening the case for the authenticity of this beautiful song.

In addition Levitan includes some of Abelard's poetry, including "Open Wide Your Eyes" (a curious "shaped" poem translated by Barbara Thorburn, which was written into its manuscript in the shape of a wheel). There is also an excerpt of the lengthy poem "To Astralabe, My Son," translated by Lombardo, which offers aphoristic advice to the young man, whose conception occasioned the secret marriage between Abelard and Heloise. Levitan provides in appendices an excerpt from the late-seventeenth-century "Letter to Philintus" (a spurious expansion of the *Historia calamitatum*) and excerpts from the so-called "Letters of Two Lovers," a medieval text that, some argue, contains early letters written by Abelard and Heloise before all the turmoil that ended in their mutilation and separation.

Levitan's translations read well and are accurate. I have, however, two reservations about some of them, ones which may be more a matter of taste than anything substantive. He is prone to add italicized emphasis on some words to create an audible voice. Here is an example from letter 3, written by Heloise (his emphasis):

But *me*—
Was it my sorry birthright to become the cause of evil,

the well-known curse of womankind
to lead the greatest men to greatest ruin?
Is *this* why the Book of Proverbs has this warning against women . . .

To impose a speaking voice on a written text is, for me, problematic. The lineation of the extract serves also as an example of the second aspect of the translations about which I have reservation. In his introduction, Levitan rightly points out that the prose of both writers, particularly that of Heloise, is rhythmic and full of rhetorical techniques. But lineating selected passages as free verse is to me a distraction, for it anachronistically aligns much of Heloise's writings and some of Abelard's with modernist and post-modernist poetics. Though many passages are written in artful prose, they are not poetry.

Another minor difficulty I have with the book concerns its cover and thus is likely something over which Levitan had little or no control. Hackett Publishing produces on the front a detail from Lucas Cranach's 1533 *Adam and Eve* that depicts the exchange of the fatal fruit. It is not so much the anachronism but the implied moral judgment on Abelard and Heloise that disturbs me. There are other ways of interpreting the love between Abelard and Heloise than summary condemnation.

These difficulties, as I said, are more about my reactions than anything substantive. Levitan's book offers a fuller table of contents than Radice's, and the effective and readable translations measure up well to her very high standards. The volume is a welcome addition to the scholarship devoted to Abelard and Heloise.

Robert E. Boenig
Texas A&M University

Iustus Lipsius, *De recta pronuntiatione Latinae linguae dialogus.* Édition, traduction française, et commentaire par Elisabeth Dévière. Hildesheim: Georg Olms Verlag, 2007. Pp. xxv, 347.

This work presents a critical edition and translation of this Dialogue of Justus Lipsius of 1586. It is based on the three editions that appeared during his lifetime (1547–1606) as well as upon a posthumous edition of 1609. It has an *index verborum non antiquorum* and an *index nominum*. The introduction situates the work in its intellectual milieu and the commentary expands upon the translation in useful ways.

*Medievalia et Humanistica*, New Series, Number 34 (Paul Maurice Clogan, ed.), Rowman & Littlefield Publishers, Inc., 2008.

The question of how to pronounce Latin goes back to the Carolingian period, when the earliest emerging vernaculars appeared to some as distorted Latin that needed to be "corrected." By the time of the Renaissance, regional if not national pronunciations of the Latin language heightened awareness of a lack of understanding of how the ancients pronounced Latin, in the same way that the humanists, realizing that Byzantine pronunciation of Greek was not that of antiquity, endeavored to pronounce Greek *recta pronuntiatione*. Amelioration of Latin orthography went hand in hand with the reform of pronunciation, and from the end of the fifteenth century much energy was addressed to these questions by a variety of scholars, including Erasmus in his *De recta Latini Graecique sermonis pronuntiatione dialogus* of 1528. Humanists including Lipsius in this work studied inscriptions and the comments of the classical and late antique grammarians in attempts to attain an archaizing purity. Nevertheless, national ways of pronouncing Latin continued to confound a drive for uniformity in the language of the Church, education, government, and the other institutions of contemporary life. Theory and practice diverged, as is so often the case in "correcting" language.

Lipsius's effort had much success, as can be seen from the various editions appearing in rapid succession. Yet at the beginning of the next century, Scaliger noted in a letter that English speakers of Latin might as well have been speaking Turkish insofar as he could grasp what they were saying. This is a bit ironic in that Lipsius dedicated his work on Latin pronunciation to Sir Philip Sidney.

Though Lipsius does not mention Erasmus, his choice of the dialogue form for his own contribution to the discussion may be owed to Erasmus's preceding work on Latin pronunciation in dialogue form. The work proceeds methodically: Letters of the alphabet, vowels, diphthongs, consonants, accents in words, all reveal the drive for systematization that Lipsius inherited from ancient grammarians, which distinguishes his work on this subject from others of his time.

An example of how very difficult it was at this period to describe the sounds of spoken language can be seen in some of the words Lipsius uses to describe these sounds: *pinguis, crassus, vastus, exilis, tenuis*. Without the living praxis of ancient rhetorical schools at hand, such adjectives are hard-put to have a limited significance. The best Lipsius and the others could do was to rely on resemblance of the way vernacular words were written to what he wanted the Latin words to sound like. Yet, of course, *loqui* and *pronuntiare* often remained at odds.

Perhaps more success from endeavors such as that of Lipsius is to be found in the area of orthography rather than in the spoken word. We are still confronted in our age with Church Latin in its spoken and sung manifestations, the Latin pronunciation of Oxford and Cambridge college graces at meals, the Latin of the American (secular) classroom, and a good many others. But of course the humanists were trying to speak Latin to each other; that they succeeded so remarkably was owed not least to great efforts such as that of Lipsius, now handsomely edited, translated, and annotated in this welcome edition.

Charles Witke
University of Michigan

Barbara Newman, *Frauenlob's Song of Songs: A Medieval German Poet and His Masterpiece*, with the critical text of Karl Stackmann and a musical performance on CD by the Ensemble Sequentia directed by Barbara Thornton and Benjamin Bagby. University Park: The Pennsylvania State University Press, 2006. Pp. xxi, 242. 7 illustrations, 1 CD.

It does not happen often that a late-medieval German poet becomes the object of study by an American scholar who is a professor of English, religion, and classics. However, Barbara Newman here turns to a fascinating and certainly underexplored thirteenth-century poet, Heinrich von Meissen (c. 1260–1318), also known by his nom de plume Frauenlob. He is particularly famous for his Marian songs in the vein of the *Song of Songs*, but the Middle High German that he used is often not easily understood, even by the experts. Nevertheless, he enjoyed the highest respect for his lyrical work for the next three hundred years, until his fame was totally eclipsed, not to ascend again until the early nineteenth century (Newman ignores, however, the treatments and translations of Frauenlob's poetry listed by Siegfried Grosse and Ursula Rautenberg, *Die Rezeption mittelalterlicher deutscher Dichtung*, 1989, 26–27). Modern German scholarship has made solid and by now actually satisfactory efforts to edit his songs and to study their spiritual meaning, their literary quality, and their reception history. Newman takes the next step to introduce Frauenlob to the Anglophone world by offering an English translation facing the original text copied from Karl Stackmann's and Karl Bertau's edition (1981).

*Medievalia et Humanistica*, New Series, Number 34 (Paul Maurice Clogan, ed.), Rowman & Littlefield Publishers, Inc., 2008.

Not content with this philologically challenging task, she explores the wider religious and philosophical meaning of Frauenlob's poems, offering detailed discussions first of the performer, his public, and his contemporary colleagues, then investigations of the poet's work altogether as a canon pertaining to the *wip-vrouwe* debate (implying the question of what constitutes a noble lady, married or not), then an analysis of his "Marienleich" (verse poems dedicated to the Virgin Mary) in a cultural-historical context, then those that aim to establish a work of art, and finally an overview of Frauenlob's reception throughout the centuries. Another major section of her book proves to be the thorough commentary of each song, which addresses linguistic, religious, historical, and simply literary aspects. Future scholarship and general readership will be well served with this detailed analysis that allows us to comprehend the larger theological context and the textual strategies realized by the poet. Newman pays particular attention to Frauenlob's reliance on the *Song of Songs* in his dedicatory songs to the Virgin Mary, then on the *Apocalypse*, and the wider wisdom literature, not to forget the extensive corpus of learned treatises and vernacular literature.

Newman embraces a concept of translation that aims for a close replication of the original not only in the lexicon, but also in the prosody, the internal rhyme, and the principle of strophic responsion, which requires translation more "sense for sense rather than word for word" (xvii). The general reader will be thankful for that because it often makes the text more comprehensible and pleasing to the Anglophone ear. The Germanist philologist will encounter problems, however, because a careful comparison demonstrates that Newman's decision comes at a considerable price. There is practically not one line in the entire translation that can be accepted as absolutely accurately rendering the Middle High German into modern English. For instance, No. 2, the second stanza, reads as follows (in a close English translation):

| | |
|---|---|
| Si tet rechte | She did correctly |
| als sie solde | as she ought to |
| ja, die holde | yes, the delightful |
| trug den blumen sam ein tolde. | carried the flowers as an umbel. |
| vrouwe, ob ir muter würdet | Lady, if would become mother |
| des lammes und der tuben, iur truben | of the lamb and the doves, you loyal ones |
| ir liezet iuch sweren? | would you allow to be burdened? |

Newman renders the same text as follows: "She did / as she should, / noble and good, / bore a flower like a scepter. / Lady, if you would be / mother of both Lamb and Dove, / could you bear the weight" and adds, inexplicably, the line "of the vineyard's grape?" I find this rather problematic, and a further examination reveals that we can hardly trust any of the translations in the narrow sense of the word, though the author certainly renders the text in a more global sense quite correctly. But clearly subjunctive forms are cut, sentence structures are changed, and the style is modernized to such an extent that I have difficulties recognizing Frauenlob's original. Two more egregious examples follow: "der kelch des suns" (8, 19), which means "the son's chalice," becomes "In this chalice / without malice," though there is no reference to "malice" in the original, and so forth; "secht, lieben, secht" (11, 26), which means "look, my dear, look," it is turned into "Dear friends, remember." That is not the same and subjectively reads into the Middle High German!

Newman is open enough to admit that she deliberately changed much in tone and expression. She states in the introduction that she "supplied literal translations of all German passages" in the commentary and the interpretations, but these short selections are hard to find and do not help to remedy the overarching problem of the translation. Therefore Newman simply refers her readers to the original text, but that would be insoucient, or a misunderstanding of her own task as translator.

Altogether, the author is to be praised for her extensive efforts to make available one of the most fascinating thirteenth-century religious Middle High German poets to the Anglophone audience. In detail, I strongly disagree with her approach to translating the poems into English, but her commentary and critical approaches to the original text in its religious and historical context deserves great respect.

Albrecht Classen
University of Arizona

Robert J. Meyer-Lee, *Poets and Power from Chaucer to Wyatt*. Cambridge: Cambridge University Press, 2007. Pp. xii, 297.

Robert J. Meyer-Lee's *Poets and Power from Chaucer to Wyatt* is an excursus through the poetry of the fifteenth through the early sixteenth centuries that emphasizes, to use the phrase so skillfully deployed by Stephen Greenblatt, "self-fashioning"—"Renaissance self-fashioning" for the poets

*Medievalia et Humanistica*, New Series, Number 34 (Paul Maurice Clogan, ed.), Rowman & Littlefield Publishers, Inc., 2008.

Meyer-Lee treats toward the end of his book and, we could say, "late medieval self-fashioning" for those he treats in his first four chapters. As Meyer-Lee asserts, the attempts to fashion a poetic self were dominated by the poets' persistent desire to situate themselves as laureates. In the late Middle Ages and early sixteenth century this term did not bear its modern meaning of an office both honorific and exclusive; instead it denoted a poet who received the patronage of the court and in varying ways served as a spokesperson for the court's interests.

Chaucerians attracted by the title of the book might be disappointed, for Chaucer plays a relatively minor role in it. He is just a starting point, the first person who employs the term "laureate" in English poetry (in the prologue to the Clerk's Tale, where the Clerk invokes Petrarch, who had himself crowned with laurel). Chaucer was appropriated as "master" by John Lydgate, who wished to align himself with Chaucer in his attempts to make patronal headway among the Lancastrian monarchs and princes in the early fifteenth century. Lydgate is the book's central figure; Meyer-Lee fashions the term "Lydgateanism" to refer to a tradition of laureate poetics he identifies as a primary concern of the fifteenth- and early sixteenth-century poets. Lydgate, the poetical monk professed at the Abbey of Bury St. Edmunds in East Anglia, established a pattern of successful engagement between poetry and patronage. It is an implied thesis of Meyer-Lee's book that subsequent poets are more Lydgatean than Chaucerian, as they are often termed. Central to the agenda of laureate poetics is the positioning of oneself in a chain of influence that includes Chaucer (and often Gower as well) because Lydgate referenced them.

Haunting the dominant Lydgateanism is a failed laureate poetics that Meyer-Lee names after Lydgate's contemporary, Thomas Hoccleve. "Hoccleveanism" is the poetics of begging, in which a failed laureate embeds pecuniary complaint within his poetry. Hoccleve was a minor civil servant who endeavored to serve the early Lancastrians with his poetry, most notably his *Regiment of Princes*, but his annuity was seemingly always in arrears, occasioning much in the way of poetic grumbling. Meyer-Lee's astute insight is that Lydgateanism is always in danger of devolving into Hoccleveanism. As Meyer-Lee puts it, "The author posing as laureate must at some point acknowledge that he will never quite be the laureate he imagines, and, as we have seen in many instances, this acknowledgment transforms laureate poetics into its mendicant [i.e., Hocclevean] other, to disclose in full view the beggar that always lurks within" (231).

After treating Lydgate and Hoccleve and explicating relevant passages from their poetry, Meyer-Lee delineates the ways the tension between Lydgateanism and Hoccleveanism play out in the careers of a number of subsequent fifteenth- and early-sixteenth-century poets— Benedict Burgh, William de la Pole (the Duke of Suffolk who married Chaucer's granddaughter Alice and writes a riposte to Lydgate), George Ashby, Steven Hawes, Alexander Barclay, and John Skelton. He concludes with a brief treatment of Sir Thomas Wyatt, who, Meyer-Lee maintains, inherits much from laureate poetics while seemingly fashioning a new individuated poetic voice.

Meyer-Lee's paradigm of a Lydgateanism haunted by Hoccleveanism is both interesting and useful. He does much in the way of presenting the careers and poetry of these poets who, with the exception of Wyatt, languish in varying degrees of mostly benign neglect. The tension between a successful laureate poetics and its "secret sharer" (225), the begging poetics of Hoccleve, provides a good way to make sense of what was going on in the century and a quarter that followed Chaucer's death. Though many poems written during this time need no such hermeneutical pattern imposed upon them, it is a good one, nevertheless.

Robert E. Boenig
Texas A&M University

Timothy Reuter, *Medieval Polities and Modern Mentalities.* Edited by Janet L. Nelson. Cambridge: Cambridge University Press, 2006. Pp. 483.

This volume brings together a number of lectures and essays by Timothy Reuter, several of which have never before appeared in English. Although Dr. Reuter passed away before the project was completed, Janet L. Nelson assumed editorial responsibilities for the remaining portions. The book covers a wide range of topics in early and central medieval history, with a particular focus on medieval Germany. The book is divided into three sections; the first deals with how "modern mentalities" have shaped our notion of medieval Europe, the second with the importance of symbolic political actions in the Middle Ages, and the third with "political structures" broadly construed.

In part 1, Dr. Reuter continually draws attention to how modern constructs, such as periodization and the rise of the nation-state, have shaped scholars' approaches to the Middle Ages, at times with ill effects. Dr. Reuter even raises the question of how the term "medieval" itself might hinder a genuine understanding of human history. Furthermore, Dr. Reuter contends that the pressure to produce a national narrative among scholars of the central and later Middle Ages has constrained the scope of their inquiries in a way that does not do justice to the political realities of the period. These methodological musings form some of the most interesting material in this volume and offer a useful framework for reading the remainder of Dr. Reuter's work.

Parts 2 and 3 are composed of a number of more narrowly focused essays spanning medieval social and political history, as well as the history of ideas. Dr. Reuter continually reexamines existing theories with an eye to exposing the anachronisms of modern pictures of the Middle Ages and the symbolic meanings of public actions. For example, when offering his interpretation of the events at Canossa, Dr. Reuter asserts that Henry IV's actions did not conform to conventional rituals of penance, but rather to *deditio*, "a ritualized surrender, which borrowed elements of public penance—especially the clothing—for a somewhat different purpose," namely, the *political* reconciliation of rebels (160). In this way, Henry's submission was primarily a political act, even on its surface. Dr. Reuter engages with several other topics, including the Becket dispute, the role of plunder in the Carolingian empire, and the "imperial church system" in a similarly thorough and innovative manner. Although these chapters all generally emphasize the importance of symbolic actions and how the proper historical context can shed new light on old issues, they do not seem to form the coherent whole that the first part of this volume does. Nevertheless, they are well researched, and several provide illustrations of the kind of scholarship Dr. Reuter calls for in part 1.

Dr. Reuter's clear and at times light-hearted style makes this collection a remarkably enjoyable read, despite the density of its subject matter. The range of topics covered is impressive, with chapters that will draw the interest of scholars of the early and high Middle Ages, political history, history of ideas, and historical methodology. This thematic variety and concern with methodological issues makes Dr. Reuter's work merit attention from medievalists of a variety of stripes.

Mary Elizabeth Sullivan
Texas A&M University

Frank Rexroth, *Deviance and Power in Late Medieval London*. Cambridge: Cambridge University Press, 2007. Pp. 411. 6 b/w illustrations.

*Deviance and Power in Late Medieval London* is the English translation of Rexroth's well-received 1999 *Das Milieu der Nacht: Obrigkeit und Randgruppen im spätmittelalterlichen London*. Rexroth's intriguing thesis, clearly summarized in the book's conclusion, is that beginning in the mid-fourteenth century with the onset of the Hundred Years' War, the government of London promoted the perception that an "immoral counter-society was operating in the city."

The emphasis here is very much on the perceived immorality and policing of what Rexroth refers to throughout the book as the "nocturnal underworld," and not on the preoccupation with political corruption, conspiracy, and the influence of Lollardy that characterized Ruth Bird's *Turbulent London of Richard II* (London: Longmans, 1949). Nevertheless, the populist mayor John Northampton is very much a central figure in Rexroth's analysis, as he was in Bird's classic study. Rexroth takes the view that Northampton was a political demagogue whose "morality campaign" against such easy targets as prostitutes was intended to augment his own power and popularity at the expense of the authority of the Council of Aldermen. This is not an evenhanded portrait of a mayor whom scholars such as Caroline Barron and Paul Strohm believe genuinely cared for the poor and who was himself a victim of the political machinations of his merchant capitalist rival Nicholas Brembre. One might do well to read Bird's older study alongside Rexroth.

The book's most important contribution is the emphasis on the marginalization of the poor and the attack on the "sturdy beggar" in the late medieval city. Rexroth convincingly documents the process by which civic leaders distinguished between the legitimate "shamefaced" poor and those morally suspect individuals who were perfectly able to work but chose to beg instead. Rexroth's examination of the criminalization of the "sturdy beggar" includes a fascinating discussion of the evolution of public punishments of vagrants such as the increasing use of the pillory to combat begging. His Foucauldian analysis of "shaming punishments" is informed by a detailed examination of civic practice, but might have been enriched by a greater emphasis on the widespread anxiety prompted by the Revolt of 1381, and not just on the local late medieval power grab by city officials.

*Medievalia et Humanistica*, New Series, Number 34 (Paul Maurice Clogan, ed.), Rowman & Littlefield Publishers, Inc., 2008.

Rexroth's point of departure for his study is the *Liber Albus*, a compilation of London laws and customs recorded in 1419 by John Carpenter under the supervision of the mayor, Richard Whittington; Rexroth convincingly demonstrates that the origins of the social conservatism of Carpenter's London can be traced back to the outbreak of the Hundred Years' War. The evidence is strongest in the careful discussion of the role of the beadle in policing the city's wards, the evolution of vocabulary for marginalized groups in civic records such as *bartours* (men who lived without rules or restraint) and *strumpetmongers* (procurers of sex), and the development of London almshouses under Whittington's mayoralty as places for the acceptable "shamefaced poor."

In sum, this is an important and fascinating portrait of the creation of London's demimonde as well as a discussion of those segments of London society that benefited from the segregation of the good poor from the bad. Scholars such as Barbara Hanawalt have compared it to Bronislaw Geremek's *The Margins of Society in Late Medieval Paris* (translated by J. Birell [Cambridge: Cambridge University Press, 1987]) with good reason. The book contains an impressive appendix of source documents that will encourage further work on a topic that has yet to receive sufficient attention from English scholars; surely the English translation itself will prompt widespread interest in London's marginalized denizens of the night.

Clementine Oliver
California State University, Northridge

Paolo Squatriti, *The Complete Works of Liudprand of Cremona*. Washington, D.C.: The Catholic University of America, 2007. Pp. vi, 296.

Liudprand (c. 920–c. 970) had a colorful career. As a child he became a pageboy for King Hugh of Italy because Hugh admired his beautiful singing voice. In 949 Liudprand went to Constantinople at the request of Berengar, successor to Hugh. Liudprand later switched to the service of Otto I and became, in 961, bishop of Cremona. In 963 he participated with Otto in an assembly that deposed Pope John XII. In 968 Otto sent him to Constantinople on a diplomatic mission. After Liudprand returned, he died about 970.

*Medievalia et Humanistica*, New Series, Number 34 (Paul Maurice Clogan, ed.), Rowman & Littlefield Publishers, Inc., 2008.

We have from Liudprand several works: *Antapodosis* ("Payback"), about events from 887 to 949; *Gesta Ottonis*, about activities of Otto from 960 to 964; a homily, largely in the form of a dialogue between a Christian and a Jew concerning the Trinity; and *Relatio de legatione Constantinopolitana*, an account of Liudprand's ambassadorial experience at Constantinople on behalf of Otto.

In the *Antapodosis* one instance of treachery follows another: Archbishop Hatto tricks Adalbert with an oath and leads him to his death; Berengar indicates that he will treat Louis of Provence mercifully but afterward has the eyes of Louis gouged out; Lambert, archbishop of Milan, pretends affection for Duke Burchard, yet Lambert is planning to kill Burchard; Romanos pledges safety to a group of nobles and then throws them into the hold of a ship.

Just as treachery is a main theme of the *Antapodosis*, so the *Relatio* has as its theme the *historia calamitatum* of Liudprand's embassy to Constantinople for Otto I. The expedition endured a series of miseries, at least from Liudprand's perspective: consider the guard placed over his house (the men would not permit anyone to enter or leave); Liudprand's dispute with Leo, brother of the emperor, about the title of Otto; tirades of Emperor Nicephorus Phocas; preferential seating of Bulgarians at a banquet; and inhospitable Byzantine bishops.

In his writings Liudprand includes many lively anecdotes, such as one about Emperor Leo of Constantinople testing his guards and mother about a show in which two boys climb a pole balanced on a man's forehead. Liudprand is not averse to recording horror, like Pope Sergius's having the body of Pope Formosus exhumed and three fingers cut away from the corpse; the death of King Arnulf by lice; Hungarians piercing food in the throats of Christians; and Giezo's punishment of loss of eyes and tongue. Nor does Liudprand shrink from subjects of sex and scandal, such as the three favorite concubines of King Hugh, Willa's infidelity, and Pope John XII's misbehavior shortly before his death.

But Liudprand is especially memorable for his unflattering remarks: Queen Willa is a second Jezebel and a child-eating witch (110–111); the tutor of two girls is a harsh barbarian, hairy and unwashed, shameless and mad (193); Liudprand's household overseer in Constantinople is one whose equal may be found in hell (239); the wine of Byzantium is an undrinkable mixture of pitch, pine sap, and plaster (239); Emperor Nicephorus is a monster, with a fat head, finger-like neck, an extended belly and scrawny buttocks, long hips but small legs (240); and his father looks 150 years old and is a walking corpse (255).

And now Paolo Squatriti, associate professor of history and of Romance languages at the University of Michigan, gives us a new English translation of the works of Liudprand. His translation is based on the Latin text of Paolo Chiesa in *Corpus Christianorum, Continuatio Mediaeualis* 156 (Turnhout, 1998), but there is a sprinkling of inaccuracies in the translation. Here is a sample of translation errors in just book 1 of the *Antapodosis* (the page references are to Squatriti's book):

(43) *distuli*: "neglected" for "postponed"

(47) *viribus*: "with their own men" for "with their own strength" (*viribus* is not *viris*)

(47) *nil*: "no one" for "nothing"

(52) *optima*: "highest" for "best"

(53) *lupanaria percurrentem*: "heading for the brothels" for "running through the brothels"

(59) *deliberat*: "he decided" for "he ponders"

(60) *properat*: "he advanced" for "he hastens"

(60) *sese . . . figerent*: "they struck each other" for "they pierced each other"

(60) *ex adverso*: "from behind" for "opposite"

(61) *utraque auris eius tinniebat*: "felt both his ears prick up" for "each of his ears gave a ringing noise"

(62) *vacuis . . . condere criptis*: "to constructing empty texts" for "to forge [metal] in empty underground chambers" (*criptis* is not *scriptis*)

(62) *pingues captare siluros*: "handling a curved fishing rod" for "to catch fat siluri [a kind of fish]"

(64) *vallo circumdatur*: "circled with a ditch" for "is circled with a palisade [made of sticks]"

(65) *vincti*: "conquered" for "put in bonds" (*vincti* is not *victi*)

(66) *redeuntem regem magna cum valetudine*: "King Arnulf retreated very laboriously" for "the king returning with great strength"

(66) *Cognatorum vero Berengarii unus*: "But one brother-in-law of Berengarius" for "But one of the kinsmen of Berengarius"

(67) *veriti ne*: "lest" for "having feared that"

(68) *medio in nemore*: "in the middle of a swamp" for "in the middle of a grove"

(68) *non passus est milites praestolari*: "would not bear to have his soldiers prepared" for "did not allow his soldiers to wait"

(69) *te scientia sua regem aut asinum facturam promisit*: "she promised you would become either a king or a donkey" for "she promised that by her knowledge she would make you a king or a donkey"

(69) *custodiae mancipantur*: "kept them in prison" for "they are delivered into custody"

On page 65, "parties" is a tame translation of *dibachationes,* which really means "orgies." And there is the wrong interpretation (65 and 280) of Vergil, *Aeneid* 3.57: in both places of Liudprand *auri sacra fames* does not mean "a holy hunger for gold" but "accursed hunger for gold." Also, some Latin expressions are untranslated—for example, *aliquando* (52); *aliquot, protinus* (53); *praesertim, poenitus* (59); *Cannabe* (62); *disponit* (66); *ferme, positum* (68); and *ilico* (69).

The introduction and notes occasionally cry out for elaboration. Squatriti says that "a twelfth-century source" claims that Liudprand died during his third voyage to Constantinople (5). Why not name the source? Squatriti declares that there is "some structural awkwardness" in the *Antapodosis.* Why not give specific instances? Likewise, Squatriti gives barest information about Boethius (44 n5), Lucian (55 n5), and Prudentius (103 n63). In saying that a meter is unusual for the tenth century (88 n31), why not identify that meter? In saying that a poem "recycles elements" from Catullus, Seneca, Boethius, and Vergil (152 n36), Squatriti should show what passages he has in mind, especially for Catullus (a very rare medieval source) and for Seneca (which Seneca?), since both writers are unmentioned in Chiesa's commentary on the poem. Squatriti (275 n105) says that "Liudprand cites his contemporary Rather . . . Virgil, and Juvenal" without reporting the passages, and by "cites" Squatriti perhaps really means "imitates or "echoes," since Liudprand neither quotes nor names these sources. Squatriti (86 n25) wrongly identifies Tartarus (truly another name for the underworld) and Flegeton (truly the burning river of the underworld) as custodians of the infernal regions.

The bibliography fails to include among the translations of Liudprand F. A. Wright's version as edited by J. J. Norwich (London, 1993). The bibliography should also notice what is said about Liudprand in Max Manitius, *Geschichte der lateinischen Literatur des Mittelalters,* vol. 2 (Munich, 1923), 166–175; F. J. E. Raby, *A History of Secular Latin Poetry in the Middle Ages,* vol. 1 (Oxford, 1957), 283–285; and F. A. Wright and T. A. Sinclair, *A History of Later Latin Literature* (London, 1969), 175–182.

Despite weaknesses, Squatriti's book will enable undergraduate students to become acquainted with an amusing and vivid medieval author. The notes are helpful for explaining Greek words in the text, geographical references, and the gods of antiquity: it is sad that some students nowadays need to learn who were Aphrodite (100 n56),

Minerva (146 n21), and the Amazons (146 n22); there should be a note too on Semele (150).

Marvin L. Colker
University of Virginia

Shogimen Takashi, *Ockham and Political Discourse in the Later Middle Ages.* Cambridge Texts in Medieval Life and Thought, 4th series. Cambridge: Cambridge University Press, 2007. Pp. 301. 10 b/w illustrations.

Lying at the base of Shogimen's study of Ockham's political thought are two questions: What prompted William Ockham to conclude that papal government was tyrannical? And what did he expect to achieve through his program of anti-papal polemics?

Ockham had had a successful, albeit contentious, career as a philosopher, but John XXII's condemnation of the Franciscan's claim to poverty had prompted him to seek the protection of Ludwig of Bavaria, who was already at loggerheads with the pope over the relation of imperial and papal authority. He was now plunged into the heart of the century's most heated political controversy, in which the Church's attachment to political authority seemed fully exposed as naked ambition, while the emperor appeared to rival Domitian in his antipathy the Church. Rather than avoiding trouble, Ockham stepped bravely into the lists, producing a body of political philosophy and polemic remarkable both for the breadth of its scope and the depth of its analysis, including *Opus nonaginta dierum, Dialogus, contra Iohannem, contra Benedictum* (attacking John XXII and Benedict XII), *Breviloquium de principatu tyrannico,* and a number of other works, enough to fill four volumes in H. S. Offler's edition of the *Opera Politica.*

The scholarship of Ockham's political thought has been rich over the past century, exploring the extent of his philosophical commitment to rights theory, the nature of ecclesiastical office and its relation to secular authority, and its overall relation to the Franciscan order that may or may not have provided Ockham a base theological identity. A defect in many of these attempts has been the tendency to base the analysis on a subset of Ockham's political works—understandable if only because of the complexity of the argument in each treatise.

*Medievalia et Humanistica,* New Series, Number 34 (Paul Maurice Clogan, ed.), Rowman & Littlefield Publishers, Inc., 2008.

Shogimen's study is the first to consider Ockham's anti-papal works as polemics, a literary genre, rather than as articulations of a political philosophy. Eschewing the traditional tendency toward classifying the body of Ockham's political works in terms of an overarching system, or a legal or philosophical paradigm, Shogimen's approach is rather to assess the content, form, and structure of Ockham's polemics against papal authority in a more concentrated analysis of the theological tension between ethics and politics as it played out in a decaying ecclesiastical structure, the result of which is a picture of Ockham as a proponent of "ecclesiastical republicanism."

Ockham's understanding of heresy is fundamental to Shogimen's argument. A. S. McGrade has famously argued that Ockham's political thought did not arise from a defense of the Franciscans against charges of heresy. Shogimen agrees, arguing that Ockham's defense of the Franciscans against papal charges of heresy was motivated more by antipathy for the legalistic maneuvering of the canonists than by an overt Franciscan ideology. After all, the poverty controversy had devolved from the earlier, theologically oriented debates between the papacy and the Minorites into a legal dispute, in which cooler Franciscan heads challenged John XXII's reversal of his predecessor Nicholas III's pro-Franciscan *Exiit qui seminat.* By the time Ockham became involved, the canonists had secured a stranglehold on the debate. Adept at manipulating law to suit their ends, Ockham argued, papal lawyers had made Catholic truth their pawn, a grievous case of confusion about priorities. The canonists' appropriation of the concept of heresy had drained all theological value from the controversy, and Ockham's desire, motivated by an earnest desire for theological argument rather than Franciscan partisanship, was to restore the proper orientation. What lay at the base of the controversy's devolution, Ockham believed, was papal heresy. Any pope ready to subvert scriptural and theological precedent to legalistic chicanery, he realized, was himself heretical. But how can the Vicar of Christ be a heretic?

Shogimen argues that Ockham's theory of papal heresy grows in I Dialogus (1334) from a more general theory of heresy, which provided the foundation for his articulation of a justified dissent against papal authority. Rather than rely upon the standard definition of heresy identified with the institutional authority of the Church, Ockham dismantled the juridical approach to heresy altogether, rescuing the health of the Church from the jealously guarded authority of the canonists. Theological exploration of heresy as such had been relatively meager; the preponderance of writings on the subject appeared in the *Decretum*, which treated heretics, not heresy itself. Theologians had actively pursued the definition of heretical belief, but again, they had not addressed heresy itself. This had heretofore been addressed only by patristic description, which was very rough indeed, given the fine analysis made possible by scholastic theology. If the philosophical nature of Christian doctrine could be so thoroughly explored, why not the foundations of heresy as well?

Ockham's definition of heresy included a strict, scripturally founded sense, and a broader sense encompassing written and oral tradition, consistent and isomorphic with his understanding of orthodoxy, which also included both strict and broad senses. Mere ecclesiastical declaration of the heresy of a given belief or individual is insufficient in itself; authority must rest on something more than papal or conciliar fiat. This represents a significant departure from precedent by shifting the power to define heresy from an ecclesiastical judge, and recasting its definition into a question of the ongoing academic perfection of an understanding of heresy at the general and specific levels.

In changing paradigms for the assessment of heresy, Ockham eliminates the subjective element in heresy accusations. A science of heresy requires a body of observable phenomena, and cannot rely on subjective interpretation of individual assertions. The phenomena of heresy are assertions concerning doctrinal matters, and either these agree with established Christian truths, or they do not. Juridical declaration of heresy on a case-by-case basis, reliant upon the learning and personal insight of the judge and his capacity to discern the integrity of the accused's assertions of orthodoxy, can no longer pass for the just examination of heresy, given Ockham's de-juridicization of the concept itself. In his paradigm-redefining analysis, Ockham does not ignore the good works of canonist and theologian; Shogimen shows how effectively Ockham incorporated both canonist distinctions and theological precedents into his construction of a general theory of heresy.

In doing so, Shogimen shows Ockham to be painstaking in his use of the term "pertinacity," an adjective crucial to the standard definition of heresy. While one cannot judge the internal pertinacity by which one might secretly adhere to heresy while asserting otherwise, external pertinacity was something else again. Ockham is indefatigable in his classification of pertinacious heterodoxy, and remarkably strict in his refusal to tolerate heresy once detected. It is especially important to make note of this, given the usual tendency to assume rather more of a modern attitude to one of modernity's progenitors than is legitimate. While determined to improve the process by which it is detected, Ockham is still convinced of heresy's threat to the faith and the faithful. The error of the heretic lies not in the offense against the Church, but in an assault on Truth itself, and the only rational tactic is to make its detection and treatment a matter for any rational reader of scripture, not the ecclesiastical hierarchy. The stage is thereby set for a scientific analysis of the heretical tendencies of anyone—convert or pope—absent the possibility of political meddling. The next logical step, namely the possibility of identifying and addressing papal heresy, leads inexorably to replacing the authority-founded order of the Church with a more universally available, knowledge-based order for the Faith itself.

Shogimen's analysis turns Ockham's movement into the dangerous realm of papal heresy, which he concluded to be a breakdown in the ecclesiastical body politic. Ockham's understanding of heresy then dictates his understanding of *plenitudo potestatis*, and ultimately on the Petrine commission and its commutability and inheritablility. Finally Shogimen describes Ockham's understanding of the relation of Church and state as mutually assisting one another, rather than either claiming authority over the other, which latter Ockham viewed as a symptom of the degeneration of the two institutions.

There has been a comparative lull in literature on Ockham's political thought during the last two decades, in large part because the scholarship of figures like A. S. McGrade had so thoroughly defined it on traditionally political grounds. Shogimen's work has likely begun a new chapter in the scholarship of Ockham's political writings by introducing more expressly theological elements into the mixture, and this book will certainly deserve a place next to the analyses of McGrade, Kilcullen, Miethke, and Tierney in the library of any student of Ockham.

Stephen E. Lahey
University of Nebraska–Lincoln

Patricia Terry and Samuel N. Rosenberg, *Lancelot and the Lord of the Distant Isles, or The Book of Galehaut Retold.* With wood engravings by Judith Jaidinger. Boston: David R. Godine, 2006. Pp. xxvii, 226.

Patricia Terry is a well-known and accomplished translator of French and Old French literature into English. She has translated, among other works, *The Song of Roland* (1965) and *Renard the Fox* (1992). She is also a poet in her own right. Samuel Rosenberg is well known among French medievalists as a powerful translator and interpreter of Old French poetry. He has translated the *Chansons de trouvères* into English (1981) as well as into modern French (1995). He has also given us an English translation of *Ami and Amile* (1996). More pertinent for the work under review is his participation in the enormous translation project under the general editorship of Norris J. Lacy, *Lancelot-Grail: The Old French Arthurian Vulgate and Post-Vulgate in Translation* (5 vols., 1992–1995). Among the various prose tales composing these two cycles, Rosenberg translated *Lancelot*, parts 1 and 3 (both of them belonging to the Vulgate cycles), and prepared a careful index of the proper names for all five volumes.

*Lancelot and the Lord of the Distant Isles* is composed of various selections from the longest component of the Lancelot-Grail cycle, that is to say, the *Lancelot Proper*. Strictly speaking, there is no such thing as a *Book of Galehaut*, but Rosenberg clearly defines his concept of this book when he presents the task that the translators set out for themselves:

> Unlike our Old French source, we have stripped the legend of everything not closely related to the development of Lancelot's affective life and the role of Galehaut in that evolution. Thus various subplots and missions involving one or another knight of the Round Table have been omitted, including some exciting magical adventures and, most notably, all the traces of the quest for the Holy Grail (an episode that occurs after Galehaut's death). We have eliminated a host of characters, reduced the presence of others, and even reshaped the trajectory of a few.
>
> All changes have been made in the interest of tightening the story without distorting the fundamentals of the original narrative. In any case, it was our intention, not to prepare either a translation or an abridgment of the Old French source, but to retell the central love drama in such a way as to restore its complexity and emotional depth for the modern reader. (xxvi–xxvii)

The work under review is thus composed of those fragments from the *Lancelot Proper* that present the relationship between Lancelot and the Lord of the Distant Isles, Galehaut (the name not to be confused with Galahad, Lancelot's son). *Lancelot and the Lord of the Distant Isles* is thus the story of a love triangle: Galehaut loves Lancelot, Lancelot loves Guenevere who loves Lancelot.

The highlights of the story can be summed up as follows: Lancelot, born of high parents, is taken care of by his fay protectress, the Lady of the Lake. The young Lancelot arrives in the court and is knighted by Arthur. As White Knight, he protects the Lady of Nahaut; later, he defeats the Lord of Dolorous Guard, which in his hands becomes Joyous

Guard. Lifting a tombstone, he learns that he is Lancelot of the Lake, the son of King Ban of Benoic. He goes to Camelot with Arthur's nephew, Gauvain; there he learns of Galehaut, Lord of the Distant Isles, son of a giantess and himself a demi-giant, who has conquered thirty kingdoms. Gauvain leads Arthur's knights in the first battle against Galehaut's huge army. The noble Galehaut, conscious of his own military superiority, offers Arthur a year's truce so that the latter can prepare his army for a more equitable encounter. In that encounter, Lancelot joins the battle as the Black Knight, and accomplishes extraordinary feats of prowess. Galehaut meets Lancelot and offers him hospitality. He loves Lancelot, and for his sake renounces the conquest of King Arthur's realm, Logres.

Later, Queen Guenevere learns that it was the Black Knight who arranged the peace between Arthur and Galehaut. She is very grateful. For the love of that knight, she says, "I would let my very honor turn to shame" (66). Galehaut fulfils Lancelot's desire, arranging a meeting between him and Guenevere. The queen and the Black Knight make a "pact of love." Lancelot bestows a kiss on the queen and his kiss is protected from the view of others by the broad shoulders of Galehaut. All Galehaut asks of the queen is that she protect his friendship with Lancelot. Galehaut and Lancelot are known to everybody as "sworn companions." Galehaut manifests his affection for Lancelot, but the latter, while remaining Galehaut's good companion, thinks only about Guenevere. Finally, as the text says: "Galehaut's sacrifice had led to this night's union, the more easily because of Arthur's indifference. As warfare and subterfuge trapped the king, Guenevere could grant her lover the unreserved fulfillment he had longed for. He had dedicated his valor to her" (116–17).

Many complications follow. Arthur, Lancelot, and Galehaut are captured by the Saxons, who are supported by magic forces. In prison, Lancelot becomes mad and so is released. But thanks to the Lady of the Lake, "[his] health is restored, and all the joys that are the privilege of lovers were his. For nine days he lived a life of perfect happiness" (129). Lancelot becomes a companion of the Round Table but after a while leaves Camelot with Galehaut, who is full of presentiments and suffers more and more from a mysterious disease. Later, Guenevere is accused of being an imposter; Lancelot saves her by fighting an extraordinary judicial combat. Many adventures follow. Finally, Lancelot is captured by Guenevere's sworn enemy, Morgan the Fay. She keeps the whereabouts of her prisoner secret. Galehaut, thinking that Lancelot is dead, dies of sorrow. The story ends with the destruction of Logres by the treacherous

Mordred and with the death of Arthur, Lancelot, and Guenevere. Lancelot is buried with Galehaut.

This beautifully printed and illustrated translation is elegant and eminently readable. The translators avoid the irritating archaisms that so often mar the translations from Old French. There is a short introduction (vii–xxvii), which acquaints us succinctly with the "Breton" tradition of Arthurian literature as developed by Geoffrey of Monmouth, Chrétien de Troyes, and their continuators of the Lancelot-Grail cycle.

I can imagine that an orthodox philologist might object to this selective translation by Terry and Rosenberg. There is, of course, a famous precedent for Lancelot and the Lord of the Distant Isles, namely Joseph Bédier's beautiful retelling of *Tristan et Iseut*. Above all, the translators have succeeded in reminding the readers of French literature of the importance of Galehaut in the Arthurian tradition. They will understand why Dante (in the fifth canto of the *Inferno*) chose Galehaut (Galeotto) as the famous intermediary between Paolo and Francesca. For Dante, Galehaut was an archetypal figure. He should not remain forgotten.

Peter Dembowski
University of Chicago

Jeff Rider, ed., *Walteri Archidiaconi Tervanensis Vita Karoli Comitis Flandrie et Vita Domni Ioannis Morinensis Episcopi*. Corpus Christianorum Continuatio Mediaevalis 217. Turnhout: Brepols, 2006. Pp. lxxx, 222.

The assassination of Charles the Good, Count of Flanders, in 1127, was one of the most shocking events of the early twelfth century. Hence, this edition of the life of Charles by Walter, Archdeacon of Thérouanne, is a mine of information about this important figure, whom Baldwin VII backed in increasing the count's political control over the south and west of Flanders, and whom he named as his successor before dying in 1119. The policy was to reduce the independence of the region's nobility and increase royal control over the finances of the region by reining in the powers of the great family of the Erembalds. Charles died without issue, and struggle for his successor involved various pretenders, with the king of France, Louis VI, finally succeeding in establishing himself as undisputed overlord of the region and appointing his own choice as

*Medievalia et Humanistica*, New Series, Number 34 (Paul Maurice Clogan, ed.), Rowman & Littlefield Publishers, Inc., 2008.

the new count: William Clito, nephew of Henry I of England. Thus Charles's work in life and his death were involved in the balance of power with not only the Holy Roman Empire but England and France as well. The fight for control was also the fight for the commercial life of the most prosperous region of Europe.

Son of a saintly martyr, Cnut of Denmark, Charles may have courted a martyr's death himself. His biographer Walter was present when Charles was warned of plots against his life awaiting him in Bruges, and quotes him as saying that no death was more glorious than that for truth. The *Vita* abounds in purported quotations such as this, and makes lively reading in this excellent edition replacing that of the Bollandists in 1668 and of the *Monumenta Germaniae Historica* of 1856.

The second life presented here is that of John of Warneton, Archdeacon of Arras from 1096 to 1099 and Bishop of Thérouanne from 1099 to 1130, achieving this post after a disputed election decided by Urban II. The see had been sorely vexed; John's four predecessors had been expelled or deposed, and John was not even the second choice of the cathedral chapter. His biography reveals a resourceful and thoughtful man, setting out to bring about reforms and networking with like-minded reforming prelates. He encouraged Benedictine houses to adopt Cluniac reforms, and he may have had the grand idea of aligning both political and ecclesiastical boundaries of Flanders, so as to expose the Flemish Church more completely to the Gregorian reform. In the year of Charles's assassination, he asked his Archdeacon Walter to write the *Vita Karoli*. Since the power bases of assassins and accomplices lay within his diocese, it has been conjectured that the work was undertaken to distance himself.

Little enough is known about the writer of these two works, Walter of Thérouanne, whom Bishop John called there in 1115 and made archdeacon of western Flanders in the following year. A collection of canons of about 1123 is attributed to him, as well as these two lives.

This volume also presents a few documents relevant to the murder of Charles, such as epitaphs and the French record of the inquest. The *De multro* by Galbert of Bruges concerning Charles the Brave was published in this series some years ago. Minor misprints include p. xiii (read "*voluissem,*" not "*voluisse*"), xxviii ("notaries," not "notary's"), and xlix ("rites," not "rights," and "communicated," not "communed"). This is a most welcome work on a major figure and his contexts.

Charles Witke<br>
University of Michigan

Trevor Dean, *Crime and Justice in Late Medieval Italy.* Cambridge: Cambridge University Press, 2007. Pp. x, 226.

For several decades now, social historians have been mining the criminal court records of Italy, as of the rest of Europe. By their very existence—and their existence in steadily increasing quantities—these records testify to the expanding reach and strengthening grasp of state institutions, making them of great interest to scholars interested in questions of state formation and social control. Because crime touched people of all classes, the records of criminal justice allow historians access to the words and deeds of people outside the social elite. And because the deeds they recorded could be lurid and the words angry, medieval criminal records hold the inherent dramatic (or prurient) interest of the sort of crime stories that dominate local television news broadcasts and furnish the matter for endless reruns of *Law and Order.*

As a corrective to the distorting effects of this taste for the outré, the microhistorical penchant for detailed study of a few exceptionally well-documented cases, the intense localism of Italian historical studies, and the tendency of Anglophone historians to focus on Florence and Venice, Trevor Dean offers this welcome overview of crime and criminal justice in Italy from the middle of the thirteenth century to the end of the fifteenth. In the first half of the book, Dean examines five different types of sources, each with its own distinctive form, construction, utility, and limitations: the trial records generated by a variety of courts; the statutes that provided the framework within which the courts operated; the legal *consilia* or expert opinions solicited by parties to court cases; the chronicles that report reactions to notorious crimes and to the exercise (and sometimes miscarriage) of justice; and short prose fiction or novelle, in which authors from Boccaccio to Sabadino degli Arienti, counting on their readers' interest in crime and familiarity with the legal system, colored their discussions of crime and justice in tones ranging from righteous outrage to sardonic amusement.

By drawing judiciously on all of these sources, and paying proper heed to the structural characteristics of each, Dean clears the way for a more solidly grounded history of criminal justice in late medieval Italy. To ensure that his is a history of Italy, and not just Florence and Venice, he draws "from the archives in Bologna, Mantua, Modena, Reggio, Savona, and Lucca; and from published documents for the whole of late

*Medievalia et Humanistica*, New Series, Number 34 (Paul Maurice Clogan, ed.), Rowman & Littlefield Publishers, Inc., 2007.

medieval Italy, from the duchy of Savoy and the Venetian *terrafirma* to the kingdoms of Naples and Sicily" (6). The printed statutes and chronicles he examines come from cities similarly scattered over the entire peninsula, including Sicily and the south, and the legal *consilia* and tale collections taken into consideration include all the major and some of the minor ones.

Dean devotes the second half of his book to a description and analysis of the incidence of criminal acts, and of responses to them, sorted into five categories: insult and revenge, sex crimes, poisoning, violence, and theft. He shows that growing alarm over many of these infractions led to more restrictive laws and heavier penalties. Though adultery and rape continued to be seen as injuries to individual honor, in many other cases the interests of public security came increasingly to the fore, as religious concerns and a sharpened sense of civic decorum inspired official intervention to cleanse and protect communities. The administration of justice changed as well: As cases initiated by accusation gave way to inquisition in some localities, prosecutions for insult declined and those for theft increased—as did crimes against the civic regimes that ordered the new criminal procedures and the judicial apparatus that enforced them. These shifts, however, were not uniform, as Dean's comparative data shows that "the character of justice—inquisitorial, accusatorial, negotiated, repressive—varies both between cities and across time" (200). The patterns, and the variations among them, that Dean has identified invite further investigations, which must now take their start from this clearly conceived, thoroughly researched, and resolutely non-sensational account of crime and justice in late medieval Italy.

Daniel Bornstein
Washington University in St. Louis

# Books Received

Abelard, Peter. *Letters of Peter Abelard: Beyond the Personal*, trans. by Jan M. Ziolkowski. Washington, D.C.: Catholic University of America Press, 2007. Pp. lii, 232. $29.95 (paper).

Alford, Stephen. *Burghley: William Cecil at the Court of Elizabeth I*. New Haven, Conn.: Yale University Press, 2008. Pp. 432, with 16 b/w illustrations. $45.00.

Ashe, Laura. *Fiction and History in England, 1066–1200*. New York: Cambridge University Press, 2008. Pp. 244. $95.00.

Bell, Adrian R., Chris Brooks, and Paul R. Dryburgh. *The English Wool Market, c. 1230–1327*. New York: Cambridge University Press, 2007. Pp. vii, 205. $90.00.

Burland, Margaret Jewett. *Strange Words: Retelling and Reception in the Medieval Roland Textual Tradition*. Notre Dame, Ind.: University of Notre Dame Press, 2007. Pp. 344. $37.00 (paper).

Burrow, J. A. *The Poetry of Praise*. New York: Cambridge University Press, 2008. Pp. 196. $90.00.

Campbell, Caroline, and Alan Chong. *Bellini and the East*. New Haven, Conn.: Yale University Press, 2006. Pp. 144, 6 b/w + 87 color illustrations. $29.95 (paper).

Carruthers, Mary. *The Book of Memory: A Study of Memory in Medieval Culture*. New York: Cambridge University Press, 1990; 2nd ed., 2008. Pp. 519. $29.99 (paper).

Cheney, Patrick. *Shakespeare's Literary Authorship*. New York: Cambridge University Press, 2008. Pp. 296. $99.00.

Costambeys, Marios. *Power and Patronage in Early Medieval Italy: Local Societies, Italian Politics and the Abbey of Farfa, c. 700–900*. Cambridge Studies in Medieval Life and Thought, Fourth Series. New York: Cambridge University Press, 2008. Pp. 388. $115.00.

De Souza, Philip, and John France, eds. *War and Peace in Ancient and Medieval History*. New York: Cambridge University Press, 2008. Pp. 247. $99.00.

Eisenbichler, Konrad, and Nicholas Terpstra, eds. *The Renaissance in the Streets: Schools and Studies. Essays in Honor of Paul F. Grendler*. Toronto:

*Medievalia et Humanistica*, New Series, Number 34 (Paul Maurice Clogan, ed.), Rowman & Littlefield Publishers, Inc., 2008.

Centre for Reformation and Renaissance Studies, 2008. Pp. 373, 15 illustrations, 8 plates.

Halsall, Guy. *Barbarian Migrations and the Roman West, 376–568.* 2007. New York: Cambridge University Press, 2008. Pp. 592. $41.99 (paper).

Hanawalt, Barbara A., and Anna Grotans, eds. *Living Dangerously: On the Margins in Medieval and Early Modern Europe.* Notre Dame, Ind.: University of Notre Dame Press, 2007. Pp. 184. $27.00 (paper).

Hanawalt, Barbara A., and Lisa J. Kiser, eds. *Engaging with Nature: Essays on the Natural World in Medieval and Early Modern Europe.* Notre Dame, Ind.: University of Notre Dame Press, 2008. Pp. 248. $30.00 (paper).

Hill, John M. *The Narrative Pulse of Beowulf: Arrivals and Departures.* Toronto: University of Toronto Press, 2008. Pp. 119.

Laiou, Angeliki E., and Cécile Morrisson. *The Byzantine Economy.* New York: Cambridge University Press, 2007. Pp. 272. $32.99 (paper).

Loud, G. A. *The Latin Church in Northern Italy.* New York: Cambridge University Press, 2008. Pp. 577. $140.00.

Lucio Paolo Rosello. *Il ritratto del vero governo del principe (1552),* ed. Matteo Salvetti. Milan: FrancoAngeli, 2008. Pp. 228.

Lyster, William, ed. *The Cave Church of Paul the Hermit: At the Monastery of St. Paul, Egypt.* New Haven, Conn.: Yale University Press, 2008. Pp. 416, 60 b/w + 250 color illus. $75.00.

Marvin, Laurence. *The Occitan War: A Military and Political History of the Albigensian Crusade, 1209–1218.* New York: Cambridge University Press, 2008. Pp. 354. $110.00.

Muir, Lynette R. *Love and Conflict in Medieval Drama: The Plays and their Legacy.* New York: Cambridge University Press, 2007. Pp. 294. $90.00.

Nutttall, Jenni. *The Creation of Lancastrian Kingship: Literature, Language, and Politics in Late Medieval England.* New York: Cambridge University Press, 2007. Pp. 200. $90.00.

Peterson, David S., and Daniel E. Bornstein, eds. *Florence and Beyond: Culture, Society, and Politics in Renaissance Italy. Essays in Honor of John M. Najemy.* Toronto: Centre for Reformation and Renaissance Studies, 2008. Pp. 518, 8 color and b/w plates.

Quester, Michael C. *Catholicism and Community in Early Modern England: Politics, Aristocratic Patronage, and Religion, c. 1550–1640.* New York: Cambridge University Press, 2006. Pp. 574.

Sawday, Jonathan. *Engines of the Imagination: Renaissance Culture and the Rise of the Machine.* New York: Routledge, 2007. Pp. 402. $33.95 (paper).

Silver, Larry, and Elizabeth Wyckoff, eds. *Grand Scale: Monumental Prints in the Age of Dürer and Titian.* New Haven, Conn.: Yale University Press, 2008. Pp. 176, 62 b/w + 45 color illus. + 2 gatefolds. $50.00.

Swanson, R. N. *Indulgences in Late Medieval England: Passports to Paradise?* New York: Cambridge University Press, 2008. Pp. 579. $120.00.

Syson, Luke, et al. *Renaissance Siena: Art for a City.* New Haven, Conn.: Yale University Press, 2008. Pp. 296, 172 color illustrations. $65.00.

Tanner, Marcus. *The Raven King: Matthias Corvinus and the Fate of His Lost Library.* New Haven, Conn.: Yale University Press. Pp. 288, 16 b/w illustrations. $35.00.

Watkins, C. S. *History and the Supernatural in Medieval England.* Cambridge Studies in Medieval Life and Thought. New York: Cambridge University Press, 2008. Pp. 271. $99.00.

Wetherbee, Winthrop. *The Ancient Flame: Dante and the Poets.* Notre Dame, Ind.: University of Notre Dame Press, 2008. Pp. 320. $35.00 (paper).

Whalen, Logan. *Marie de France and the Poetics of Memory.* Washington, D.C.: Catholic University of America Press, 2008. Pp. xii, 208. $59.95.

Ziolkowski, Jan M. *Nota Bene: Reading Classics and Writing Melodies in the Early Middle Ages.* Publications of the Journal of Medieval Latin 7. Turnhout: Brepols, 2007. Pp. 362 (paper). 14 b/w plates. €55.00.